MOTORCYCLE ROAD TRIPS ACROSS NEW ZEALAND

Molly

MOTORCYCLE ROAD TRIPS ACROSS NEW ZEALAND

RIDE 20 BREATHTAKING ROUTES

KIM JOHNSTON

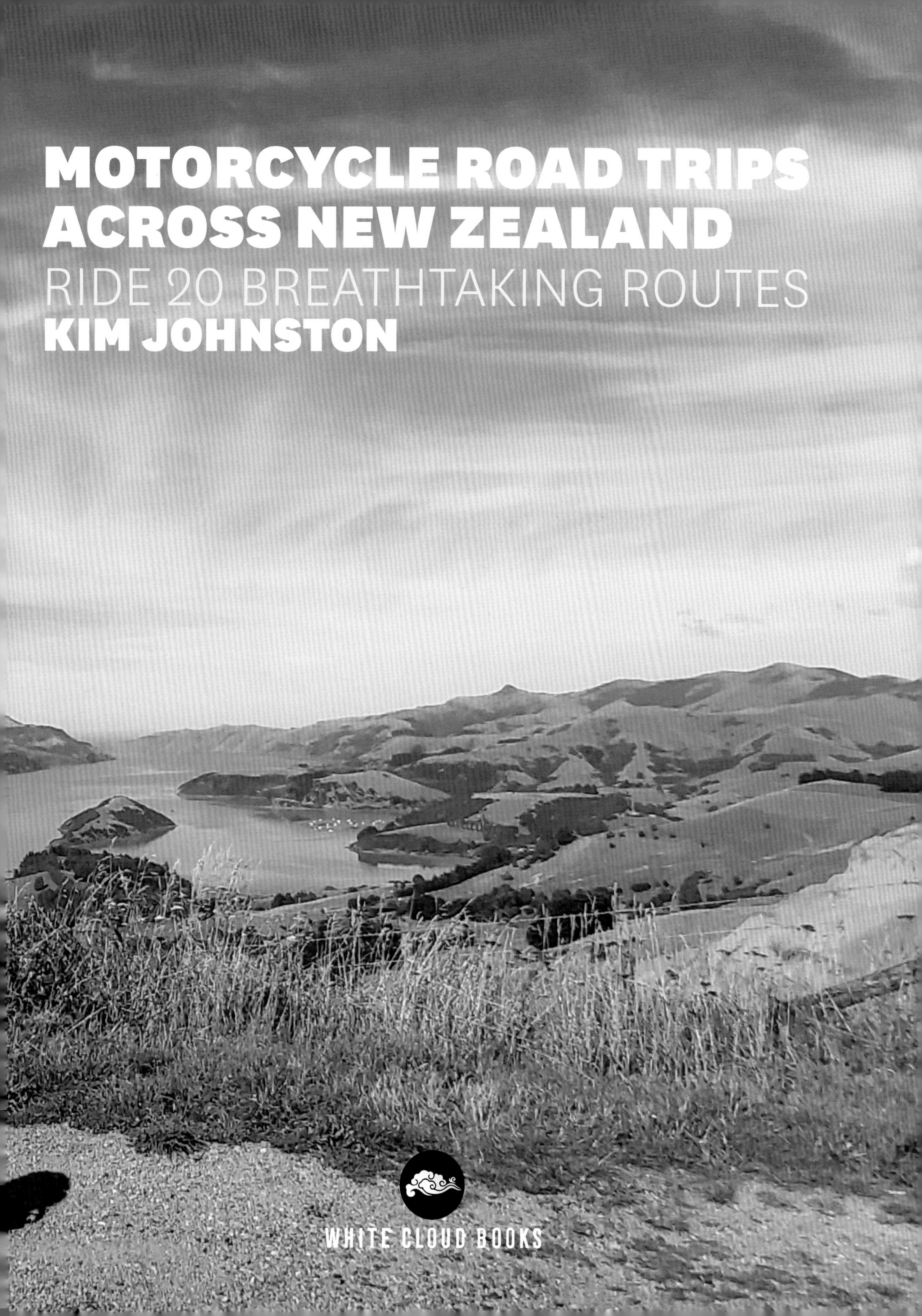

WHITE CLOUD BOOKS

Contents

Kim Johnston with John Munro

Foreword

If you love travelling by motorcycles and want to see the REAL New Zealand then reading and planning with this detailed travel book is a must.

I am often asked why I don't write a book about my life experiences on bikes and all the other bike related things I have been privileged to experience both in New Zealand and on overseas events. The simple answer is that I wouldn't know where to start so thank you Kim for saving me the trouble!

My father, Herbert James Munro, (World's Fastest Indian) never wrote a book about his life experiences. If he had then I could hand on a copy of it to answer the many questions I get about him on his travels.

In this book the details provided of routes and side trips will assist you in your planning whether you are intending to travel on your own, with mates or as part of a tour group.

I have often said that, if you choose to spend the time to travel around our country, you will have seen the sights of a round the world trip. Mountains, glaciers, ancient forests, geysers, deserts, vineyards, rivers, caves and many of the other scenes and places as detailed in this book. Of course most of these features here are on a smaller scale in New Zealand but they are all for you to see in a couple or four weeks on a bike (or in a car for that matter). The main routes covered here are some 4,000 km and some 60 hours riding. Allow 200 km per day riding and this will be accomplished in a leisurely 20 days. With side trips it is easy to add another 2,000 km or more if time is on your side.

During the late 1950's and through to the late 1960's I spent many kilometres on the roads of New Zealand exploring the back blocks and out of the way places. Many of the roads I rode then would be classed as trail rides now.

Kim, as Operations Manager of South Pacific Motorcycle Tours Ltd, has done an excellent job of covering the roads, trails and visual wonders of New Zealand's two main islands.

She is well qualified in her position with racing in her blood. Her father, Robert (Bob) Johnston, built and raced Formula Fords and was the South Island Champion in 1972.

South Pacific Motorcycle Tours Ltd was brought to life in April 2003 by Kim's Step Father Mike and Mother Carole Lester. Mike, who has been a lifelong rider of bikes, together with Carole and Kim have created a reliable tour service for local riders and many overseas visitors. Kim has travelled most of these routes herself and the balance is from Mike and Carole based on their experiences of touring Godzone on a bike.

Thank you Kim for saving me the trouble of answering questions about my travels of where to go and what to see while riding New Zealand. I can now pass on a copy of your excellent travel book *Motorcycle Road Trips Across New Zealand*.

JOHN MUNRO

Introduction

This book started as a way to catalogue the work my parents have put in over 20 years of motorcycle touring around New Zealand. South Pacific Motorcycle Tours began in 2003 and can boast years of hiring top quality motorbikes to international and local riders who rely on their knowledge and advice on riding tried and tested roads. These are some of the best on-road riding routes that New Zealand has to offer, and depending on your duration, whether it be a day ride, or 3 week adventure, these routes will ensure the best riding experience possible.

The routes outlined in this book focus on sealed roads for top motorcycle touring, so you don't have to go off-road or adventure riding to see the best of New Zealand. You can still experience the breathtaking and unspoilt scenery from well-maintained sealed roads. However, there are multiple back-country and adventure riding routes that can easily link up with these routes if you are wanting a more challenging off-road ride.

Writing this book has been a fabulous emotional experience, in the sense that the information in this book has been gathered by my wonderful mother, stepfather and by myself over the past 20 plus years of riding around New Zealand. With their help, we have put together our best suggested routes to explore and enjoy.

Our family business model has been to build a company that provides riders with top quality motorcycles on which to live out their dream to 'ride New Zealand'. To provide tour routes so that visitors can experience the best of the best, built from their own personal experiences.

We have met thousands of riders and expanded our biker family worldwide. This includes the most well-known family name in New Zealand motorcycling history, Munro. John Munro is the son of Kiwi motorcycle legend, Burt Munro (World's Fastest Indian) and has been kind enough to write the foreword for this book. A legend in his own right, John has explored New Zealand by motorcycle and is not only a trusted friend but has certainly made us feel like extended members of the Munro family. His understanding of passing on family legacy was inspirational in writing this book.

Running a business that sends riders out around ones own country to experience some of their most memorable riding is a true privilege. Passing on our advice and knowledge, sharing stories and suggestions from a personal perspective with riders before they embark on their trip of a lifetime is magical.

When approached to share our family legacy with a wider audience in literary form, I was proud to put our family knowledge to print. To inspire more riders to explore New Zealand and add to our world-wide biker family.

KIM JOHNSTON — 2023

Kim Johnston, Mike and Carole Lester
South Pacific Motorcyle Tours

Riding in New Zealand

Riding anywhere in New Zealand is a wonderful adventure, and there is a surprise around every corner. Packed with a kaleidoscope of scenery and rich in culture, you will enjoy the route as much as your destination. Some of the very best motorcycling roads in the world are to be found in the South Island of New Zealand thanks to the Southern Alps' spine that runs virtually down the middle. Roads are often empty, with fantastic sweeping bends and great visibility. In contrast the North Island also offers great riding, with its volcanic plateaus, rolling hills, beach-lined peninsulas, and thermal highways.

Road Conditions

The famous New Zealand motorcycle touring roads make for terrific riding. Due to a small population, the roads have less traffic than most countries and are well maintained in most places, however following wild weather or rockfalls, the roads can become damaged and extra care is needed to navigate any potholes, cracks, or rocks. 'Metal' roads are gravel, not tarmac. Many side roads in New Zealand will show a sign stating metal road.

Road Riding

Motorcycle riding in New Zealand is generally relaxed, so you can take in the scenery and see this wonderful country at a comfortable pace. Make sure all fluids are checked on your bike, you regularly top up your tank with fuel to avoid any unwanted fuel gauge watching and that your tyres have sufficient tread for the distance you are riding. If you have space, take a puncture repair kit with you somewhere on your bike just in case.

Weather Conditions

New Zealand's North Island is subtropical and the South Island temperate, to get the most enjoyment out of the weather December through to March is the best time to visit. June, July and August are the coldest months and the mountainous areas often close due to snow.

During our summer our temperatures range between 20–40c(68F–104F)

During winter it can be anything between 0–20c (32F–68F)

The summer sun can be fierce so sun screen is highly recommended, also wear layers and be prepared to ride in both hot and colder weather. Check out the Met Service website for more details about New Zealand weather. This is also a great site to follow when you are riding around the island to avoid any unwanted rain.

Travelling times

It's easy to underestimate travelling times in New Zealand. Although distances may seem short on paper, New Zealand roads may be narrower than you are used to, cover hilly terrain and vary from highways to unsealed gravel roads. If you're tired you're much more likely to have a crash. Here are some tips to help you stay alert:-

- Get lots of rest before a long ride;
- Take a break from riding every two hours;
- Drink plenty of fluid;
- If you begin to feel sleepy, stop. If you're feeling very tired, find a place to stay over-night.

Fuel

In some parts of rural New Zealand fuel stations are few, so topping up each morning before you head off is recommended. There are manned and un-manned stations around both Islands.

Emergency Services

For Fire, Medical and Police the Phone Number is 111.

Animals on the road

Watch out for farm animals and horses on the road, particularly in rural areas. When you see them slow down and do not sound your horn - it may startle them. You may need to stop and let the animals go past you or move slowly up behind and follow the farmer's instructions.

Keep left

Always drive on the left side of the road. If you drive on the right hand side in your own country, please take a moment to re-familiarise yourself with this rule before pulling out onto the road after a break - it's easy to forget where you are!

Giving way at intersections

Always use your indicators when turning. Stop completely then give way (yield) to all traffic. Slow down and be ready to stop and give way to all traffic.

Driving speeds

Speed limit signs show the maximum speed you can travel. However, at times you may need to drive at a slower speed due to road or weather conditions. Different speed limits apply throughout New Zealand, look out for the speed limit signs. On most of New Zealand's main roads the speed limit is 100 km/h unless a sign says a lower speed applies. In urban areas, the speed limit is usually 50 km/h unless a sign says otherwise.

Alcohol

Do not drink and ride, the laws against this are strictly enforced in New Zealand and penalties are severe. The legal limit for over 20 years and over is 250 micrograms of alcohol per litre of breath and 20 and under the limit is zero. This information is from Waka Kotahi, the NZ Transport Agency. Check out their website for more detailed information.

Overtaking

Most roads in New Zealand have a single lane each way, but provide passing lanes at regular intervals, these should be used where possible. You must not cross a solid yellow line on your side of the centre-line, as this indicates it's too dangerous to overtake.

One lane bridges

Many roads in New Zealand have one lane bridges on them. At one lane bridges, vehicles travelling in one direction must give way to vehicles going in the other direction. Slow down and check for traffic coming the other way. The larger arrow shows which direction has the right of way.

Basic Road Rules

It is important to view the road rules before you ride, below are some brief tips, but for the official New Zealand road code visit the NZ Transport Agency website.

- **Speed Limits:** Vary between 50 km/h in built up areas and 100 km/h max on the open road. All speed limits are well signposted.
- **Giving Way:** In general give way to the right. When at a STOP sign you must stop completely and give way to all traffic until it is clear to proceed.
  - Traffic not turning at cross junctions (going straight) have the right of way over turning traffic.
  - Signs at single lane bridges advise of who has right of way, slow down and be prepared to stop.
- **Corner Speed:** There are speed recommendation signs on most bends in New Zealand and can be used as a rough guide to judge your speed into corners.
- **Driving Licence:** You must hold a current motorcycle licence to be able to legally ride in New Zealand.
- **Clothing:** When riding in New Zealand you are required to wear a helmet by law. For your own

safety wear armoured clothing with multiple layers in case the weather gets cooler. Motorcycle jackets, pants and boots that are wind and waterproof and able to withstand abrasion are also recommended.

- **Overtaking:** You may not cross a solid yellow line to overtake, they are there to warn of hidden dangers so abide by this rigidly. Broken white lines are fine and you should stay within the speed limit. You are not allowed to cross the centre line if you are not overtaking and must keep left when driving normally.
- **Parking:** Consider your parking carefully, for your convenience remember to park the back wheel down to the kerb, this will make it easier to ride away, it also illegal to park on the opposite side of the road facing onto traffic.
- **Road Camber:** The road camber in New Zealand is fairly high so when pulling over, make sure to double check your footing and that the bike is stable before putting your stand down.
- **Kea Parrots.** Keas are alpine parrots that live above the snowline and prefer the cooler landscapes. If you are near the mountains keep an eye out for these birds as they will happily peck a hole in your seat within seconds and their sharp talons will instantly damage your seat if they land on it.
- **Roadworks:** Roadworks are seldom motorcycle friendly in NZ. Whilst some are easy to navigate, others can be a little daunting as deep gravel may hinder progress.

1. Twin Coast Discovery Highway Part 1
Kauri Coast

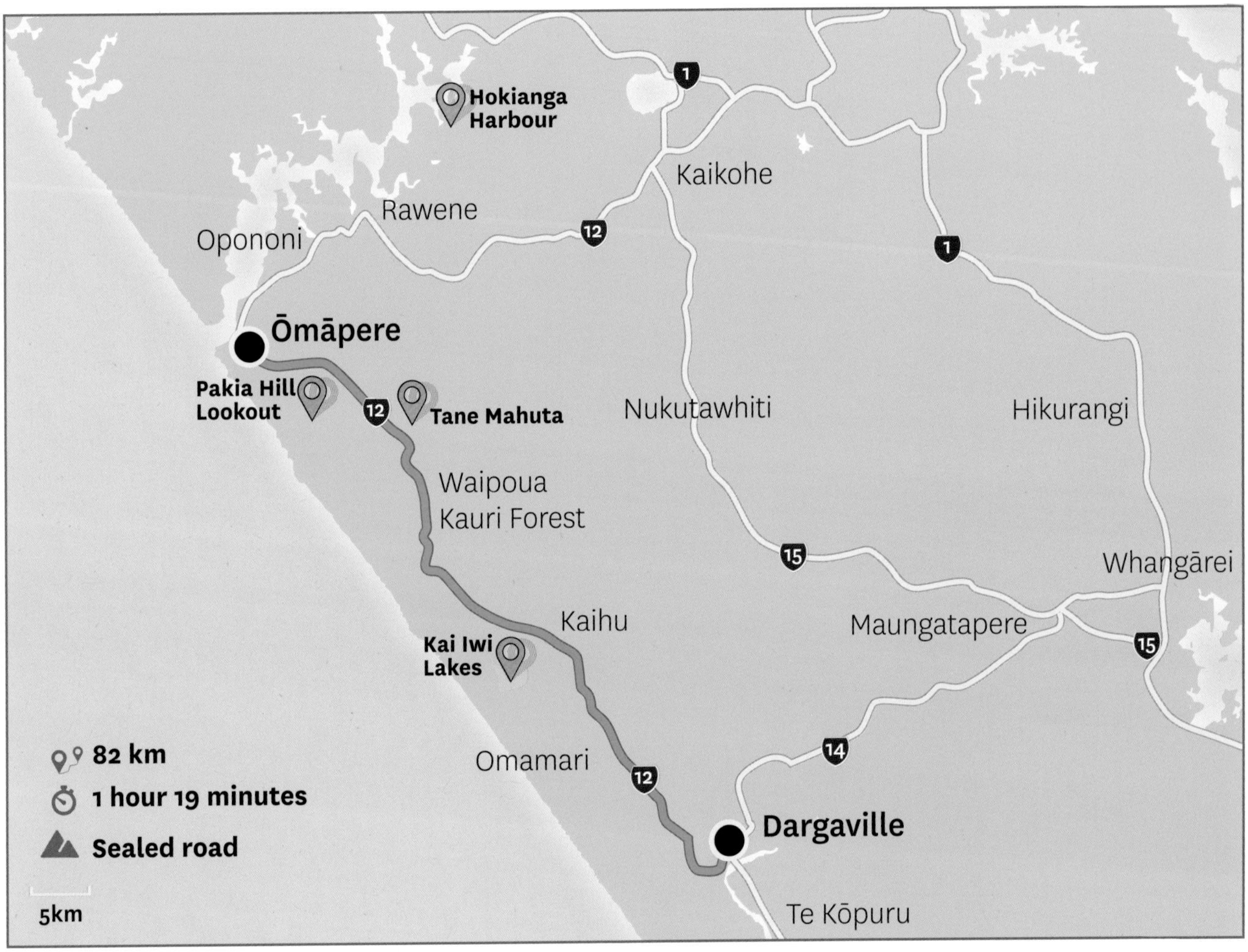

Route Overview

Exploring the 'Winterless North' as it is known, is a must do ride for any biker, and getting there is half the fun. With endless twisty, densely forested roads all the way to the white sand beaches of Hokianga Harbour, this ride is a fabulous treat for any motorcyclist.

Check out the **Detour to the Kauri Museum** if you have time on your way to Dargaville to learn more about this incredible environment. The kauri is the largest native tree in New Zealand. Growing over 50 m tall and living for over 1,000 years, these mighty trees used to be plentiful and tower above the coastal landscape, covering most of Northland in dense, ancient, semitropical forest.

Considered a taonga (treasure) in Aotearoa, the kauri holds cultural significance for Māori. The arrival of Europeans meant these majestic monoliths were cut down and harvested for their wood and the resin they secreted.

The kauri you see on this trip are still there today largely due to their inaccessibility, so have managed to escape being felled. These incredible forests are now being painstakingly preserved for future generations and there are numerous restrictions in place before you step foot into the forests. Rinsing shoes helps to prevent the spread of Kauri dieback; this disease affects the trunk and roots of the tree causing it to starve and die.

As you ride through the Kaipara District, there are many beaches that can be accessed from the highway. Most of these are via gravel roads so worth a look if you are confident riding on this terrain.

This route will take you past 'God of The Forest',

Tane Mahuta

Tāne Mahuta, the tallest kauri tree. Well worth the stop to stretch your legs along the way and experience these immense giants up close.

This road trip finishes at the pretty harbourside town of Ōmāpere in Hokianga Harbour. Stop and learn more about the cultural and historical significance of the area and its coastal landscape at 'Manea Footprints of Kupe'. There are various accommodation options if you choose to stay here, or optional detours continue heading north via the Rawene Ferry to Kaitāia and Cape Reinga, continuing along the Twin Coast Discovery Highway, or east across Northland straight to Paihia.

Start Your Engines!

Although a short ride, the Kauri Coast is one of the best bike trips in New Zealand and is part of the Twin Coast Discovery Highway. This route can be extended and joined from either direction to create a longer ride should you wish to spend a little more time exploring Northland. Check out the Twin Coast Discovery Highway Part 2 to lengthen this route into a 2 or 3-day road trip and take in the Bay of Islands.

Just two and a half hours from Auckland, starting this trip from Dargaville means you can ride and join up with the Twin Coast Discovery Highway from any direction. Heading north, follow State Highway 12 out of Dargaville through rural pastures and dairy farms with paddocks full of livestock. Dairy farming is the main industry of the area so it is common to be held up by cattle crossing the road. They do make the road messy and slippery once they have passed, so be vigilant if you see any telltale signs on the road.

The road begins to serpentine its way through hills lined with stunning native toetoe and tī kōuka or cabbage trees. These undulating and sweeping bends, together with the lush green landscape, makes this highway a joy to ride as you fall easily into the counter steering rhythm of this coastal road.

Twenty minutes riding north of Dargaville will bring you to Kaihū Valley. Check out the **Detour to Kai Iwi Lakes** if you have the time.

The environment will change as you spy Waipoua Kauri Forest blanketing the terrain on the horizon. This incredible ancient forest boasts the towering kauri this route is famous for, as well as rare native birds and an abundance of jaw-dropping prehistoric nature trails, all free for the public to explore.

The road becomes thick with dense bush on either side as you lean into the next lot of tighter twists and turns before crossing the Waipoua River. The immense kauri trees suddenly appear towering over the forest canopy and you will feel like you have travelled back in time as you ride through this unspoiled natural forest. A magical place to stop, crack open your visor and enjoy the fresh air.

The next 15 minutes of riding is a biker's dream with serpentine sweeps that will have you grinning from ear to ear all the way to your next stop.

Signposted on the left as you approach is Tāne Mahuta. Park up and take the short walk to this incredible monolithic tree. Meaning 'God of the Forest', Tāne Mahuta towers over the surrounding canopy at 45.2 m high and has been dated at approximately 2,000 years old.

More fabulous hairpin bends snake their way through the Waipoua Forest as the sunlight touches the tops of the trees. The dense forest shade over the road makes riding in the cooler months a little slower going due to potential frosty patches and slippery moss-covered ground at the sides of the road.

Civilisation begins to appear again and you will emerge out of the forest to the rolling hills. There is a small fuel station at Waimamaku if you need to top up the tank.

As you crest the hill and get your first glimpse of the Tasman Sea in the distance, you will have reached the outskirts of Ōmāpere. You are treated to a few more hairpin bends as you wind your way up Pakia Hill where a breathtaking view out across Hokianga Habour awaits you and you can enjoy stunning seaside riding along white sand beaches before deciding on the direction of your next adventure.

Check out the 'Twin Coast Discovery Highway — Bay of Islands Part 2' to extend this route further by taking the Rawene Ferry to the far north.

Biker-friendly stops along the way

Kauri Museum at Matakohe — 5 Church Road, Matakohe, 0593
Gumdiggers Cafe, Matakohe — 5 Church Road, Matakohe, 0593
Kaihu Tavern — 3065 State Highway 12, Kaihu, 0379

Scenic highlights along the way

Kai Iwi Lakes
Kauri Coast Beaches
Tāne Mahuta Kauri Tree
Pakia Hill Lookout
Hokianga Harbour

Why this is such a great ride

Being part of a longer ride means this trip can be extended if needed. This route transports the rider back in time to discover how the New Zealand landscape may have looked in the past. Boasting a densely forested subtropical environment with towering trees overhead and multiple long twisting roads through the incredible lush green hills. All this while enjoying a landscape of important preserved culture and heritage.

Detour 1

Kauri Museum

If you have time, before heading to Dargaville and the Kauri Coast, take this detour to the Kauri Museum to learn more about the history and culture of this ancient landscape when it was still covered in native kauri forest. You can start the Twin Coast Discovery Highway from State Highway 12 at Brynderwyn. Veering left up Church Road at Matakohe, The Kauri Museum is a quick turn off the main road and well worth the visit to understand more about the incredible landscape you are about to ride through. Rejoin State Highway 12 following signs to Dargaville.

Detour 2

Kai Iwi Lakes

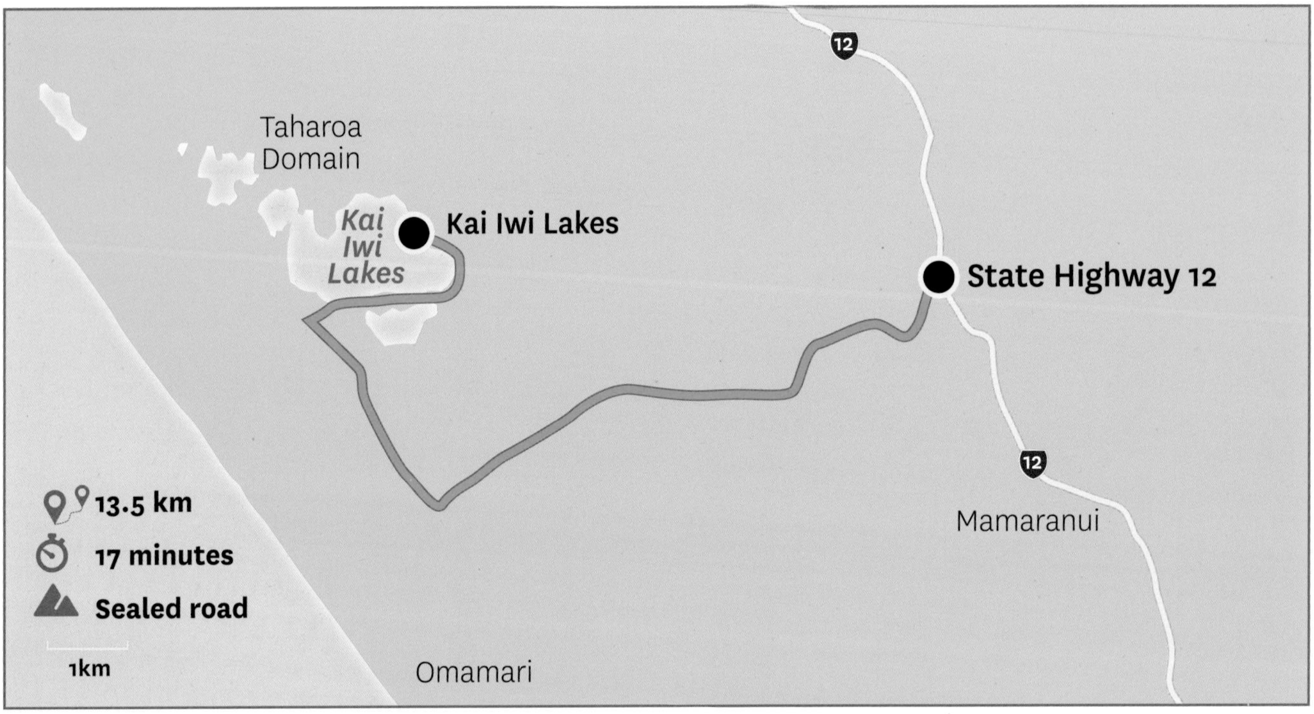

This quick detour is 17 minutes from Dargaville. Taharoa Domain is a popular recreation reserve and boasts the crystal clear blue freshwater Kai Iwi Lakes.

Perfect for safe swimming, kayaking, boating and other water-based activities, the lakes are surrounded by white sand dunes and are a drawcard for locals and tourists.

Kai Iwi Lakes

Detour 3

Inland loop via Kaikohe

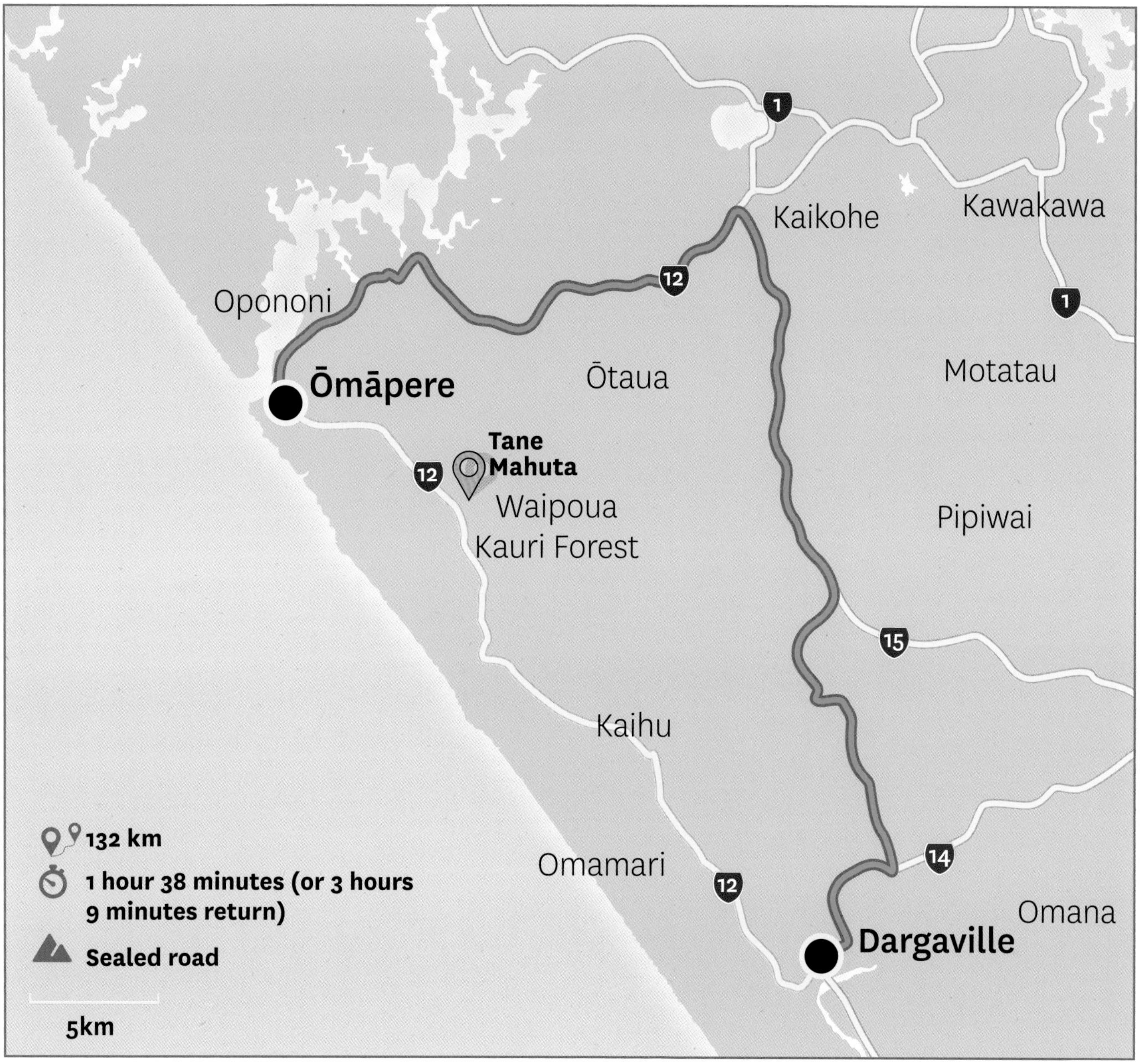

To extend this trip to a longer, enjoyable loop ride, and take in a little more of the far north before heading back down south, continue along State Highway 12 following signs to Kaikohe.

This inland road is also used by freight and logging companies so you may get stuck behind the odd truck at some point. At Kaikohe township, turn right on to State Highway 15 along Mangakahia Road and follow signs to Dargaville. Enjoying subtropical surroundings and vast forested hills, this route follows the twists and turns in the same direction of the Awarua River before it joins the Mangakahia River at the Twin Bridges.

When reaching Pakotai, you can either turn right to head towards Dargaville to complete the loop or continue on State Highway 15 towards Auckland.

2. Twin Coast Discovery Highway Part 2
Bay of Islands

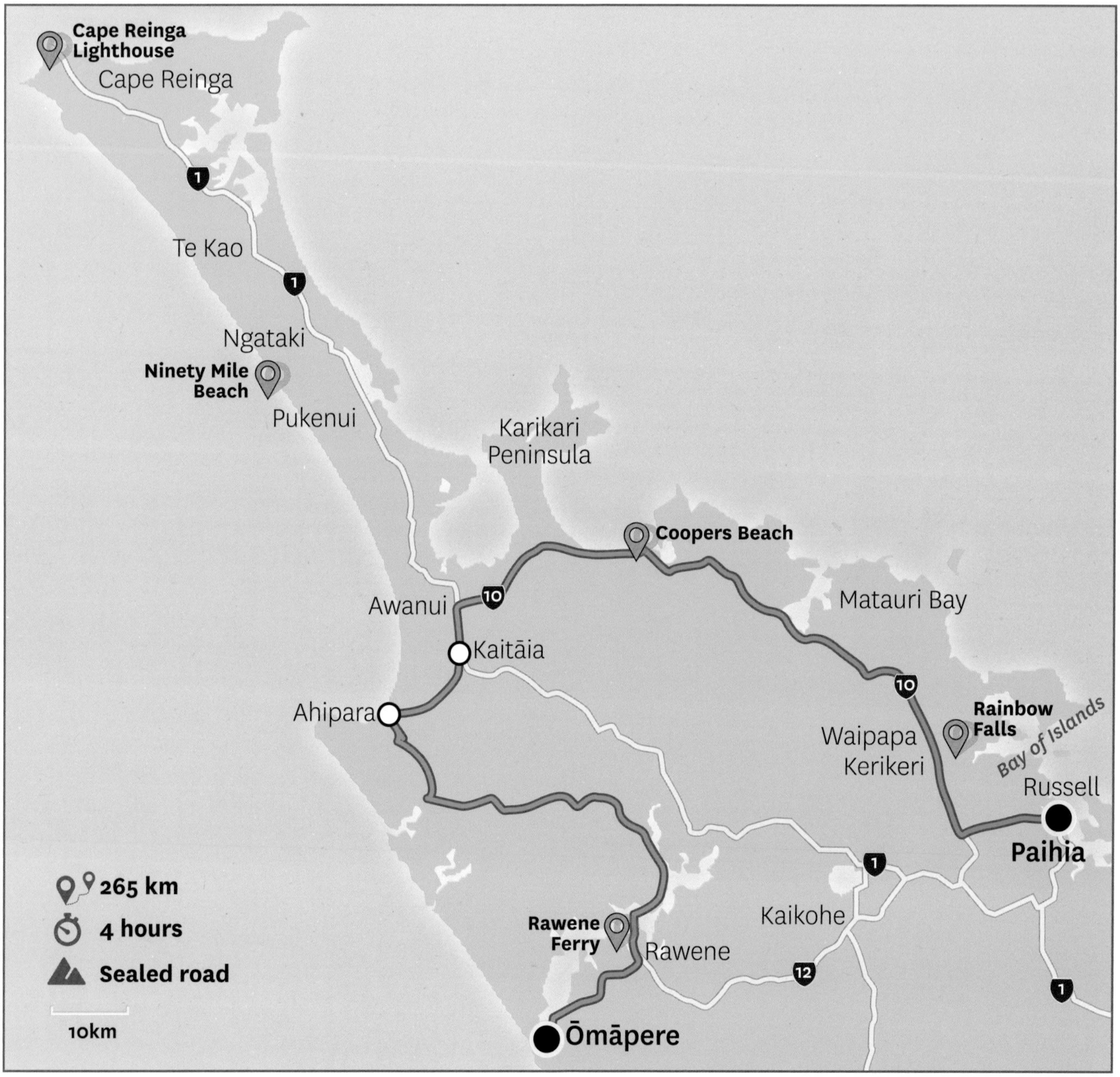

Route Overview

This journey to the far north begins at Ōmāpere, finishes at Paihia and can take anywhere between 3 to 5 hours depending on your speed and stops along the way. Enjoy over 200 plus kilometres of fantastic non-stop riding, or more if you decide to explore further taking one or more of the recommended detours.

The Far North District stretches between Hokianga Harbour, on the western side of the North Island, up to Cape Reinga at its most northerly tip, and across to the beautiful Bay of Islands on the eastern side. With minimal traffic and a total population of no more than 70,000 people, it's easy to see why this route is one of New Zealand's best motorcycle road trips.

This region is a paradise for boaties and hikers, with mile upon mile of intriguing coastline to explore, the most famous of which is Ninety Mile Beach that in fact stretches for only 58 miles from Ahipara to Scott Point.

Cape Reinga

This long stretch of golden sand offers superb fishing, breathtaking sunsets, and excellent waves for surfing. Other than suitable four-wheel drive vehicles and special tourist coach trips, there is limited access to this beach by vehicle.

Cape Reinga is the northernmost top of New Zealand's mainland and boasts a stunning coastal track that can be easily accessed from the main car park. Cape Reinga Lighthouse towers over the coast and looks down over a spiritually significant location for Māori, Spirits Bay. According to ancient Māori beliefs, this is the place where the spirits of all people who have passed gather in readiness for their final voyage back to their ancestors' land known as Hawaiki.

Head inland to find an equally appealing landscape of lush, rolling hillsides and native forest-clad mountains, all intertwined by a spiderweb of incredible biking roads encircled by two state highways that provide the perfect playground for motorcyclists. Temperatures in the far north are much warmer than the 'Deep South' with an almost subtropical climate. Cape Reinga lies almost parallel with Sydney, Australia so the climate is perfect for fruits such as avocados, kiwi fruit and citrus to grow.

The stunning Bay of Islands boasts over 140 completely unspoiled islands with multiple boat trips

Bay of Islands

departing from the main township of Paihia heading daily out to the iconic 'Hole in the Rock'. You will be spoilt for choice with activities in the area: scuba diving, fishing, snorkelling, nature cruises, and jet boating draw tourists year-round to this picture-perfect paradise.

European and American whalers first settled here around 1820 and Te Tiriti o Waitangi/The Treaty of Waitangi was signed in 1840, outlining the promise of protection for Māori by the British Crown. A visit to the Treaty Grounds at Paihia is well worth a visit to discover more about this prominent piece of New Zealand History.

Start Your Engines!

Fuel up at Ōmāpere before setting off in a northerly direction on State Highway 12. After crossing the Omanaia River, the Twin Coast Discovery Highway makes a left to Kohukohu via the Rawene Ferry.

Check out the **Detour to Paihia**, a shortcut across to the east coast.

The Rawene Vehicle Ferry boat only carries around 20 or so vehicles and takes a few minutes to cross the inlet, but it's well worth the interesting journey as it saves a lengthy long way round trip inland. When you disembark, follow the signs to continue on the Twin Coast Discovery Highway and enjoy waterside riding along the Hokianga Harbour following Kohukohu Road.

The roads here are relatively flat and offer fabulous sweeping corners to keep you entertained all the way to Herekino. The road then begins to steadily climb into Herekino forest. Enjoy the undulations of the road as you make your way north with native feather-like toetoe scattering the sides of the road as you fly by before arriving at Ahipara. This small seaside village is situated at the very southern tip of the famous Ninety Mile Beach.

The larger township of Kaitāia is a good place to top up the fuel tank. Follow the signs to State Highway 1 to continue along the Twin Coast Discovery Highway to Awanui. From here you can either turn right and join State Highway 10 or **check out the Detour to Cape Reinga** if you have the time.

Half an hour's ride from Awanui on a long straight you'll see a sign on your left to Matthews Vintage Collection. For any petrol heads and classic car enthusiasts, this museum collection houses an incredible display of old cars, tractors, stationary engines and other farming memorabilia.

The ride from Kaitāia to Paihia is only 117 km but you are spoilt with picture postcard views around every corner combined with undulating roads as well as tempting bays and beaches to stop at and discover along the way. Endless curves set the scene, ducking out every now and then for glimpses of Doubtless and Whangaroa Bays. Check out the **Detour to Matauri Bay** if you have the time.

The Twin Coast Discovery Highway now provides easy riding towards the stunning Bay of Islands. When reaching Waipapa, the Twin Coast Discovery Highway turns left at the roundabout and heads out to Kerikeri Inlet following the Heritage Bypass. On your right you will see the sign to Rainbow Falls, a beautiful short walk and one of the many scenic treats here in the Bay of Islands. Follow the sign to the Stone Store and park up in this stunning inlet with its heritage waterfront. Retrace your steps a little on your way out of Kerikeri and turn left to rejoin State Highway 10 to get you back on your way. Delightful riding through rolling farmland will bring you to the large roundabout at Puketona. The Twin Coast Discovery Highway to Paihia is clearly signposted left. Check out the Haruru Falls and the Waitangi Treaty Grounds via Haruru Falls Road before settling in at the subtropical golden beaches of Paihia. Check out the **Detour to Russell** if you have the time.

Biker-friendly stops along the way

Kohukohu Hotel — 1372 Kohukohu Road, Kohukohu 0491
North Drift Cafe, Ahipara — 250 Ahipara Road, Ahipara 0481
Matthews Vintage Collection — 4365 State Highway 10, Kaitāia 0483
Gumstore Bar & Grill — Totara North, 250 Totara North Road, Totara North 0479
Mussel Rock Cafe & Bar — Paihia, 75 Commerce Street, Kaitāia 0441
Duke of Marlborough Hotel, Russell — 35 The Strand, Russell 0202

Scenic highlights along the way

Rawene Ferry
Ninety Mile Beach
Sand Dunes
Cape Reinga
Cape Reinga Lighthouse
Coopers Beach
Rainbow Falls
Kerikeri Inlet
Haruru Falls

Why this is such a great ride

This excellent route provides uninterrupted riding with limited traffic and a variety of quality two-lane highways and narrow biking lanes. All topped off with a stunning selection of detours and bays at which to stop and stretch your legs and explore the picturesque perfection of the subtropical far north.

Detour 1

Rawene to Paihia Shortcut

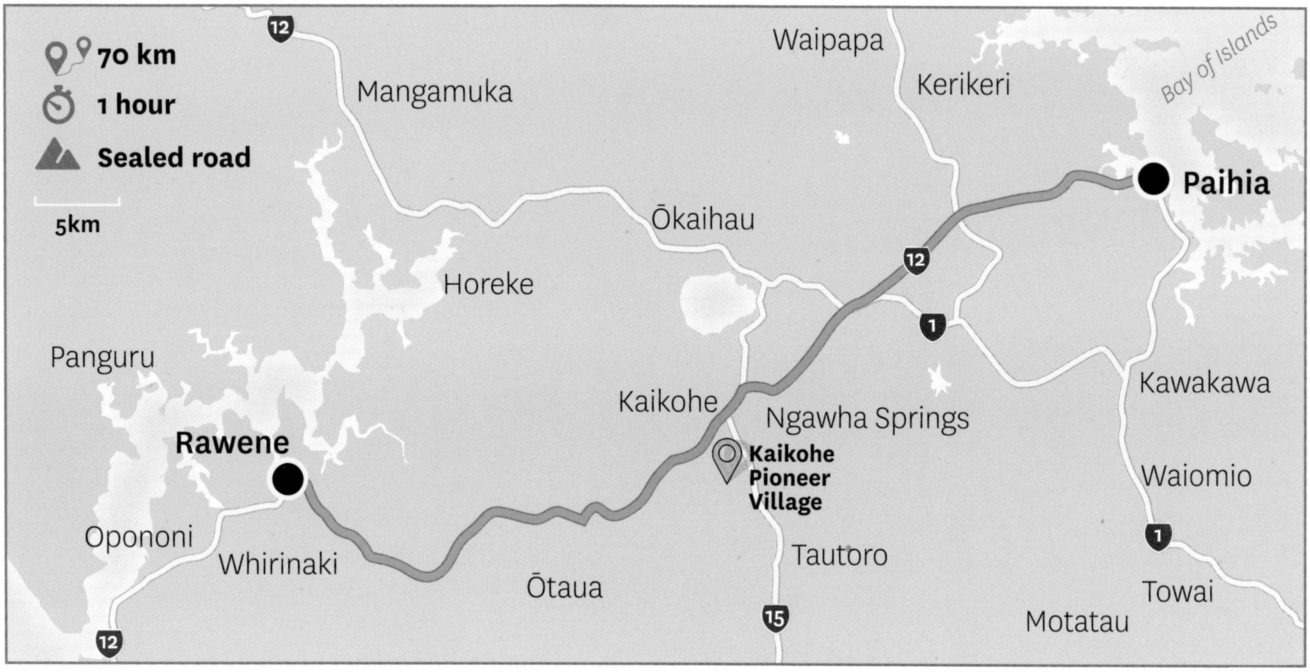

This is a good 'coast-to-coast' option if you are pressed for time and still want to check out the Bay of Islands.

Following State Highway 12 and 11 for most of the way, this route has fabulous uninterrupted riding the entire way. From Rawene to Kaikohe enjoy long sweeping bends and good visibility, little traffic, and no roundabouts or traffic lights to worry about. Kaikohe is the largest inland town of this region, but still relatively small with a population of approximately only 17,000 people. Grab a coffee at the local bakehouse and visit the replica Pioneer Village. When you reach Pakaraka, veer off left to follow signs to Kerikeri and State Highway 10 for more easy riding. After five minutes heading north, take the right turn on State Highway 11 until you reach the stunning east coast and Paihia.

Detour 2
Kaitāia to Cape Reinga Return

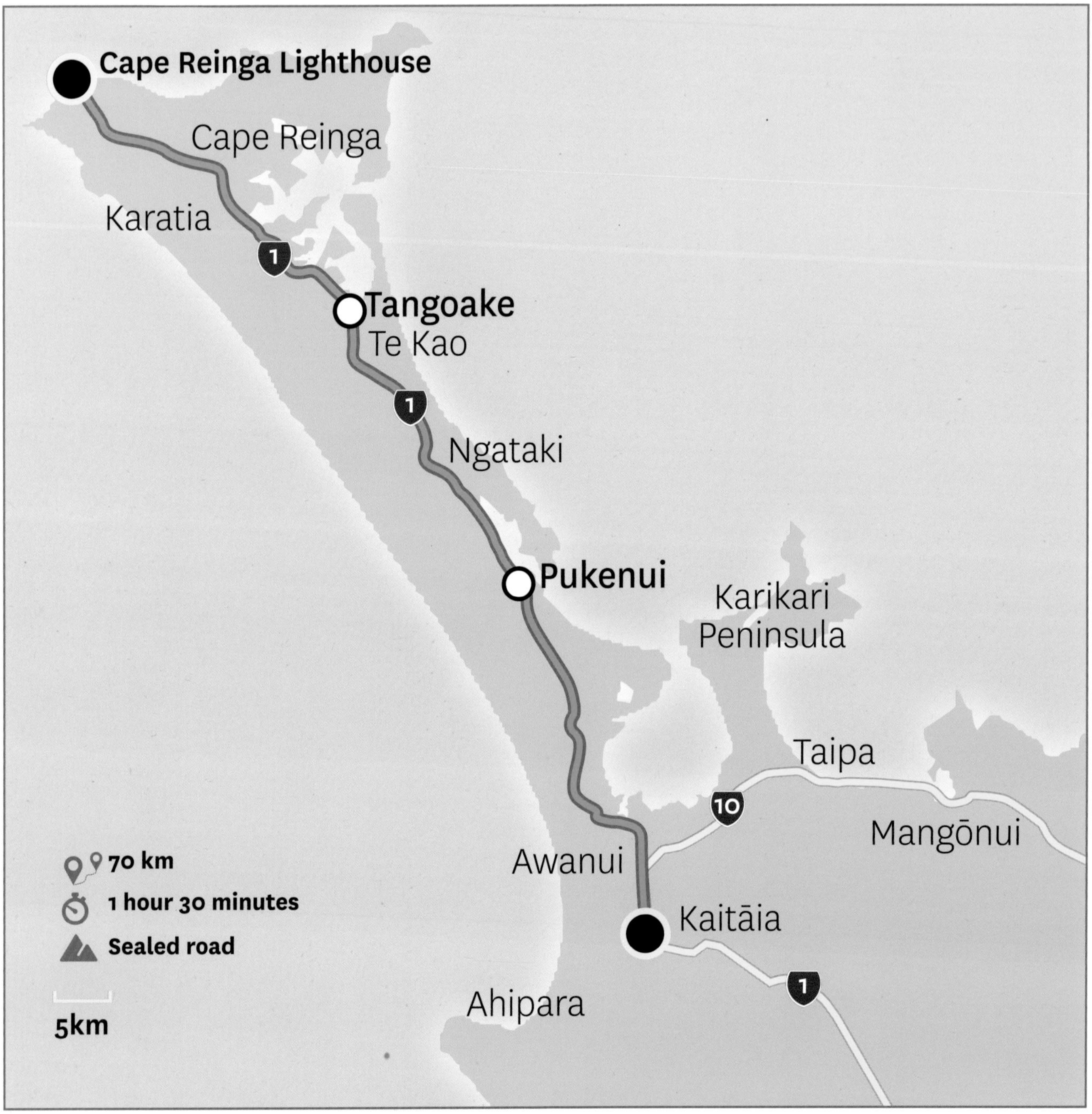

For many motorcyclists the trip up to Cape Reinga is a must-do pilgrimage. New Zealand's most northerly point where the Tasman Sea and Pacific Ocean collide. Fuel up before you leave Kaitāia as petrol stations are few and far between. The two-lane State Highway 1 is now fully tar sealed and the first 40 km between Kaitāia to Pukenui offers non-stop, long, sweeping bends through open farmland with fantastic views.

Take a break at Pukenui, nestled in the pretty Houhora Harbour before the adrenaline kicks in once more for the superb roller-coaster ride to the lighthouse.

Cape Reinga is packed with adventure and nature activities. Four-wheel drive adventures, sand dune surfing and incredible walkways mean you will be spoiled for choice on this detour.

A short walk from the Cape Reinga car park brings you to the iconic lighthouse and from here you can enjoy the most spectacular views of this wonderful northern coastline.

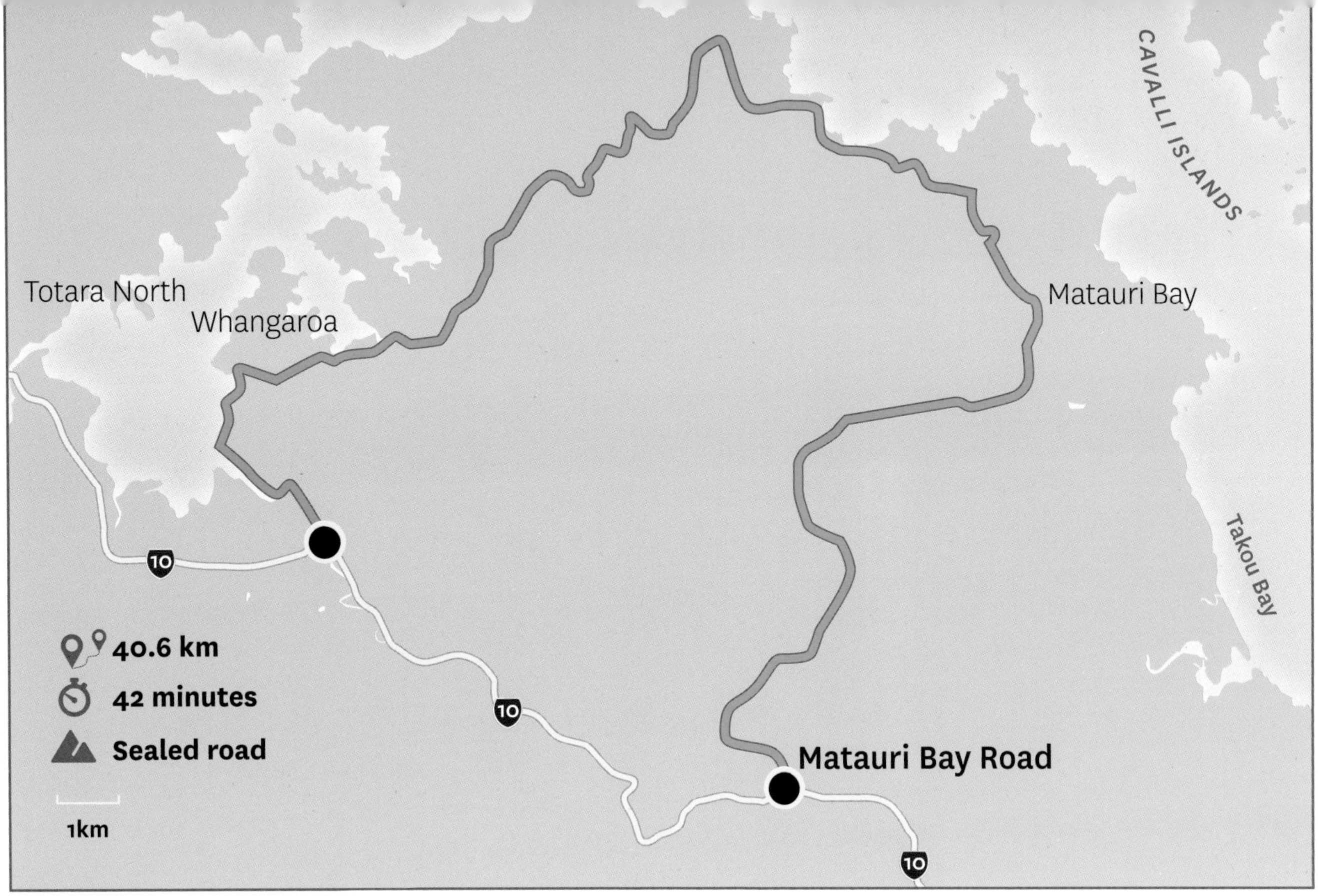

Detour 3
Matauri Bay Loop

This detour to Matauri Bay offers an extra boost of awesome riding in the far north. From Kaitāia, after 68 km, cross the Kaeo River, turn left to follow signs to Tauranga Bay along the Tourist Drive. Getting off the state highway allows you to extend your ride to enjoy over 40 km of uninterrupted riding over green hills and stopping at numerous bays and beaches along the way. Enjoy panoramic views looking towards the Cavalli Islands and grab a steak and cheese pie or hokey pokey ice-cream at one of the beachside cafes.

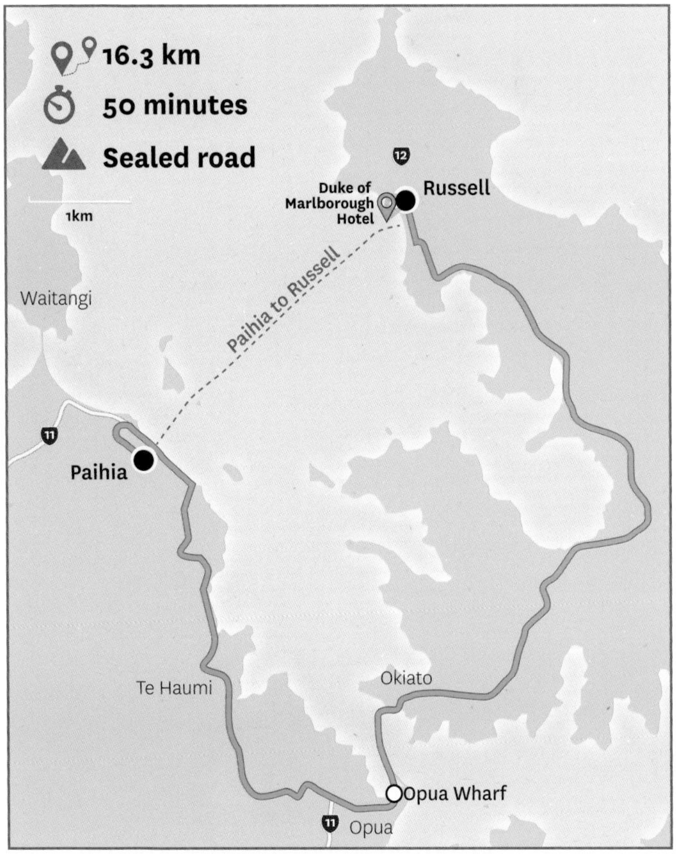

Detour 4
Paihia to Russell via the Opua Ferry

From Paihia continue south on the Twin Coast Discovery Highway along the beach and over the Haumi River. Within ten minutes you'll see signs to Opua Wharf. Take your motorcycle with you on to the ferry and enjoy the 20-minute boat ride across the Waikare Inlet to Okiato. Enjoy easy riding through evergreen native forests until you arrive at the historic township of Russell. Rich in history and dating back to 1843, Russell's street layout and street names are original, giving the whole town a colonial feel. The Duke of Marlborough Hotel, situated on the waterfront and dating back to 1827, provides visitors with excellent food, drink, and accommodation, and is the perfect detour destination.

3. The Coromandel Peninsula

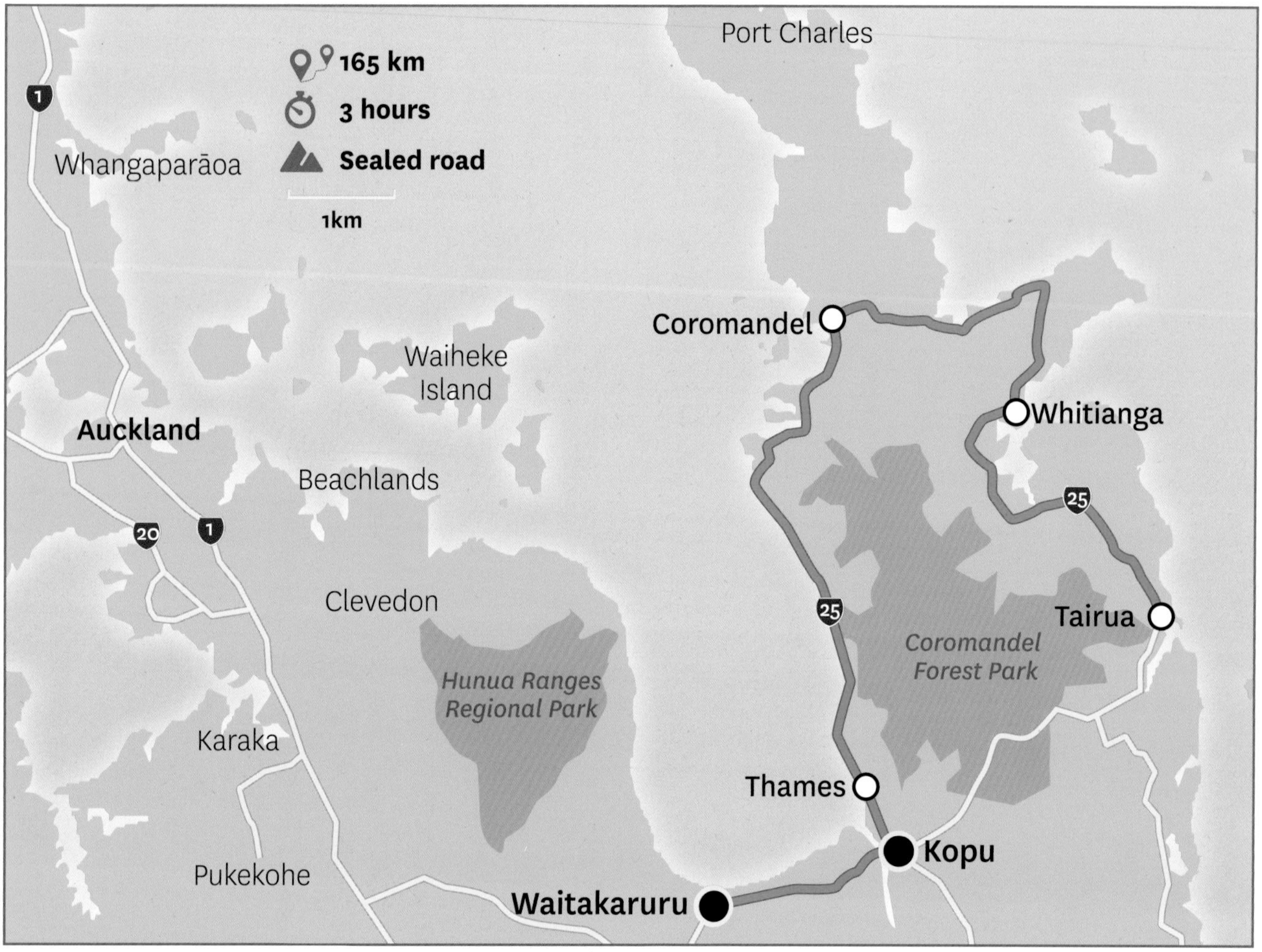

Route Overview

The Coromandel Peninsula ride will rank high on your top ride list and is a favourite destination for local bikers to saddle up and escape the hustle and bustle of Auckland. Within a few hours from the city this peninsula is a biker's paradise, with glorious white sand beaches, quaint coves, great fishing spots, and most importantly, superb biking lanes.

If you can spare a few days to explore Auckland before doing this loop, the village of Devonport is situated at the southern point of Auckland's North Shore and perfectly positioned to leave your bike behind and hop across the harbour via a 20-minute ferry crossing to Auckland's major hotspots. including the vibrant Viaduct Harbour and Sky Tower. Or you can take another ferry to one of the amazing nearby Hauraki Gulf islands including Waiheke, famous for its superb wineries, the volcano island of Rangitoto, or Mototapu, rich in cultural history and birdlife.

The Coromandel Peninsula is a popular destination for local holidaymakers who flock here in the summer to enjoy its quiet bays and soak up the natural beauty and peace of the coastline.

Upon the discovery of gold in 1852 Coromandel town quickly became popular, with the population ballooning to around 10,000 at the time. Today, with only around 1,700 inhabitants, the town has a bohemian feel about it with creative people being attracted to the tranquillity: artists, craftspeople and those looking for a more peaceful and alternative lifestyle.

The beautiful Coromandel Peninsula is Auckland's very own motorcycle mecca and can be accessed via the main motorways or by following the Pōhutukawa Coast from Auckland City, around Maraetai and the coastal bays and beaches, along East Coast Road.

Whitianga is a destination town for the locals looking for a beach or fishing holiday due to its sheltered bays and safe bathing areas. The explorer Kupe, from

Polynesia, apparently discovered this area calling it 'Te Whitianga-o-Kupe' meaning the 'crossing place of Kupe'. By the time Captain Cook first visited in 1769 there was a Māori settlement here with a most impressive Māori pā. There's a great little passenger ferry that takes you across the harbour to visit this historic landing site.

On beginning the Coromandel ride, this spectacular route is part of the Pacific Coast Highway which stretches along the entire east coast of the North Island. It has multiple roads which leave the main highway and take you to the many inlets and beaches.

Cathedral Cove and Hot Water Beach make for great detours to discover this geothermal landscape. Taking the time to explore these many offshoots of the Coromandel ride, you'll find yourself riding more fabulous roads, discovering some spectacular secluded bays on your way and enjoying one of the best motorcycle routes in New Zealand.

Start Your Engines!

From Waitakaruru follow State Highway 25 to Kopu, following signs to Thames and Coromandel Town. Top up the tank in Thames before embarking on this great Ride to make sure you aren't checking the fuel gauge every other second. Enjoy the following 54 km of ribbon road that winds its way along the Pacific Coast Highway hugging the waterline. Trees cascade down the cliffs and their branches reach out over the road, providing welcome shade on the hot summer days. Wind your way slowly around the bays at water level before reaching Wilsons Bay, where the road begins to climb up and into the hills to the Manaia Road Saddle and Lookout before snaking its way back down. These undulations make for great riding as you continue through to the peninsula's main township and route namesake of Coromandel.

This pretty seaside town boasts great cafes and quirky little shops with heritage storefronts, galleries and coastal walking tracks as well as the Driving Creek Railway which attracts tourists and locals alike. It's easy to see why this is a favourite biker's destination along such a fantastic riding route and is well worth the stop.

As you leave Coromandel town, the road begins to climb again into the lush tree-covered hills of the Maraetotara Reserve. Overlooking the peninsula, riding beside native ponga, and with totara dotting the canopy, enjoy 50 km of excellent serpentine and hairpin bends on well-maintained roads which are a true joy to ride.

Continue along State Highway 25 and you will come to the flat of Warekaho/Simpsons Beach before the view of Mercury Bay appears on your left and you ride in to Whitianga. Follow the road ahead to Whitianga Wharf to check out this harbourside town. Whitianga is a great halfway location to stop if you want to split up this trip into two days as well.

Further south of Whitianga there are a few detours for fabulous well-known activities and attractions such as Cathedral Cove and Hot Water Beach. Check out the **Detour to Hahei and Hot Water Beach** if you have the time. Hot Water Beach is famous for its thermal waters. Dig your own bathing hole in the sand and enjoy a soak in the heated seawater. Or pre-book a scenic boat cruise to Cathedral Cove if you are wanting to explore this beautiful landscape by sea. The cove is an impressive rock archway that juts out from the sandy beach of the Te Whanganui-A-Hei Marine Reserve.

Continue south and enjoy a further hour of spectacular riding alongside the Tairua River inlet.

Biker-friendly stops along the way

Minos Mussel Kitchen, Coromandel — 309 Road, Preece Point, Coromandel 3581
Stoked Restaurant & Bar, Whitianga — 19 Esplanade, Whitianga 3510
Coroglen Tavern, Whitianga — 1937 Tairua Whitianga Road, Coroglen 3591
Colenso Country Café & Gift Shop Whenuakite — 895 State Highway 25, Whenuakite 3591

Scenic highlights along the way

Driving Creek Railway
Cathedral Cove, Whitianga
Hot Water Beach

Why this is such a great ride

Well-known by local riders as the great escape from the city of Auckland. This ride takes in fabulous sweeping roads with oceanside riding and dotted with small-town charm all the way around the peninsula.

Whitianga

Coromandel curves

Detour 1

Hahei Beach/Cathedral Cove/Hot Water Beach

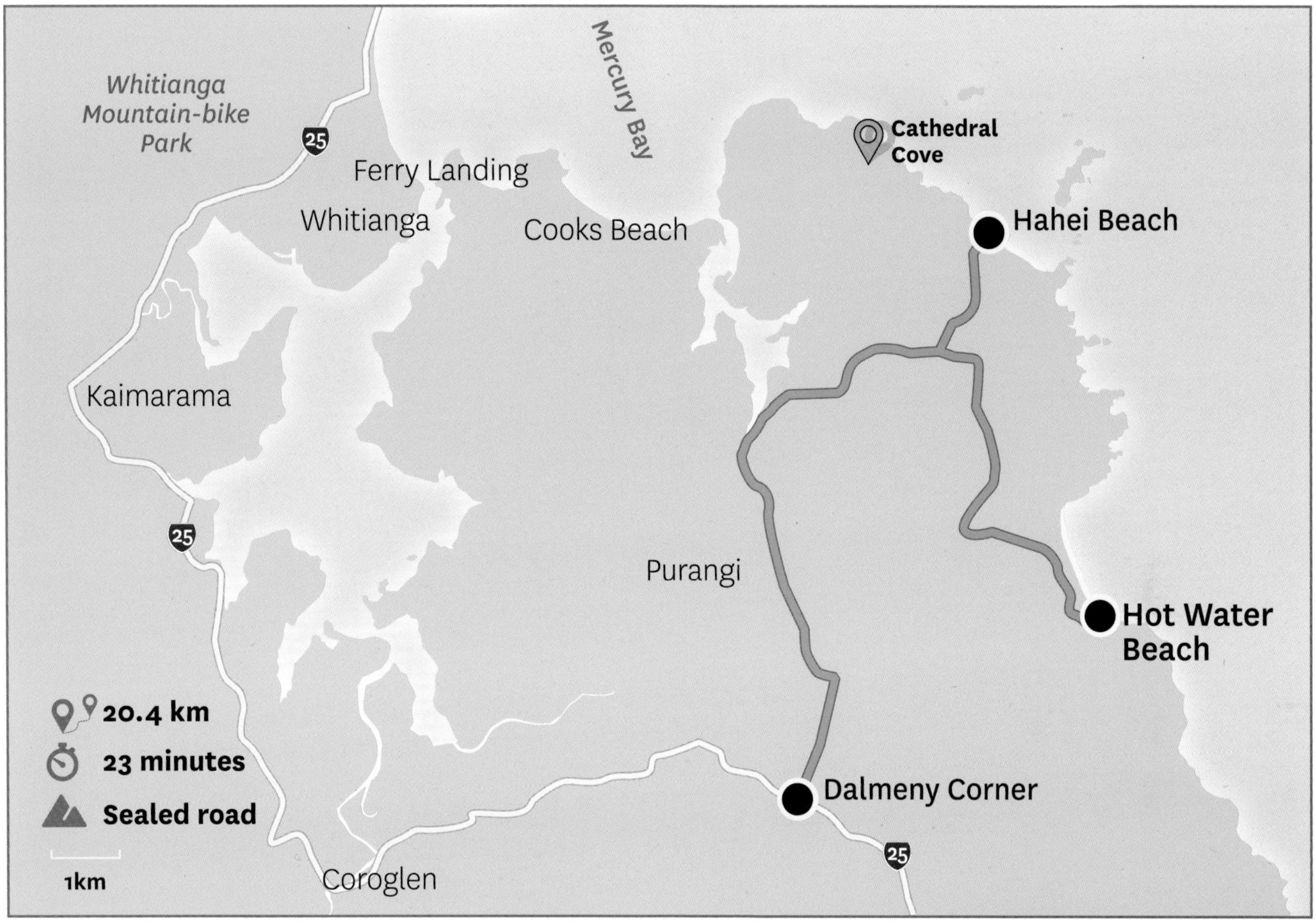

Heading along State Highway 25 in a southerly direction, take the Hot Water Beach Road turn-off to Hahei/Hot Water Beach. To visit Cathedral Cove and Hahei Beach first, turn left at the sign to Cooks Beach and follow Hahei Road all the way to the main seafront. You can book boat cruises from here to see Cathedral Cove and surrounding spectacular bays, take out a kayak to explore at your own pace, or simply relax at the edge of the ocean in paradise.

Meeting back up with Link Road on your way out of Hahei Beach, follow the sign to turn left to Hot Water Beach. A short walk along the beachfront will bring you to one of New Zealand's favourite unique, natural, and free attractions. The sand on top of the beach happens to be above two freshwater springs, thermally heated from below, so the seawater is like soaking in a hot bath.

At low tide, you can hire a bucket and spade and find yourself a spot on the beach. Start digging and low and behold, you have your own open-air natural thermal hot spring. A great detour to stop and relax if you have the time.

Relaxing at the Coroglen Tavern

4. Thermal Explorer Highway

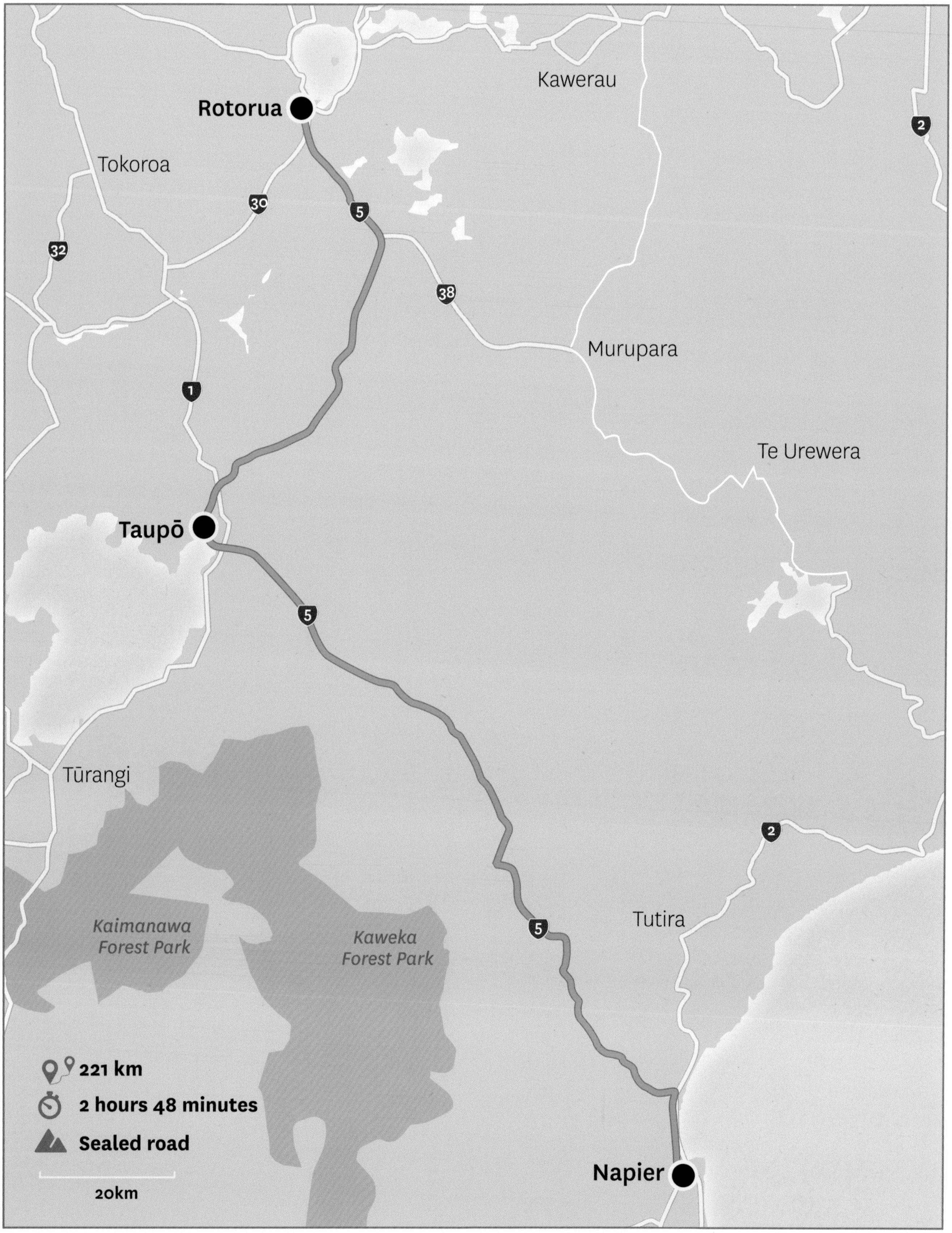

Tongariro National Park

Route Overview

The Thermal Explorer Highway is named for its route through the breathtaking geothermal and volcanic landscapes that make up the unique panorama of Te Ika-a-Māui, the North Island. Stretching from Napier on the lower east coast to Auckland, this road trip takes in half of the highway and has lots of optional detours to extend or adapt your trip along the way.

The artdeco city of Napier is located in the spectacular Hawke's Bay Region. Surrounded by world-renowned wineries, and considered an architecturally and historically significant location in New Zealand's history, makes Napier a great place to start this route. Alternatively, if you're coming down from the north it's easy to start from either end and join up to others.

Following a large earthquake that rocked the city in 1931, Napier was rebuilt in the fabulous art deco style of the time, and this seaside resort town now boasts colourful, charismatic Great Gatsby style buildings which draw locals and tourists alike.

The flat, low-lying hills and plains of Hawke's Bay are covered with award winning vineyards which thrive in the temperate climate. The further north and inland you travel, the landscape morphs into a mountainous geothermal wonderland and the region is a prime example of how natural forces shaped the landscape into what we see today. Historically, Māori utilised these forces, and the area is culturally significant. Tours and excursions are available to learn more about this rich geothermal environment and how it has changed through the ages.

Lake Taupō is the largest lake in New Zealand and is located in the middle of the North Island. The remnants of volcanic craters, the lake is a caldera (collapsed volcano) and spans 46 km, 237 sq mi. This vast expanse of water attracts those looking to enjoy recreational water-based activities and surrounding geothermal landscapes, as well as experiencing incredible ancient contemporary Māori rock carvings at Mine Bay which can only be accessed by boat or kayak.

Riding around Lake Taupō and further will take you along the Volcanic Loop Highway, through the Desert Road and Tongariro National Park, and around Mount Ruapehu; an active volcano which attracts outdoor enthusiasts all year round, with activities such as snow sports, hiking, fishing, and cycling to name a few. Riding this detour will give you unrivalled viewing of this incredible peak with it's towering presence which dominates the landscape for miles.

Heading north from Taupō, through the Bay of Plenty region, Huka Falls showcases the power of nature and attracts thrill seekers with its jet boat and whitewater rafting activities. Rotorua is renowned for its incredible preservation of Māori culture and is a premier tourist destination. With bubbling mud pools, steaming geysers, lunar landscapes, towering trees, adventure activities, rejuvenating treatments, and outstanding natural beauty, Rotorua is not to be missed.

Start Your Engines!

Leaving Napier, head north to follow State Highway 2 and the Pacific Coast Highway for a short time before veering left on to State Highway 5, following signs to Taupō and Rotorua. You are now on the Thermal Explorer Highway and one of the great touring routes of New Zealand.

As you head inland through Hawke's Bay, long sweeping bends snake through rolling hills and countryside, perfect for enjoying both the ride and scenery at the same time. As you pass through vineyards, orchards and small towns, the road climbs into the hills and snakes through lush livestock dotted pastures with crystal clear streams. With views reminiscent of Hobbiton, in *The Lord of The Rings* movies, it is easy to see why Peter Jackson chose the North Island as a location for his world-class films.

These roads are a joy to ride and, with multiple passing lanes along the way, you won't be stuck behind campervans or trucks for very long.

When you reach Te Hāroto, the speed limit drops down to 80 km and the tree-lined road eventually cuts its way through stone cliff with a slight descent. It pays to be vigilant here and watch for small slips and rockfalls which may wash gravel and scree into the road. Keep an eye out for signs showing the speed changes as this route also has a high crash rate.

Enjoy the endless kilometres of emerald hillside undulations and perfect bends all the way through the Eastern Bay of Plenty to the Central Plateau. The environment changes to rows of radiata pine trees, with forestry being the main export of this area. Eventually finding signs of civilisation you'll view Lake Taupō on the horizon. Check out the **Detour to the Volcanic Loop** if you have the time.

Follow signs to Taupō **along Napier Road** and head for the lakefront along Lake Terrace. The azure blue of New Zealand's largest lake stretches out in front of you. There are numerous cafes and accommodation options along this picturesque waterfront, and in the main town centre, making it a great stopover option. Natural geothermal landscapes can be accessed from multiple walks around the area if you have time to explore.

If you're riding on through, continue to follow the road around and over the Waikato River on Wairakei Drive. Huka Falls is a great place to watch the power of the Waikato River in action, as it thunders over an 11 m high waterfall. Thrill seekers can take an action-filled ride on a jet boat and get up close to this impressive natural wonder. Just take the right turn on to Huka Falls Road all the way to the car park at the end. The road eventually meets back up with Wairakei Road so you can continue on your way.

Joining up with State Highway 5, follow signs to Rotorua to continue on the Thermal Explorer Highway up and over the rolling hills once again for another 40 km. Signs to Waiotapu Thermal Wonderland may pique your interest and is well worth the turn-off to check out the volcanic zone of New Zealand in more detail. Free to enter, there are various short walks and viewing areas to experience this surreal local landscape with its craters, sulphur vents, geysers and steaming pools.

Riding on, you'll come to the outskirts of Whakarewarewa Forest Park with its incredible towering Redwoods. The distinct sulphur smell in the air will signify your arrival in Rotorua. Check out the **Detour around Lake Rotorua** if you have the time.

Biker-friendly stops along the way

Cafe Baku, Taupō — 42 Roberts Street, Taupō, 3330
Pig & Whistle Historic Pub, Rotorua — 1182 Tutanekai Street, Rotorua, 3010

Scenic highlights along the way

Lake Taupō
Huka Falls
Craters of The Moon
Waiotapu Thermal Wonderland
Te Puia
The Redwoods, Whakarewarewa Forest
Rotorua Lakes, Lake Tarawera, Lake Rotoiti

Why this is such a great riding route

Riding one of the great tourist routes in New Zealand means you experience the best parts of this magical country. This road is well maintained and has long, sweeping bends that makes riding a joy. With fabulous destinations to break up the ride, as well as numerous exciting detours boasting more incredible riding, means you are spoilt for choice.

Detour 1

Volcanic Loop Highway/Tongariro National Park

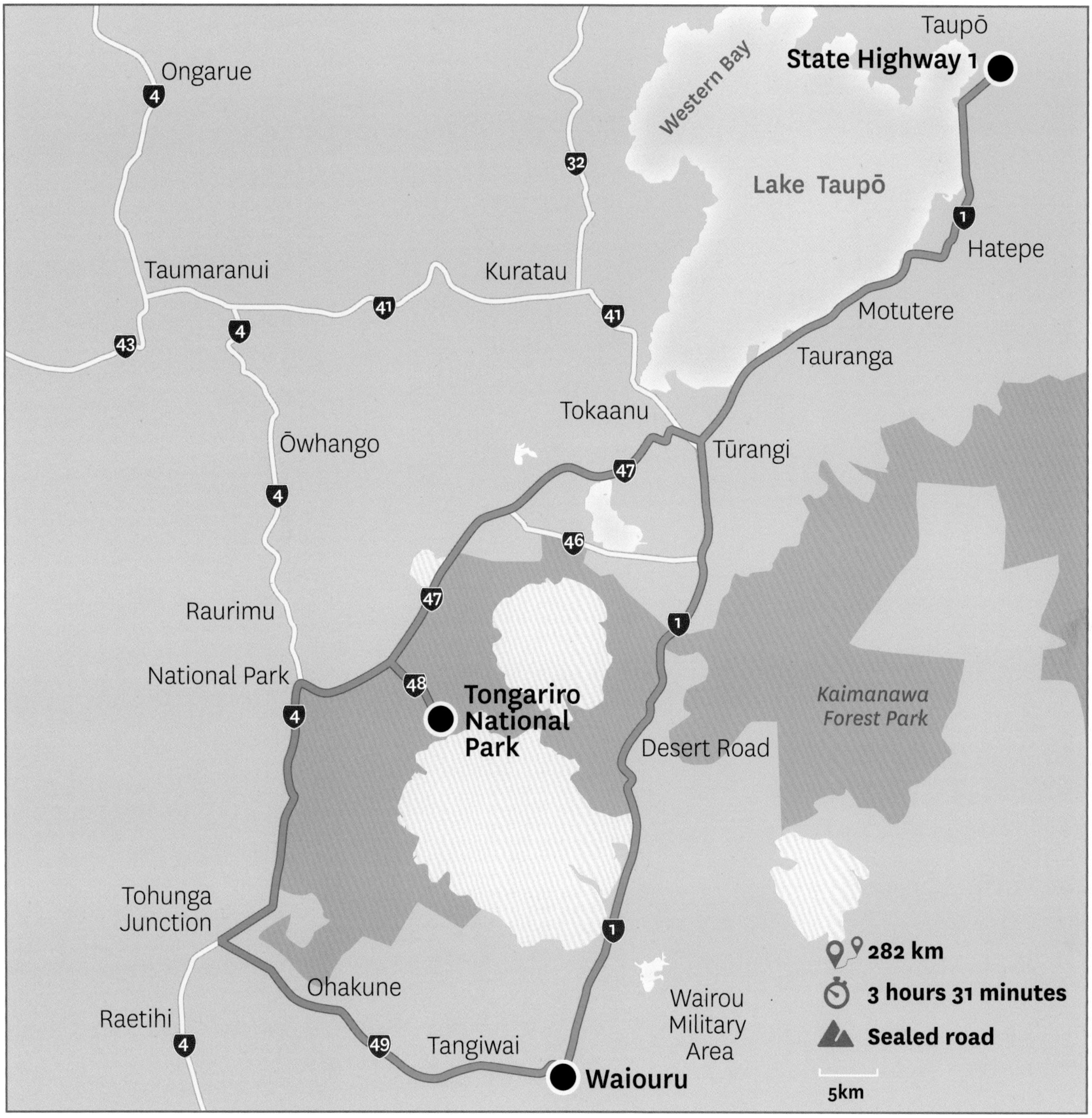

This detour takes in the incredible North Island Volcanic Plateau. The loop ride skirts beside the caldera of Lake Taupō and continues on to encircle Tongariro National Park and Mount Ruapehu.

As part of the 'Pacific Ring of Fire', New Zealand's volcanic activity is a constant source of fascination and Mount Ruapehu is the largest active volcano in New Zealand. Following State Highway 1, through the remote twists of the alpine terrain and over Desert Road, to see Mount Tongariro and then Mount Ruapehu emerge to your right; the ever-present watchers in the distance as you ride through vast tussock-covered landscape. Turn right at Waiōuru and follow signs to Ohakune National Park to take in the southern view of Mount Ruapehu. At Tohunga Junction turn right to take State Highway 4 to National Park. Further along the ride, if you are wanting to get closer to the Volcano, State Highway 47 then 48 will take you to the Tongariro National Park Visitor Centre and options to explore this incredible area. A haven for snow sports in the winter months, tourists flock here to make

Relaxing in Rotorua

Towards Taupō

the most of some of the best ski fields New Zealand has to offer State Highway 47 continues around and the road climbs back into the mountains and snakes its way to join up with Highway 41 then State Highway 1 in Tūrangi where you will loop to head back in to Rotorua.

Detour 2

Lake Rotorua Loop

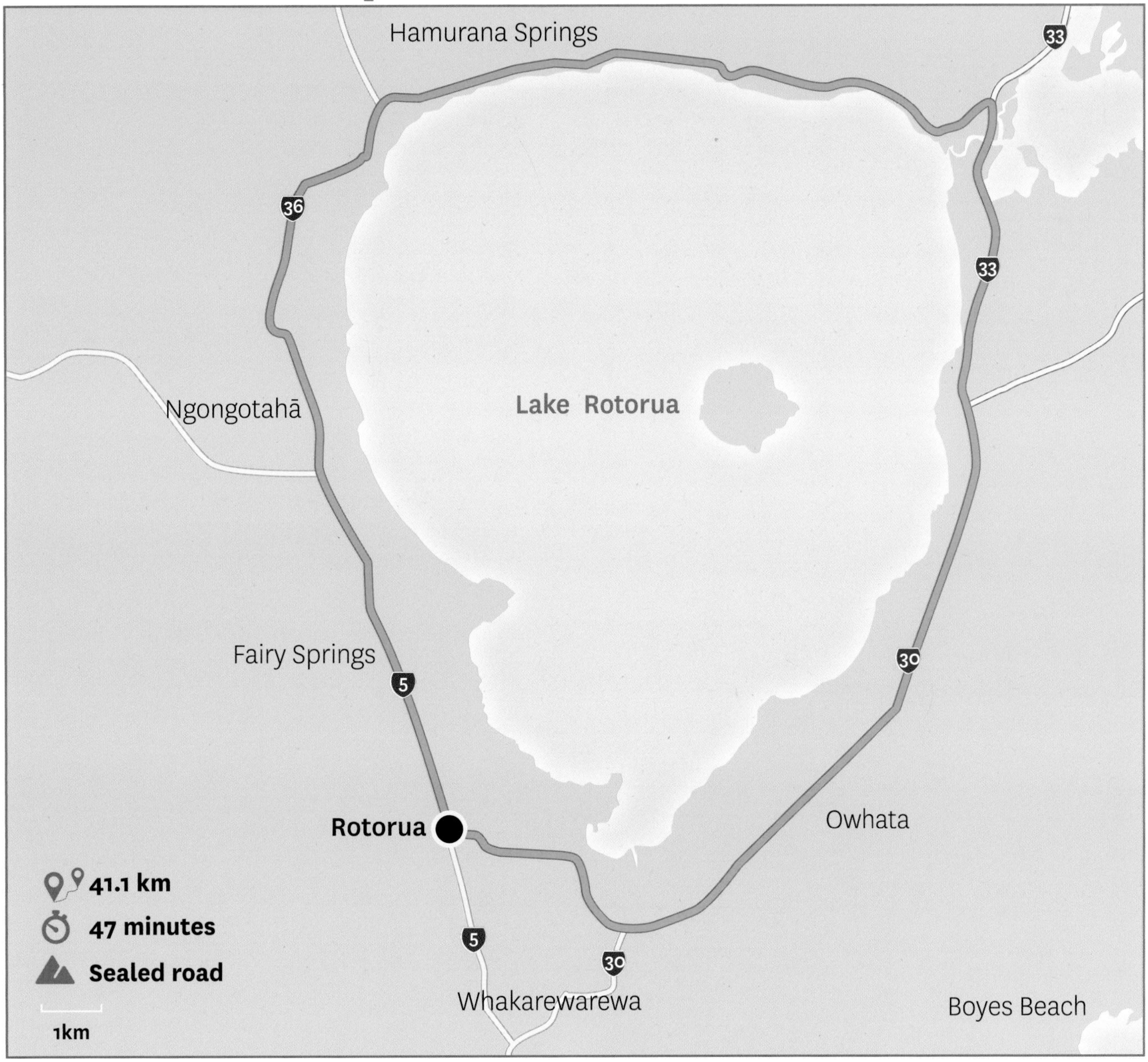

This picturesque loop ride skirts the waterside of Lake Rotorua and its surrounding towns. Heading north to follow State Highway 5, you will see numerous signs for activities and excursions to tempt everyone. From relaxing mud pools, to hurtling yourself down a hill in a plastic bubble, Rotorua boasts an array of fantastic treats for tourists, and the surrounding roads are a joy for riding and exploring. After approximately 7 km outside of town, continue along the lake to follow State Highway 36 to Hamurana. After a long, sweeping bend, the speed drops to 80 km and the road continues around to the right along Hamurana Road, where the speed drops again to 60 km. Hamurana Reserve is a great place to stop and look out across the lake to Rotorua from the opposite side. Hamurana Road continues to snake around the top of the lake until meeting up with State Highway 33 where you turn right to follow the signs back to Rotorua.

5. The Forgotten World Highway

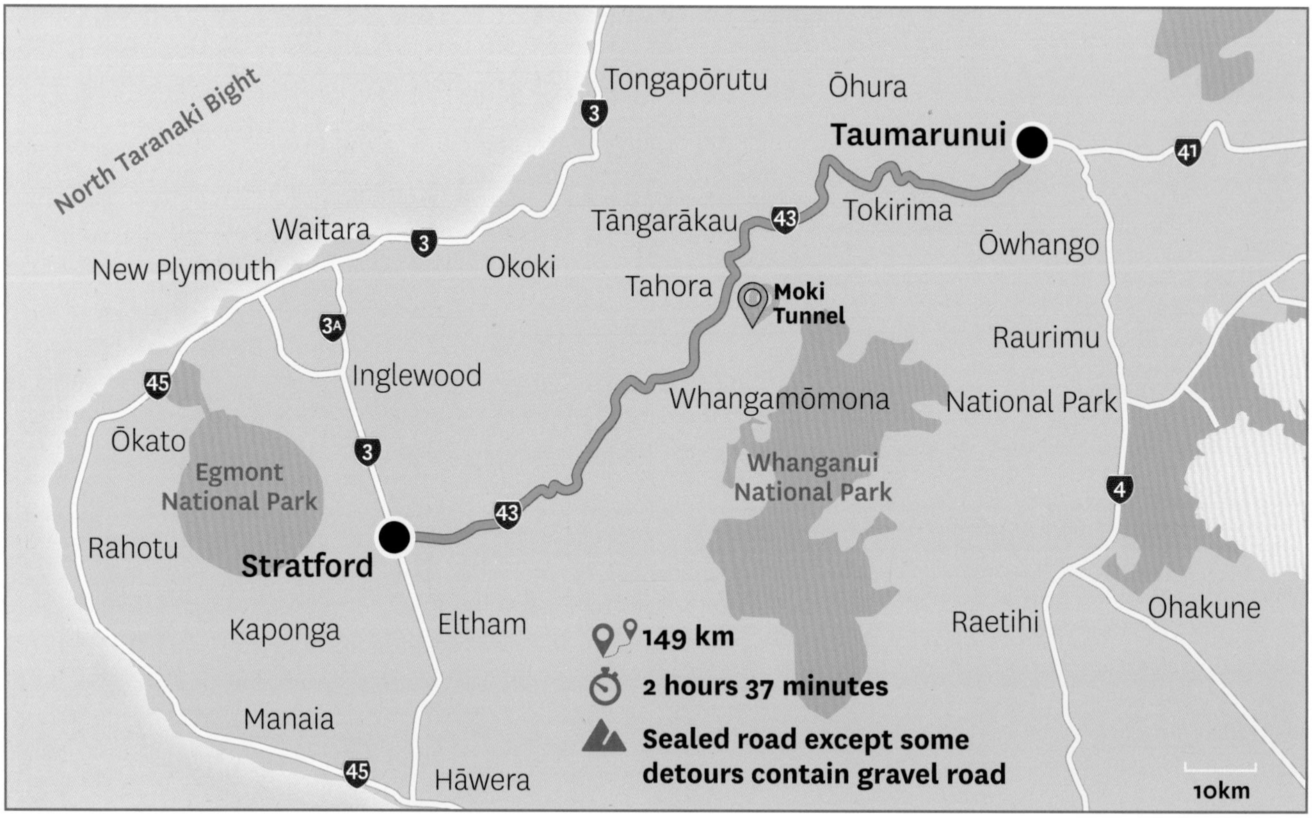

Route Overview

Imagine a biker's paradise with no sign of civilisation, endless rolling green hills, twists and bends and all topped off with a magnificent volcano being your starting point. This is the Forgotten World Highway and it feels like exactly that — a forgotten world. Rainforests of Jurassic-like tree ferns shelter the road as you pass, gigantic gorges, beech-covered ridge tops, canyons and gushing waterfalls are all ribbon wrapped with a road that must have been made in motorcycle heaven.

The Highway is nothing short of magical for the motorcyclist keen for adventure and a challenge, and the road is often referred to as one of the most scenic rides in the world. Following the lines of an old bridle path from pioneering days the road was all but abandoned. In early 2000 it was deemed a State Highway and renamed The Forgotten World Highway due to the wild and remote nature of the landscape. The road was relatively dangerous with no passing lanes, no services, and old tunnels and wooden bridges in disrepair. Approximately 12 km of the highway was still unsealed too, creating a muddy and hazardous route in wet weather conditions, but things have changed. The New Zealand Government finally announced provision of funding to the New Zealand Transport Agency, Waka Kotahi, to embark upon a two-year upgrade to repair and fully seal the Highway, making it safer for the locals, more accessible for tourists, and more importantly an excellent road for riding.

Starting this route in Stratford, this small town is situated in the shadows of Mount Taranaki on its eastern slopes. The town was named after William Shakespeare's birthplace, Stratford-upon-Avon, in England, and today you can see many street names and areas also dedicated to Shakespeare and his characters. One of these is the Clock Tower situated on Broadway. A unique landmark built in the 1990s from which Romeo and Juliet emerge from small doors on the tower and re-enact Shakespearean scenes with recordings of the famous balcony scene.

Egmont National Park is a great place to explore before this trip if you have the time. The Park includes Mount Taranaki, also known as Mount Egmont, and was named by Captain Cook in honour of his patron, the Earl of Egmont. Mount Taranaki is a dormant volcano

Mount Taranaki

and has been erupting every few hundred years on a regular basis for the last several million years. At just over 2,500 m high this colossal, natural landmark is a sight to behold. A perfectly formed 'stratovolcano' with a perfect cone that is often dusted with snow of various depths, depending on the seasons.

Midway along this route, and the best place to stop for a break, is Whangamōmona. This town has a very interesting history; in 1988 the New Zealand Government decided to change the district boundary, splitting the town into two regions. The lack of consultation with residents caused an uproar and resulted in the locals announcing their independence completely from the rest of the country. They declared themselves a Republic and elected themselves as president. This very unusual event is, to this day, celebrated every other January with a 'Republic Day' festival. The little town swells in size with those wishing to participate in such frivolities as gumboot throwing, shooting, and possum skinning, and to hear about who, or what, will be the next 'president'. In the past this has been a goat, a poodle, and even a turtle.

A great highlight of The Forgotten World Highway is Moki Tunnel, usually the poster picture for tourism for the entire route. This gothic-style tunnel was completed in 1936 and like all the other tunnels in this area, was dug out by hand using pickaxes and shovels. Originally the tunnel was only five metres tall, and in 1989 the tunnel floor needed to be lowered to create a more manageable height of seven metres. Until 2022 the gorge was unsealed and a real talking point amongst discerning motorcyclists as to whether or not the highway should be ridden at all, due to the fact that in poor weather conditions this stretch of road was earmarked as one of the most dangerous roads in New Zealand, with no road markings or safety barriers,

Whangamomona Hotel

and very muddy if wet. Today it is fully tar sealed with good road markings providing an excellent route for all motorists and cyclists alike.

The Forgotten World Highway is just 150 km long but will take you a good three hours to navigate, so allow yourself plenty of time for this ride. The isolation of this route allows for very little activities and attractions along the way so make sure your tank is full before you head off. Taumaranui translates roughly to 'place of abundant shade' in Māori and marks the end of the Forgotten World Highway where it meets up with the 'Adventure Highway' of State Highway 4. This town provides a good base to continue your journey in any direction.

Head north to the Hobbit-style lands of Waitomo, south to explore the mountains of the volcanic Central Plateau, or east to Lake Taupō and the geothermal wonderlands around Rotorua.

Start Your Engines!

The isolation of this road needs mentioning again. Before starting off, make sure you are well prepared and the tank is full. There's absolutely nothing along this route for most of the trip until you reach Whangamōmona, except for completely unspoiled natural scenic beauty and an awesome road packed to the gunnels with twists and bends to keep the adrenaline pumping for many a mile.

In some places, visibility is limited due to the thick native forest that lines the road. Tight hairpins that lead up and around high gorges will mean taking your time and reading the road conditions.

Heading in an easterly direction from Stratford, following State Highway 43, enjoy a good half an hour of pleasant, easy riding through the hills and dairy farmlands, until you begin the climb up and around the fabulous sweeping bends of the Strathmore Saddle.

This route is also well known for having plenty of narrow scenic tunnels and bridges along the way, perfect for that all important photo shoot. At Strathmore you will see the sign to Mākāhu. Check out the **Detour to the Makahu Tunnel** if you have time to see one of these historic engineering marvels.

For the next 30 km, riding up and over firstly the Pohokura Saddle, where the road is cut into the limestone cliff with vegetation packed with ferns, trees and roots clinging onto the rocky outcrops as you pass. Followed by the Whangamōmona Saddle. The scenic viewpoint at Whangamōmona is a great place to stop and read about the trials and tribulations of the first

settlers who dug out the track back in the 1880s.

The grin will widen on your face as the road twists and winds its way up to 270 m above sea level. This fabulous serpentine road is magnificent, and as you descend, the tight hairpins will keep you on your toes.

Your reward for successful navigation is a refreshment at Whangamōmona. The Whangamomona Hotel is a favourite biker's watering hole here, so park up for some good food and coffee, and step inside to look around at all the memorabilia that decorates the walls. The grand old lady is one of many historic 'hotels' dotted around New Zealand that have been lovingly restored to provide refreshment and accommodation. The original hotel burned down in 1911. the one still standing today was built in 1912 and now well-loved amongst the motorcycle fraternity as she's always a welcome sight after so many kilometres of isolation.

Climbing up the Tahora Saddle you are treated to breathtaking scenic views. On a clear day, the volcanoes of Taranaki to the east, and the Tongariro National Park to the west are quite visible, providing a spectacular sight.

When you first approach the narrow, arch-shaped hole of Moki Tunnel, it may seem like even you and your motorbike might be too large to get through, but as you draw closer it's evident that there's no other way. Also referred to as the 'Hobbit's Hole' this tunnel is a highlight of the Forgotten World Highway and, at 180 m long with no lights and a single lane, headlights are a must.

Emerging from the Moki Tunnel continue for eight kilometres and look for the signs to Joshua Morgan's Grave, taking a very short walk through dense bush to see his tomb that lies next to the Tangarakau Stream. This is a memorial to the pioneers who dug out the Forgotten World Highway with their bare hands back in the 1890s.

The last hour of this ride, from the Tāngarākau Gorge to Taumaranui, entails nothing but you, your motorbike, the long and winding road that twists and bends its way between the ponga tree ferns and native beech of the stunning New Zealand wilderness. The challenging hairpins make another appearance to give you another boost of adrenaline before the Whanganui River appears to your right and escorts you in to your destination of Taumaranui. From here you can follow the 'Adventure Highway' of State Highway 4, north or south, depending on which adventure you choose next.

Check out the **Detour to Waitomo Caves** via the Adventure Highway, State Highway 4.

Detour 1

Strathmore to Makahu Tunnel

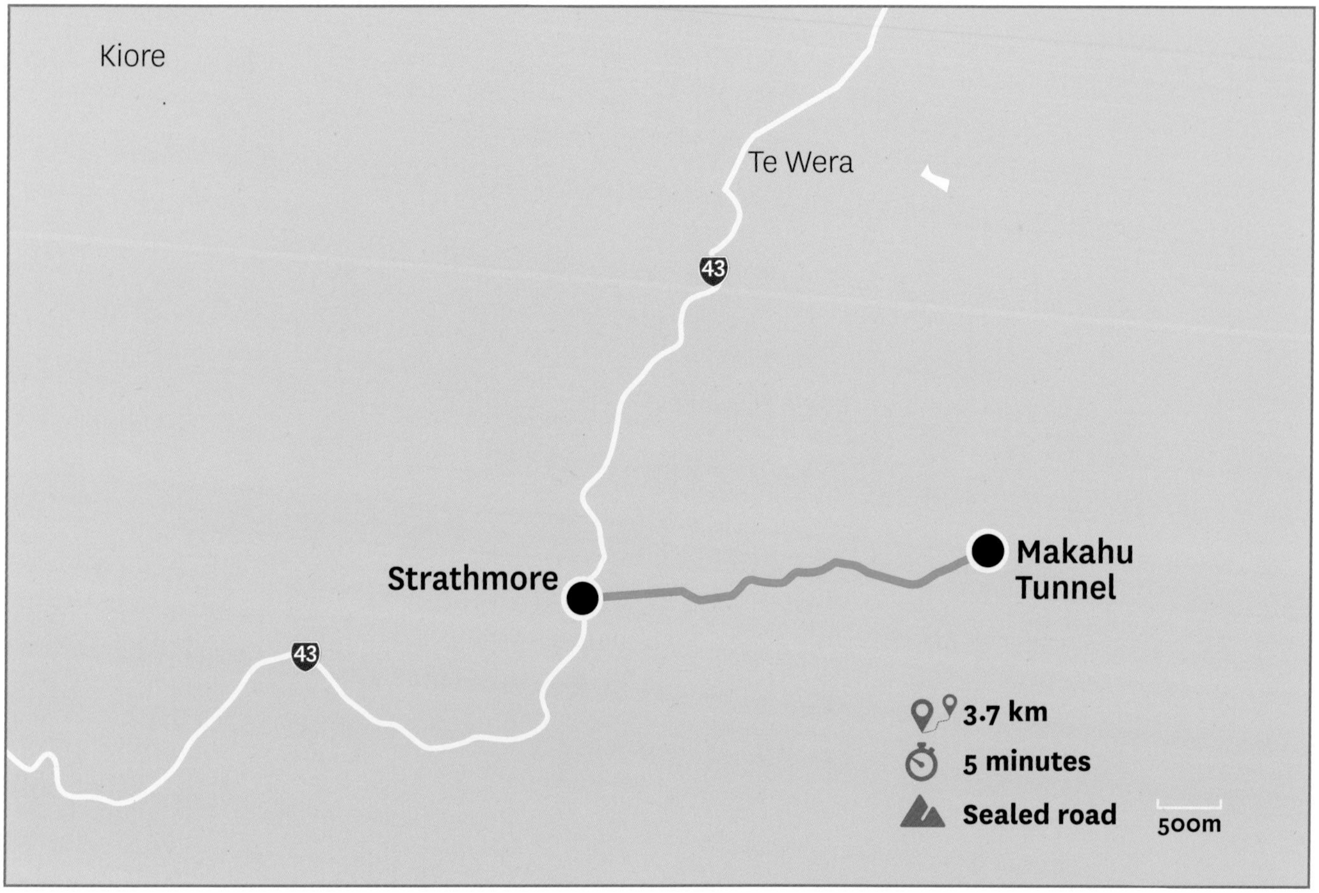

After about half an hour from Stratford you arrive at Strathmore. Turn left and ride for 4 km to the Makahu Tunnel, one of ten built by the pioneers of yesteryear, all dug by hand with pickaxes and shovels.

This tunnel was originally built in 1907 to make life easier for the thriving community here trying to earn a living by carting their dairy produce through to Strathmore. The wooden tunnel collapsed and was replaced in 1921 with sturdy concrete pillars.

Biker-friendly stops along the way

The Whangamomona Hotel — 6018 Ohura Road, Whangamōmona, 4396
Lauren's Lavender Farm, Café & Store — 1381 River Road, State Highway 43, 3991

Scenic highlights along the way

The Tāngarākau Gorge
Tahora Saddle
Moki Tunnel
Whangamomona Hotel
Joshua Morgan's Grave

Why this is such a great ride

Due to its isolation, this route has minimal traffic which makes for a fabulous ride. Narrow roads and twisting bends amongst rainforest add that extra grin factor when exploring this forgotten highway.

Detour 2
Adventure Highway to Waitomo Caves

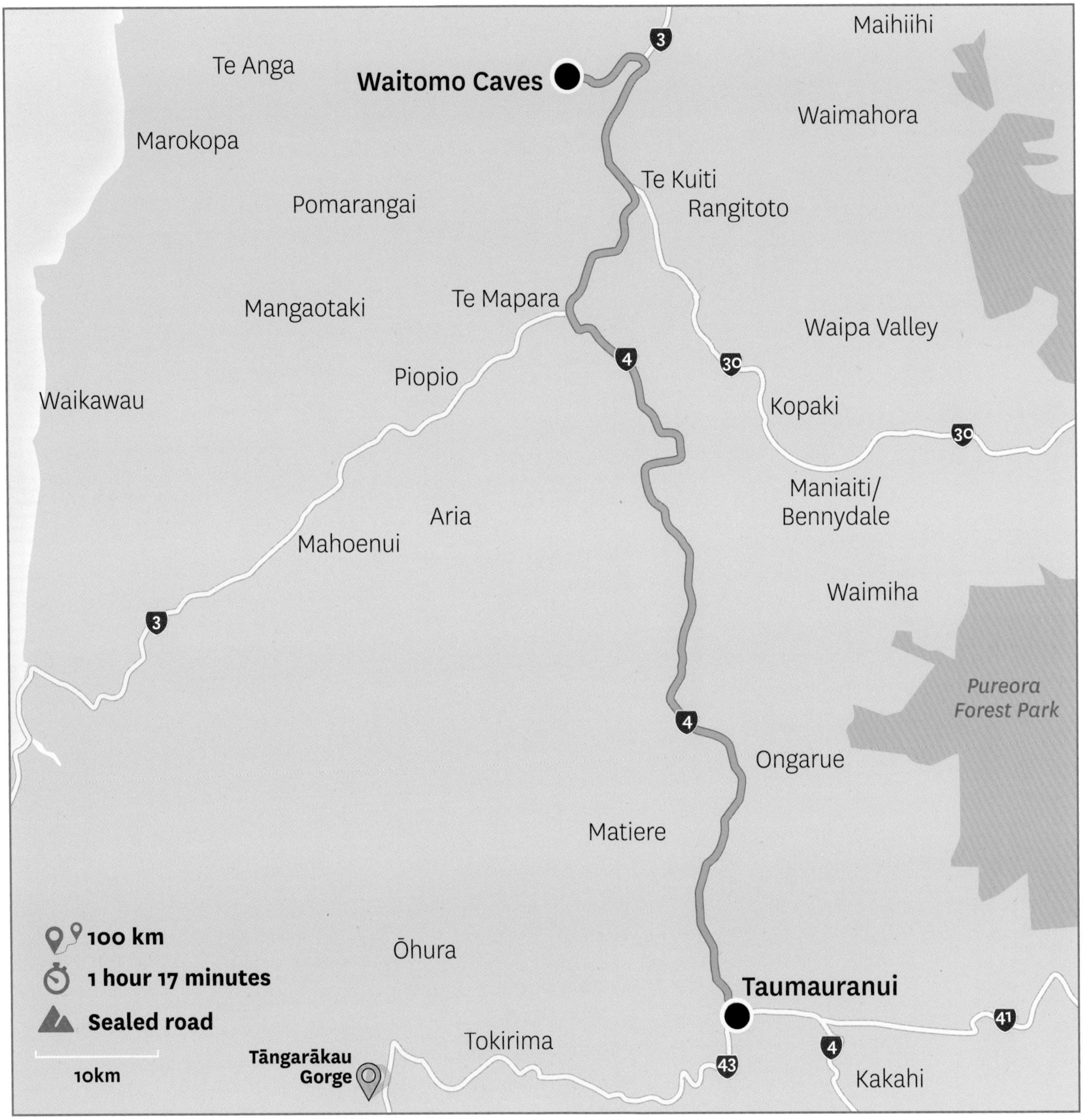

From Taumaranui, head north on State Highway 4, the 'Adventure Highway', for 100 km to visit Waitomo Caves. Although this will take you around an hour and a half with a superb ride on an extremely well-maintained road that runs between gorgeous rolling hills.

Long sweeps and bends and great visibility make for an enjoyable trip. The Waitomo area is known for its large system of underground caves, and guided tours are available here. For the more adventurous, the activities available are endless. With caving, canyoning, blackwater rafting and zip-lining through the caves just a few activities on offer.

The Waitomo caves themselves are a true natural wonder and are illuminated by millions of glow-worms. Relax in the pitch darkness as a small boat transports you through the immense cave systems and learn about the magnificence of one of New Zealand's unspoilt natural wonders.

6. Top of The South — Nelson to Collingwood (via Tākaka Hill)

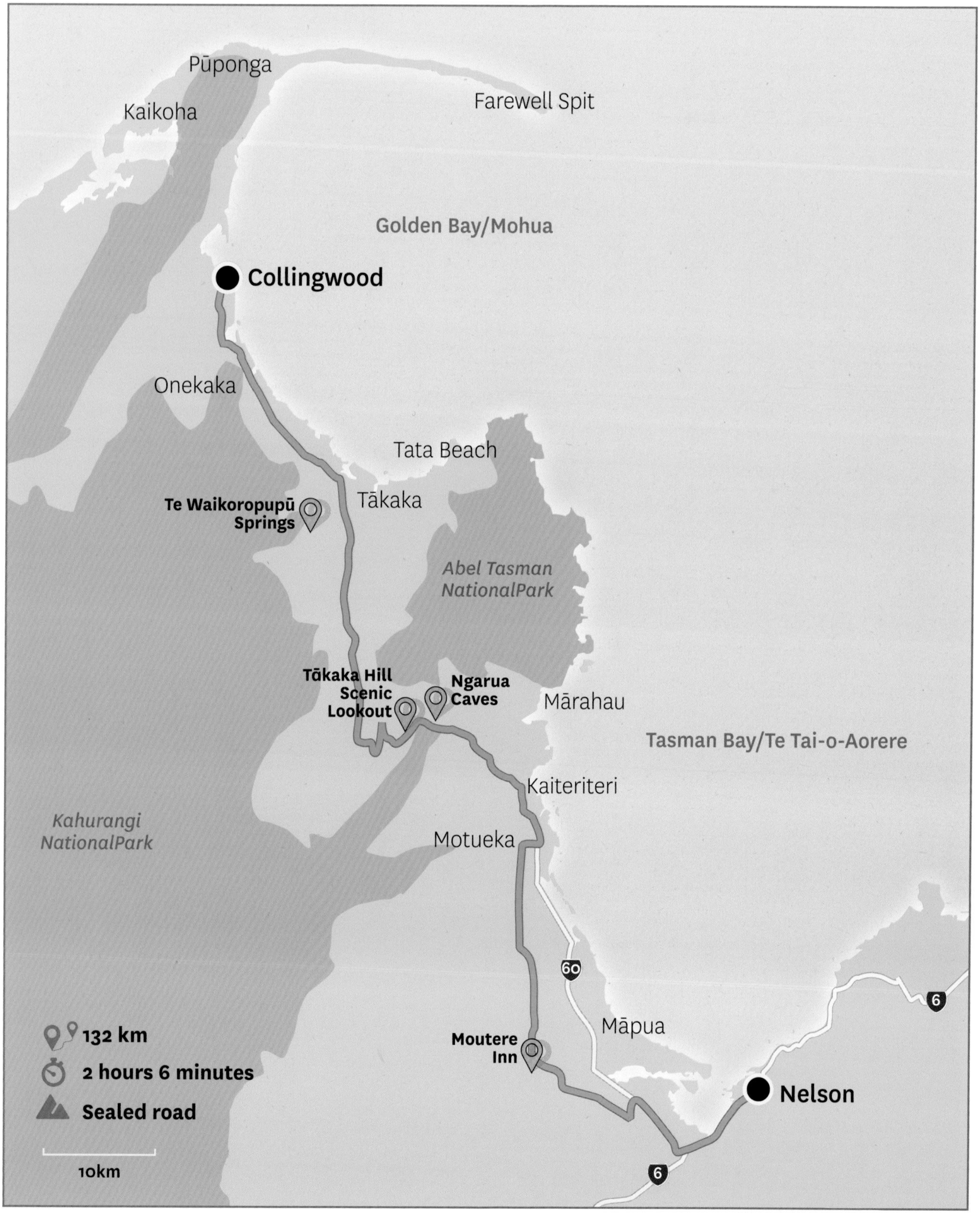

Twists and turns on Tākaka Hill

Route Overview

This ride encompasses part of the 'Top of the South' roads in the stunning Tasman District. Starting in Nelson, a vibrant and exciting city in an area full of creativity, arts, and crafts. Located east of the Tasman Bay, Nelson is surrounded by orchards, wineries and incredible landscapes that alter with each turn in the road.

Nelson's creativity is showcased in events such as the Nelson Arts Festival and the annual World of Wearable Art, an event which highlights designers and their outstanding creations each year. These incredible garments are on display along with other fascinating exhibits in the World of Wearable Art and Classic Car Museum, where more than 150 cars, from Cadillacs to Ferraris, are sure to make any petrol head stop and take a second look.

For the movie buffs out there, Nelson's own local jeweller, Jens Hansen, is the maker of the world's most famous ring, The One Ring, from *The Lord of The Rings*. You can purchase your own and even have it engraved for a precious loved one back home.

This trip skirts the incredible Abel Tasman National Park, named after the Dutch explorer and the first European to reach New Zealand. The National Park is a drawcard for the adventurous, such as hikers looking to test their endurance on the many tracks and walks, or the bravest of explorers and cavers who want to challenge themselves by descending into the depths of Harwoods Hole, the deepest vertical shaft in New Zealand.

Tākaka Hill bridges the divide between Nelson and Golden Bay and is a well-earned treat for any biker.

Golden Bay, as its name gives away, is a golden, sandy mecca for those looking to escape and find a piece of paradise at the end of a long journey. The Tasman region boasts many Mediterranean-style beaches such as Kaiteriteri, as well-hidden gems, just waiting to be discovered from the water by kayak or on an activity tour. A great place to stop midway, or on your way back for the night, to break up this ride into two or three days to explore the area.

Collingwood is the end of the ride but the beginning of a true eco-tourism gateway. Farewell Spit Nature Reserve and the South Island's northernmost point, Collingwood is small with vast views out to the Spit, so you'll feel like your ride has truly ended at the edge of the world.

Savour the ride through forests of ancient beech trees, twisting the throttle into rolling meadows and orchards, testing the bends through eerie granite rock formations then emerging over mountains to vistas of golden beaches where the sky meets the sea for a breath of sweet ocean air. All this while the ride itself tests your skills and concentration. It will bombard you with the riding experience that only this kind of challenging ride can give you. A delightful shove out of your comfort zone in this ancient and untouched part of New Zealand.

Start Your Engines!

Starting from Nelson City, head west on State Highway 6 towards Richmond, then turn on to State Highway 60 for a brief distance before turning left onto the well signposted Moutere Highway. The traffic should reduce dramatically so that you can enjoy this pleasant country road that winds over lush rolling hills. Ride through the quaint villages of Upper and Lower Moutere which were first settled in the 1840s by German immigrants, and are today frequented by crafts people who make beers, wines, cheeses and olive oil. The Moutere Inn historic pub is a well-known biker's destination and stopping here is a must to take a look at some of the motorcycles parked up, chat with other riders, and of course to enjoy one of the many craft beers on tap.

Merge back onto State Highway 60, and when you get to Motueka, lovingly known simply as 'Mot' by the locals, check your brakes, fuel up, and prepare yourself for Tākaka Hill.

Check out the **Detour to Kaiteriteri beach** if you have the time.

Local motorcyclists refer to this route as riding 'over The Hill' and it is well known for being one of the most challenging and thrilling rides of the top part of the South Island. The hill being referred to is the Tākaka Hill, but it is in fact a mountain, known as Marble Mountain for its history as a main quarry location in the early 1900s. The mountain pass is the only way to get to Golden Bay. Due to the area's unspoiled natural scenic beauty of secluded golden beaches for swimming and kayaking, tranquil rivers for fishing, and alpine valleys for walking and trekking, it's no wonder Golden Bay is one of New Zealand's most popular holiday destinations.

Navigating Tākaka Hill entails some challenging twists, bends, hairpins, climbs and descents to keep the adrenaline of even the most experienced rider pumping. The climb up will have you using every gear available, all your wits, and all your concentration as you enjoy the curves. At the top of the hill stop and survey your progress before checking out the views over Golden Bay, as you won't have time for this on the way down. If you are lucky enough to have an extra hour to spare, visit the Ngārua Cave also situated at the summit. You can't see much from the road but don't be deceived, follow the short track down to the car park and you will be pleasantly surprised by this interesting stop.

Back on the road and time for the descent into the sweeps and bends with a series of tight hairpins. You will finally be back down to earth and welcomed to the small vibrant town of Tākaka, with its cool bohemian vibe, marking your arrival into the serene Golden Bay.

Continuing just six kilometres further north, you'll discover the Te Waikoropupū Springs, New Zealand's largest freshwater springs, and arguably the clearest ever measured. Lovingly known as 'Pupu' Springs, you can walk around the area via a small track and boardwalk surrounded by native bushes and trees, with plenty of information panels to tell you more about the place. Just 14 km further north, the Mussel Inn is a quirky woolshed style building famous for freshly steamed mussels on the menu, as well as awesome

Biker-friendly stops along the way

The Moutere Inn Historic Pub — 1406 Moutere Highway, Upper Moutere, 7175
The Mussel Inn — 1259 State Highway 60, Onekaka, 7182
Nelson Classic Car Museum — 23 View Mount, Stoke, Nelson, 7011

Scenic highlights along the way

Moutere Highway
Tākaka Hill Scenic Lookouts
Ngarua Caves
Te Waikoropupū Springs
Split Apple Rock
Abel Tasman National Park
Kaiteriteri Beach

Why this is such a great ride

The route includes Tākaka Hill — a 50 km tar-sealed, two-lane pass and climbing to 791 m at its summit. Over 250 corners made up of twists, turns and tight hairpin bends make this a magical ride which seems to go on forever, and if you are fortunate enough to do this ride without too much traffic, it's a must do on the biker bucket list.

craft beers, ales and ciders, all made in a small brewery adjacent to the pub.

This fabulous empty ribbon road continues northwards for another 11 km until you reach the small township of Collingwood. Collingwood is the main supply town for visitors and residents of Golden Bay. Aptly named, Golden Bay is remote but stunningly beautiful. In addition to motorcycling, outdoor sports such as horse-trekking, fishing, kayaking, swimming and hiking are popular pastimes. But one of the top attractions here is to take a thrilling bus trip onto Farewell Spit — a 30 km long 'finger' of land made up of hilly sand dunes that jut out from the tip of the South Island into the Tasman Sea, protecting Golden Bay from the rougher weather on the other side. The Spit is famous for its kiwi-like appearance on the map and the nature reserve is strictly protected. Eco-tours and adventure flights are available if you want to explore this area more.

Detour

Kaiteriteri Beach Loop

Shortly after crossing the Riwaka River on SH60 (before riding over the Tākaka Hill), turn right onto the Riwaka-Kaiteriteri Road, following the signs to Kaiteriteri Beach. This idyllic golden sand beach is likened to the Mediterranean and is the summer holiday spot for many New Zealanders. Stop for a swim and an ice cream or jump on a kayak or tour to see the iconic 'Split Apple Rock'.

The loop road virtually finishes where you started, so you won't miss out on riding 'The Hill'!

7. Marlborough Magic — Queen Charlotte Drive

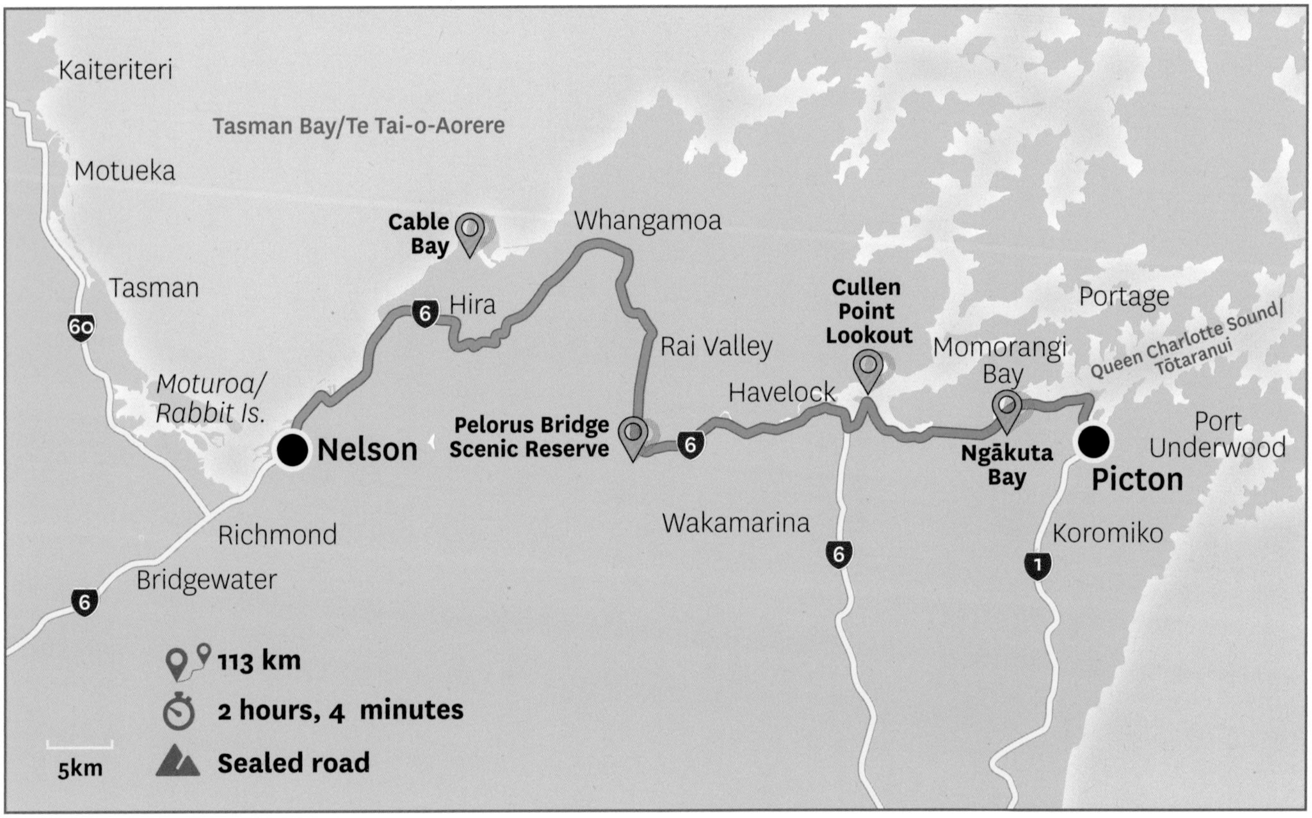

Route Overview

The Marlborough region at the top of the South Island is an exciting destination for any rider. With a multitude of destinations to explore and experience, Marlborough is interlinked with superb riding roads that will keep that glorious grin etched permanently on your face.

This great trip links the Alpine Pacific Triangle and Top of the South nicely and starts from the small city of Nelson, the oldest city in the South Island. Named after the British Admiral Lord Nelson, the main industry here is fishing, closely followed by forestry, and of course tourism. Nelson oozes an awesome arts and crafts vibe, resulting in a bohemian-style atmosphere. On a Saturday morning you can sample the wares of cottage industry owners from around the region who have set up their stalls full of handmade arts and crafts, cheeses, and super-fresh market garden produce.

Nelson tourist attractions include a heritage park, a trip into the Abel Tasman National Park and the Nelson Classic Car Museum, situated just to the west of the city which is well worth a visit, with over 150 cars on display ranging from the early 20th century onwards. Up until 2016 it also housed a large private collection of motorcycles, but these were moved to Invercargill, at the bottom of the South Island, and are now displayed at New Zealand's Classic Motorcycle Mecca.

The Marlborough Sounds are a group of waterways that have filled the area's lush green valleys, creating the perfect playground for boaties, tourists, and those wanting to escape into an untouched, remote paradise.

The highlight of this ride is the Queen Charlotte Drive. With 40 km of winding, narrow road set amongst the most spectacular scenery, take your time and enjoy this challenging route to test your counter steering skills, the Queen Charlotte Drive is a must do for any biker.

Heading south, continue your adventure for just 28 km to the larger town of Blenheim, and notice that the usual farmlands have now turned into mile upon mile of vineyards. The Marlborough District is recognised as New Zealand's best wine region, with the soil and climate here just perfect for the creation of

award-winning Sauvignon Blanc. Marlborough has now attracted so many discerning vintners that over 75% of all New Zealand wines are now produced here.

At the seaside town of Waitohi/Picton, boats and yachts of all descriptions are moored up patiently waiting for their owners to embark upon yet another fishing or boating adventure around the Sounds. The main gateway to the South Island, the Interislander and Bluebridge ferries navigate their way into this pretty port.

Start Your Engines!

Head east along the coastal road overlooking Tasman Bay on the well maintained two-lane State Highway 6. The usual city traffic soon diminishes and you'll find yourself powering up to enjoy a great ride further north. An hour and a half's ride will bring you to the Cable Bay turn-off. The Cable Bay Adventure Park is jam-packed with activities such as the Skywire, a thrilling zip line above the forest canopy. As well as quad biking, paintball and archery, and is well worth a stop.

From this point the road starts to climb up and over the Whangamoa Saddle which rises to an elevation of 466 m. Enjoy a selection of challenging twists and turns through the forest-covered mountains. You may encounter a steady supply of logging trucks, milk tankers and other large vehicles coming down hill in the opposite direction so be vigilant on this stretch of twists and utilise the many passing lanes available along the route. The recommended corner speed signs are a great way to gauge the approaching corners.

No place on earth compares to New Zealand when it comes to offering so many distinctly different landscapes within such a small area. After riding through Whangamoa, you leave the Nelson District and cruise into Marlborough District, with its intricate waterways, vineyards, forests, and tussock-clad rolling hills. This highway treats riders to continuous sweeps and bends with great visibility of the surrounding hills, following the Rai River.

The landscape changes now from pine-clad hills to an area of native bush laced with huge Jurassic-like ferns, ponga, kahikatea, and the Pelorus Bridge Scenic Reserve is well worth a stop. The speed limit reduces dramatically as you slowly take the corner before crossing the river via a one-way bridge. A sharp right after the bridge will take you to the Pelorus Bridge Cafe. Here you can view the crystal clear Te Hoiere River, explore some short walks, and grab a coffee and homemade pie.

After another 20 km of easy riding through farmlands and alongside the Te Hoiere River you'll come across the small fishing town of Havelock, marking the beginning of your adventure into the Marlborough Sounds. At Havelock in particular, the green-lipped mussel beds nestled in the nearby sheltered bay inlets mean that this town is also the perfect place to stop to sample these famous delicacies at the waterfront. On your way out of Havelock, turn right to follow the sign to Queen Charlotte Drive.

Classed as one of New Zealand's most scenic 'drives', this narrow, fully tar-sealed road hugs the coast that overlooks the beautiful Marlborough Sounds. The result is an adrenaline pumping series of twists, bends and hairpins all the way to Picton which will have you grinning from ear to ear for some 40 km, as you navigate over 300 tight bends in the course of an hour. Cullen Point is the first lookout you will come to and is a safe viewpoint via a ten-minute loop walk to get your photos before the fun sets in.

The lush, subtropical rainforest plants that line the road give you the feeling of riding through paradise, and frequent glimpses of stunning vistas across the Sounds peak into view as you navigate the constant hairpin bends.

Continue winding your way around the Mahakipawa Arm until you reach Linkwater. There is a small fuel station here for a top up, then a three kilometre stretch of straight road before embarking upon yet more twists and bends along unparalleled waterside riding, and over the hill to the next inlet of Grove Arm with its many stunning bays. Easy riding until the next series of twists and bends starts the adrenaline pumping all over again down to Shakespeare Bay. Pulling over at Picton Harbour Lookout, you may spot the Interislander and Bluebridge ferries that link New Zealand by weaving their way between the Sounds and out into Cook Strait, then heading for Wellington on North Island. Coming back down to earth you will reach the harbour town of Picton, from which to decide the direction of your next adventure.

Biker-friendly stops along the way

Nelson Classic Car Museum — 23 View Mount, Stoke, Nelson, 7011
Cable Bay Adventure Park — 194 Cable Bay Road, Nelson 7071
Captain's Daughter — 72 Main Road, Havelock 7100
Seamus' Bar — 25 Wellington Street, Picton 7220

Scenic highlights along the way

Cable Bay
Pelorus Bridge
Cullen Point, Marlborough Sounds
Ngākuta Bay
Picton Waterfront

Why this is such a great ride

The last 33 km, known as the Queen Charlotte Drive, is what makes this such a good route. With no traffic lights, no roundabouts, and no side roads to watch out for, except the odd holidaymaker's 'bach' driveway, this narrow, winding road hugs the Marlborough Sound hillside, starting just south of Havelock and finishing at Picton. With over 300 corners, twists, turns and hairpins and unparalleled views across the Sounds, this delightful ribbon road will delight every rider looking for adrenaline-pumping action.

Detour 1

Havelock to Renwick

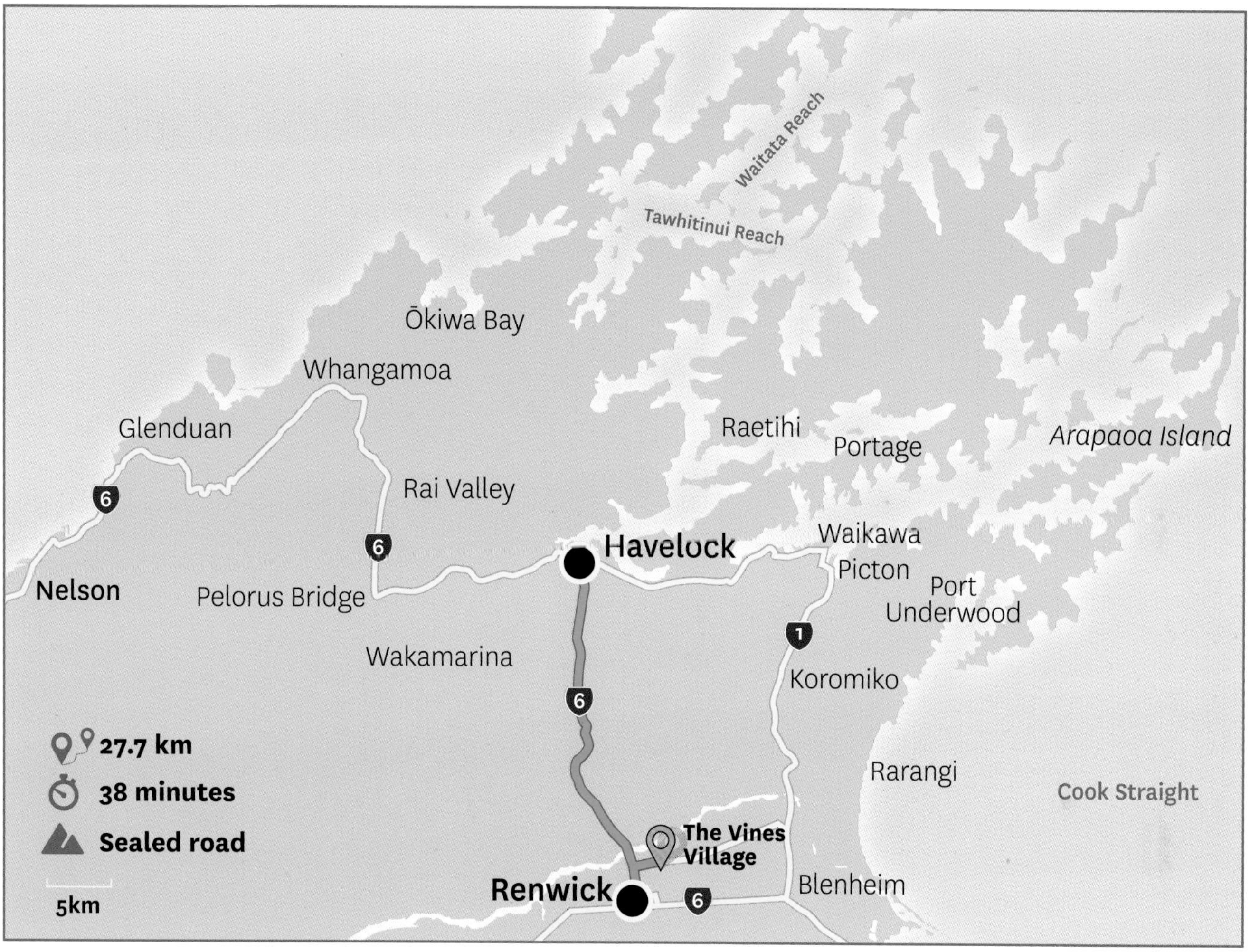

If the challenging and narrow Queen Charlotte Drive doesn't 'float your boat' and you're looking for good visibility with long sweeps, then simply continue on State Highway 6 from Havelock all the way to Renwick. This stretch of road follows the line of the Kaituna River, that flows from the heights of Mount Richmond Forest Park, all the way down into Havelock Marina. Enjoy your ride alongside green pastures and forest and when you cross over the Wairau River, turn left onto Rapaura Road, following the signs to the Vines Village at Renwick. This location isn't a village at all, rather a delightful precinct of artisan shops including a great cafe overlooking the vineyards, and a cellar door for wine tasting. A drawcard is also the surrounding wineries and vineyards that entice discerning wine lovers here from around the world.

Detour 2

Picton to Kaikōura

This is a continuation of your journey around the north-eastern part of the South Island. Although the route uses 'State Highway 1' the entire way, the ride is quite tantalising since the terrain changes from vineyards to dry, tussock rolling hills, then again to wonderful Pacific coast vistas and yet again as the awe-inspiring seaward Kaikōura Ranges of the Southern Alps come into view.

If you have a few hours to spare at Blenheim, visit the Omaka Aviation Heritage Centre which showcases a fabulous collection of film producer Peter Jackson's WWI aircraft and artefacts; or for any chocolate lovers, the Makana Chocolate Factory. Gliding your way alongside the tracks of the Coastal Pacific scenic railway the place to stop after an hour or so is the cafe at Kekerengu known as 'The Store'. Perfectly perched overlooking the beach and azure blue waters of the Pacific. The second half of your ride into Kaikōura is equally as good as the first half, but if you did decide to break up the fun you could have a quick break at 'Nins Bin', an iconic landmark of this area; a small old caravan from which the freshest local delicacy of crayfish is served.

Kaikōura's main attraction is whale watching. From the safety of your boat or from the air by plane, you can view these magnificent, giant sperm whales, dolphins and seals up close. Having the Kaikōura Ranges as the backdrop to this stunning ride, makes it all the more impressive.

Kaikōura Coast Road

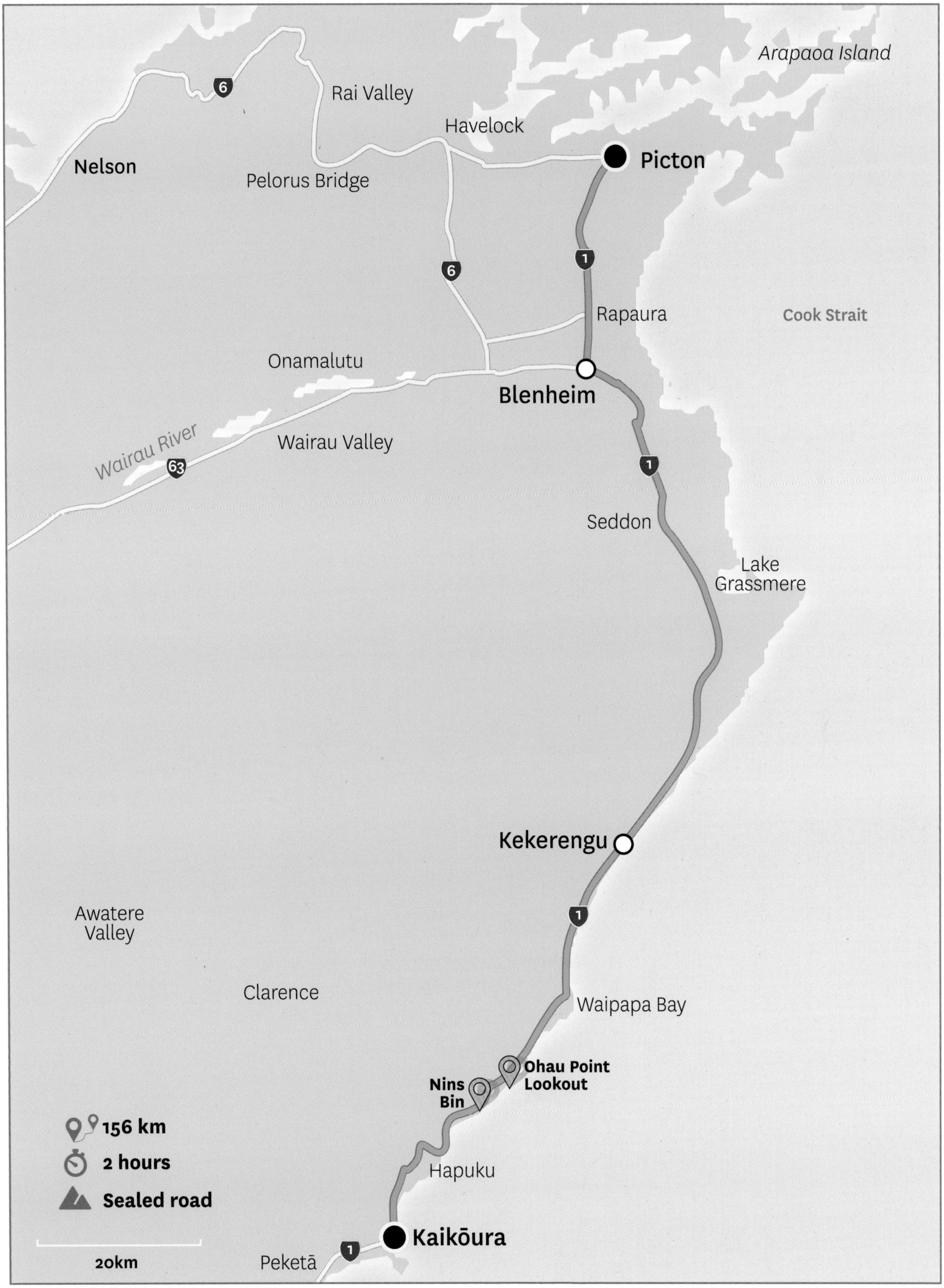
Arapaoa Island
Rai Valley
Havelock
Picton
Nelson
Pelorus Bridge
6
6
1
Rapaura
Cook Strait
Onamalutu
Blenheim
Wairau River
Wairau Valley
63
1
Seddon
Lake Grassmere
Kekerengu
1
Awatere Valley
Clarence
Waipapa Bay
Ohau Point Lookout
Nins Bin
156 km
2 hours
Sealed road
Hapuku
Kaikōura
1
20km
Peketā

8. West Coast to Tasman Bay

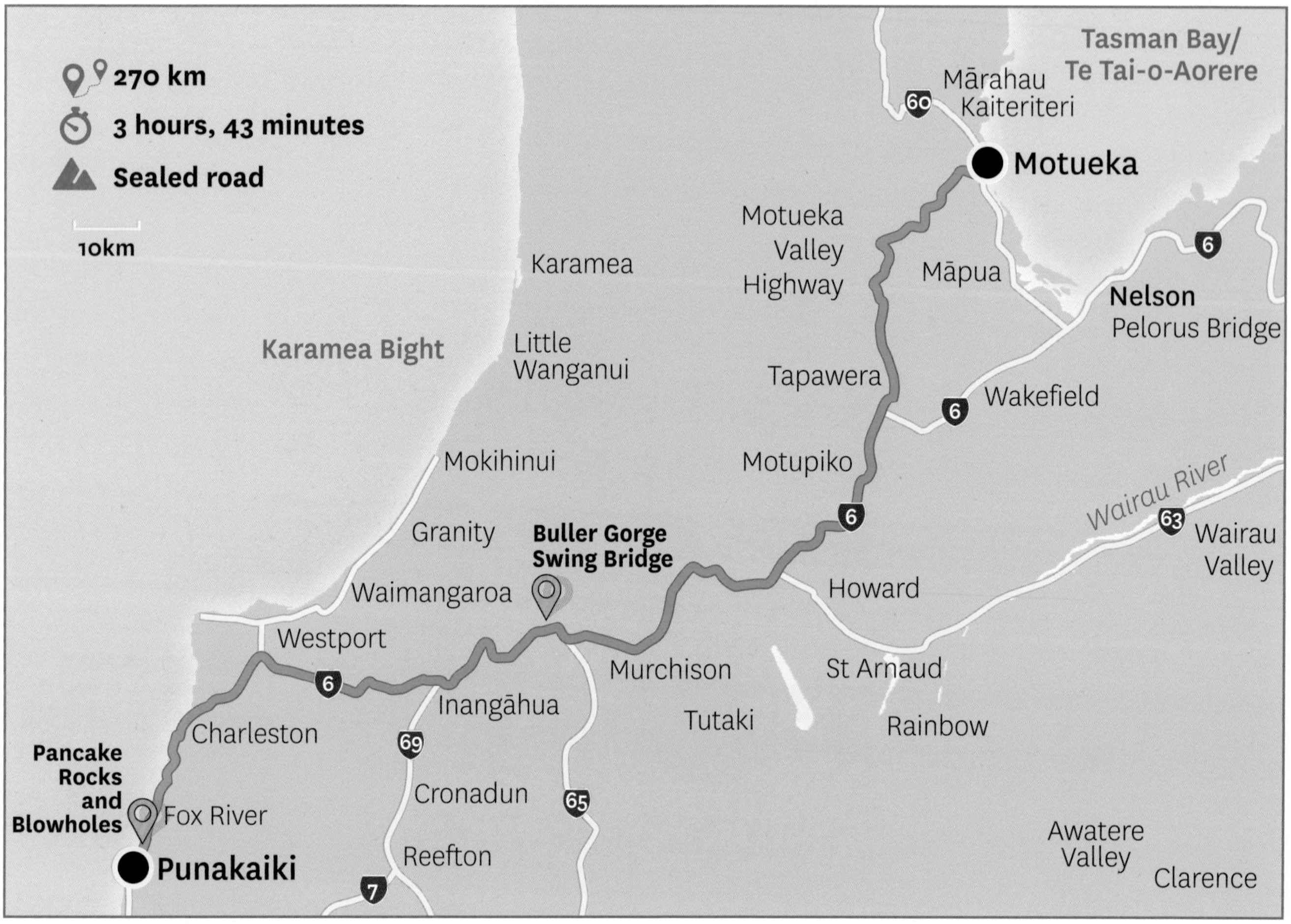

Route Overview

This stunning ride includes part of the wild west coast, traversing phenomenal mountain ranges, and weaving through incredible valleys with idyllic twists and turns neatly sandwiched in between.

Whichever way around you choose to ride, this trip ticks all the boxes and beginning the ride at Punakaiki offers the chance to join up from other trips in the book.

The West Coast of New Zealand always conjures up scenes of wild and Jurassic-like imagery for travellers. Towering nikau palm trees scatter the ancient coast and the road cuts through native bush like a modern scar stretching out before you.

The 'Great Coast Road' is a spectacular ride and Punakaiki is a great place to stop over on the West Coast as it is unspoiled and secluded. Just far enough away from the larger towns, and with numerous places to explore twisty coastal roads while you are here. Boasting its own subtropical climate this area offers different styles of accommodation, from hotels, beachfront cottages, motels, and a friendly local tavern as well. Each being treated to the most incredible west coast sunsets each evening.

Situated in Paparoa National Park, Punakaiki Pancake Rocks and Blowholes are a natural wonder which you can access for free. Nestled in lush coastal rainforest these breathtaking rock formations resemble stacks of pancakes. The pure force of the ocean has blasted these limestone cliffs over time to create spectacular blowholes that erupt from natural fissures and tubes with the moving tides in clouds of salty sea spray. Well worth the visit if you have the time.

This ride will take you back inland into the mountains and through the Buller District, following the largest river on the West Coast — the spectacular Buller River. You are treated to densely forested landscapes as you enjoy fern-covered cliffside riding before crossing over into the Tasman District.

This route veers off and travels through the Motueka Valley for more fabulous riding before reaching Tasman

Riders at the Kilkenny Lookout

Bay at the top of the south and Motueka. Gateway to Abel Tasman National Park, this area is known for its horticultural crops with orchards of kiwifruit, olives and hops made abundant and sweet by the warmer climate. Tasman Bay boasts golden beaches as well as adventure activities such as caving, sea kayaking and tramping and is a great base to check out other trips that link with it in this book. The fun-filled twists and turns of Tākaka Hill are just a short blast away and are a favourite destination ride for New Zealanders.

Start your Engines!

Before you depart, make sure you've checked out the Punakaiki Pancake Rocks and Blowholes. From Punakaiki, head north and follow State Highway 6. The crashing waves of the Tasman Sea meet with deserted beaches, and on your right is the Paparoa National Park filled with lush native palm trees, grasses, and fern-covered cliffs. The well maintained two-lane tar-sealed road snakes and winds its way along the coast, ducking and diving to cross the many rivers and navigating bluffs via narrow one-way bridges with fabulous coastal views as your backdrop. Forget the traffic lights, roundabouts and traffic as you will leave them all in your wing mirrors. The few road signs you will see around you include those to caution you about penguins that hop from the beach and cross the road to roost.

The road heads inland after riding through Charleston, a tiny gold mining village founded back in 1867 during the gold rush days, but the riding remains ideal with a continual flow of uninterrupted sweeps and bends. Just 20 km north of Charleston is the Cape Foulwind seal colony. Check out the **Detour to Cape Foulwind** and also the **Detour to Karamea** if you have time.

Heading inland, the next 100 km provide some of the very best riding in New Zealand, as the road meanders alongside the mighty Buller River and snakes its way through the Lower Buller Gorge as you enter the Tasman District.

Slow down at the Kilkenny Lookout to navigate the one-way road that literally cuts into the craggy rocks that drop into the Buller River below. Pull over and look back for a great photo of the overhanging mossy rocks, the road below, and the stunning surrounding scenery.

Berlins Cafe makes for a great biker-friendly place to stretch your legs and grab a bite to eat. The cafe is easy to spot with its giant, metal sadfly out front and stunning gorge views

Kick into gear once again for more adrenaline-pumping riding, turning left at Īnangahua to remain on SH6/Upper Buller Gorge Road. There are no side roads or residential areas to worry about, just mile upon mile of ribbon road lined with lush ferns and beech forest.

Just 15 km before your arrival into the small township of Murchison is the Buller Gorge Swing Bridge, Adventure and Heritage Park. The activities here ar numerous if you have a little time to spare and want to try out New Zealand's longest swingbridge, zip-lining on the high-speed Comet Line or take a jet-boat ride through the Buller River canyons. Murchison is the perfect half-way point for refuelling both yourself and your bike with its many cafes and quirky vintage stores.

Continue along SH6, still following the Buller River in a north easterly direction, to enjoy over an hour of superb riding through farmland and pine-forest bedecked rolling hills until reaching Kawatiri.

Check out the **Detour via Tophouse Road** if you have the time.

The next five kilometres is relatively flat riding before you begin to climb Hope Saddle, then enjoy the hairpins on the descent. After approximately an hour you'll arrive at the Kohatu Flat Rock Cafe, perched on the corner, marking the beginning of your last leg of this journey. To think the ride could get even better than what you've just done is hard to imagine, but the awesome Motueka Valley Highway is surely your highway to heaven.

The last sector of this ride on the 'Mot Valley Highway' provides an hour of wonderful, smooth, easy riding. With no side roads, stops, give ways, or tee junctions, and hopefully not even a farm tractor to get in the way, you can stay in fourth and fifth gear for many a mile to keep that smile on your dial. The surrounding forest-covered ranges provide natural scenic beauty and the clouds hang low here, epitomising the Māori description of New Zealand: Aotearoa, 'Land of the Long White Cloud'. Cruise through farmland until you arrive at the tiny village of Tapawera. The main attraction here is the Tapawera Hop Bar, a country hotel offering comfortable accommodation and excellent craft beers due to this region's vibrant hop growing climate.

The two-lane, well-maintained road continues in a northerly direction alongside the Motueka River, making for a great ride with good curves and excellent progress through the regions stunning countryside. The odd farmhouse and campsite eventually marks the beginning of civilisation as the wonderful Motueka Valley Highway finally gives way to straighter roads. College Street will take you into the township of Motueka itself.

Biker-friendly stops along the way

Berlins Cafe — 1205 Lower Buller Gorge Road, Westport 7866

Rivers Café, Murchison — 51 Fairfax Street, Murchison 7007

Dust and Rust — 35 Fairfax Street, Murchison 7007

Kohatu Flat Rock Cafe — 5087 Motueka Valley Highway, RD2 Wakefield

Hop Bar & Restaurant — 84 Main Road, Tapawera, 7096

Scenic highlights along the way

Truman Track

Irimahuwhero Lookout

Buller Gorge Swing Bridge

Why this is such a great ride

The variety of riding along this route will keep you on your toes. Riding part of the Great Coast Road through mountains and narrow gorges will keep you alert as you traverse the different landscapes. Enjoy 270 km of relatively empty, uninterrupted ribbon road that feels like it's made just for motorcycling.

Welcome to the top of the South Island. From here you can choose to head left towards Golden Bay via the hairpin bends of Tākaka Hill, or right to Nelson and beyond. The top of the south has some great biking roads, so if you have an extra day or two to explore you won't regret it. Boasting golden beaches, stunning national parks, and friendly locals, after a long day in the saddle you can relax and enjoy this incredible part of New Zealand.

Detour 1
Cape Foulwind Seal Colony

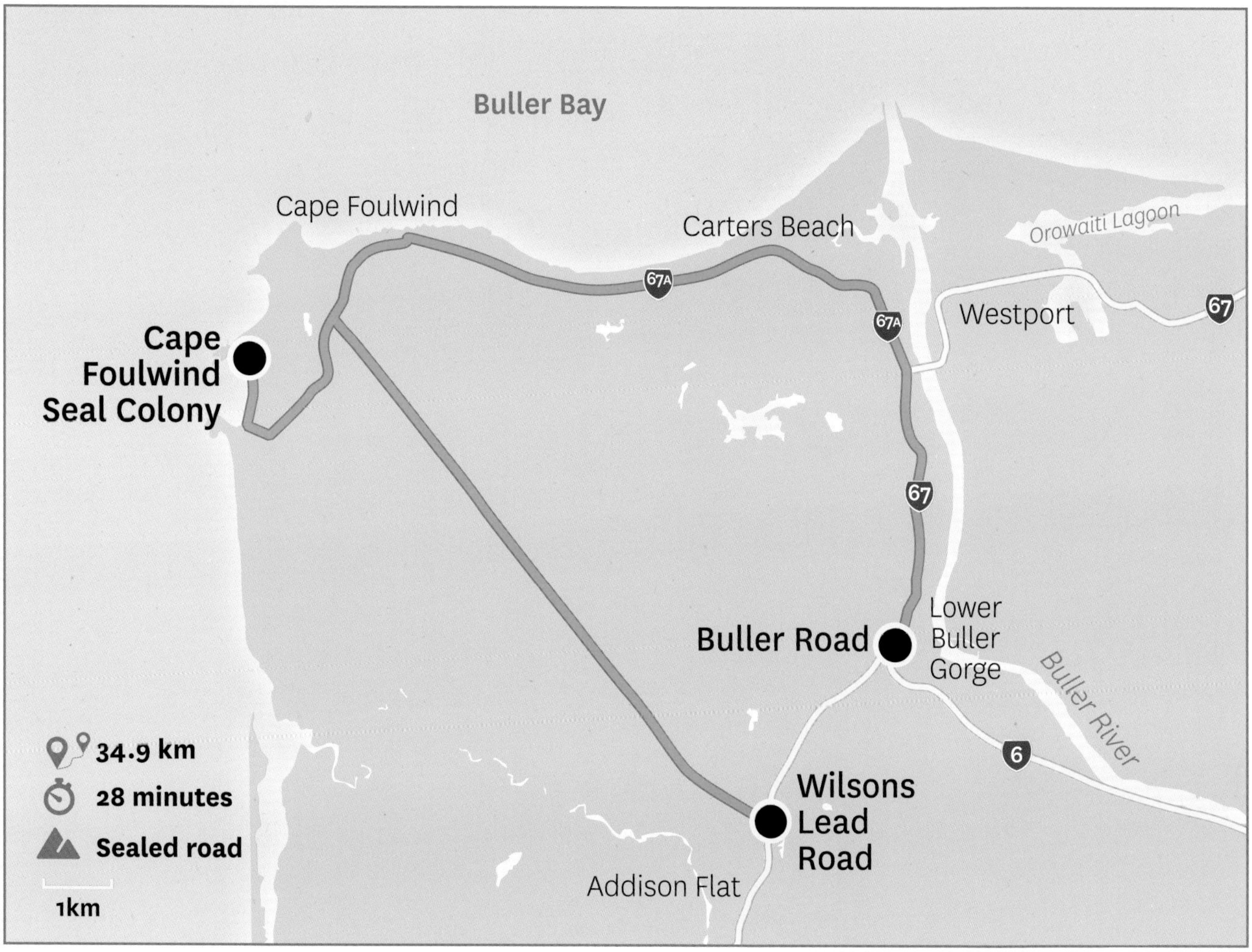

Turn off from State Highway 6 onto Wilsons Lead Road. Easy riding to the Cape Foulwind seal colony and walkway may be rewarded by glimpses of weka. These are native flightless birds often mistaken for kiwi, and about the size of a chicken. At the car park there is often a coffee caravan for a well-earned break.

The ten minute walkway to the seal colony viewpoint is well signposted and makes for a good stop before continuing along State Highway 67A, Buller Bay to Carters Beach, and then to the town of Westport, a recommended place to top up the tank if you are running low. Merge back onto State Highway 6 again looking out for the signposts to Christchurch and Murchison.

Detour 2

Karamea Highway and Coast Road

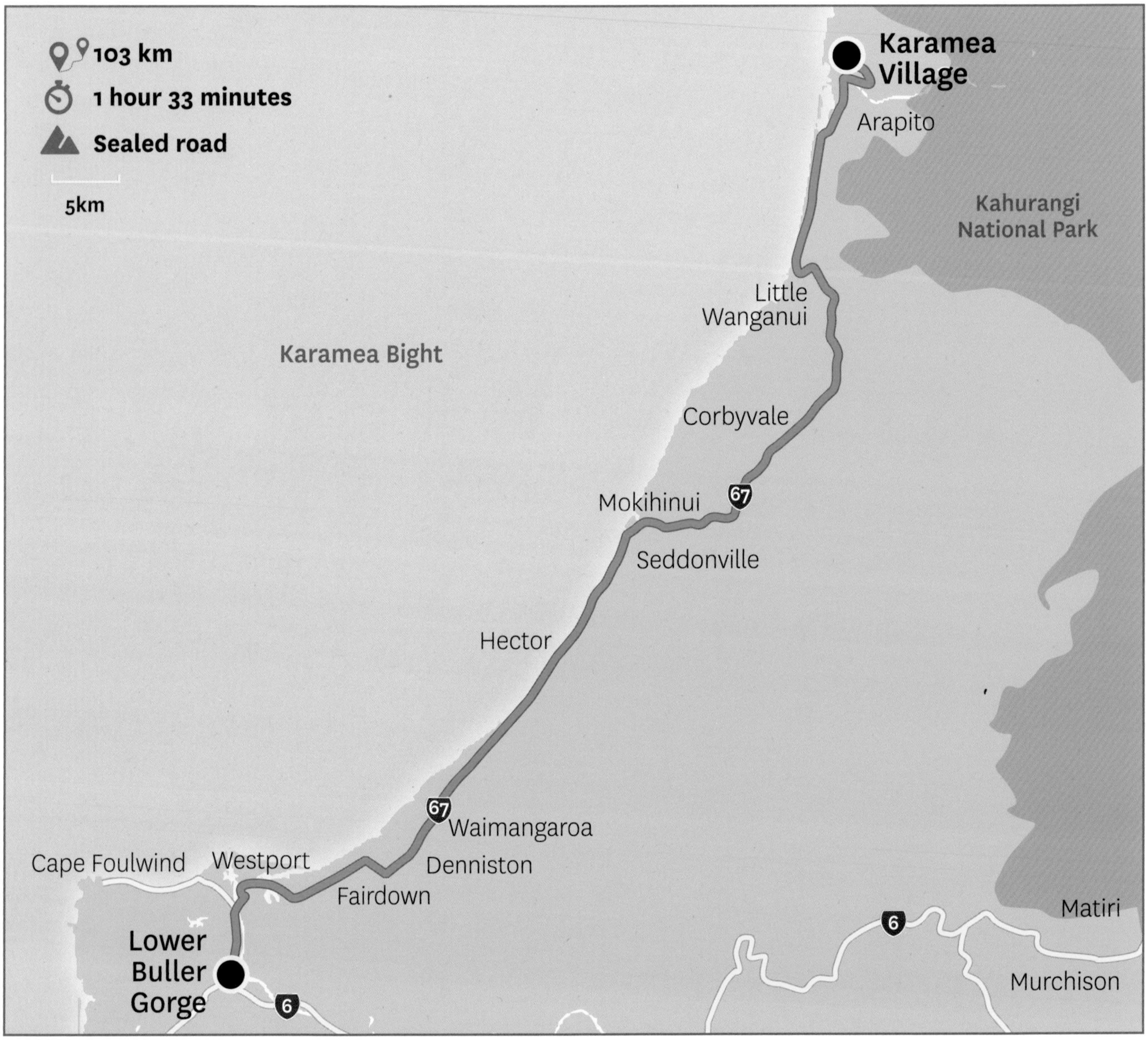

Before continuing along State Highway 6, turn left onto State Highway 67, following signs to Westport and Karamea.

There is a fair amount of straight and coastal riding before you reach the Karamea Highway which begins at Mōkihinui. This is where the fun begins. The hairpin bends and tight twists are sure to put a smile on any biker's face here. Surrounded by West Coast forest with lush ferns, nīkau palms and moss covered fauna you'll want to crack open your helmet a little to breathe in this fresh coast air.

Karamea and its unsurpassed natural beauty is the West Coast's best kept secret and is a destination in itself. With hiking, fishing, caving, and adventure activities all on the doorstep of the Kahurangi National Park. Add a world-class twisty forest ride to this and you've got yourself one must-do detour.

Detour 3
Tophouse Road

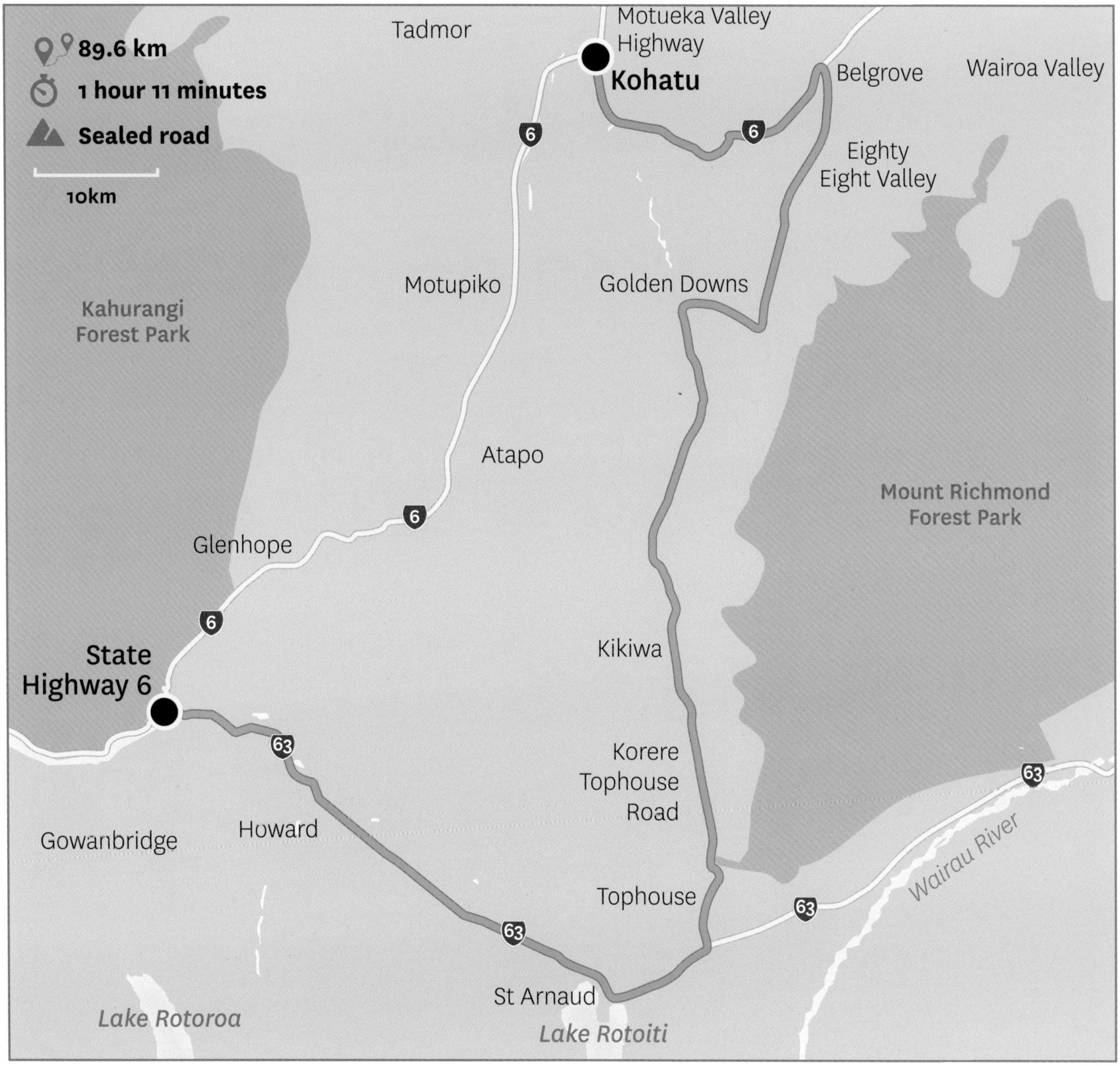

This one hour detour adds some more time to this route but includes the long, sweeping bends that make riding a true joy. Turn sharp right off Highway 6 when you reach Kawatiri and follow signs for State Highway 63 and St Arnaud. You'll continue to follow the Buller River and criss-cross it at various points.

After a short, straight stretch through farmland you'll reach the village of St Arnaud, located beside stunning Lake Rotoiti. This vast, blue mountain lake is a great place to stop before veering off left on to Korere-Tophouse Road, following signs to Nelson.

Enjoy the next 30 minutes of high grin factor riding along this detour. As you follow the road it'll become Kerr-Hill Road, Stock Road then Wai-iti Valley Road before joining back up with State Highway 6 at Belgrove. Turn left following signs to Murchison to get back on track on this route, or head right to Nelson if you're joining this detour with another route in this book.

9. Alpine Pacific Triangle

Kaikōura Ranges

Route Overview

You can begin this high grin factor ride from either Christchurch, Kaikōura or Hanmer Springs and choose to ride whichever way around you prefer. The detour options available mean you can also make the route as long or short as you wish.

Splitting this route into three days means you will be able to enjoy each destination and explore what it has to offer, as well as taking your time getting there and enjoying the ride along the way.

Christchurch boasts English heritage that has been preserved, restored, and improved following substantial devastating earthquakes in 2010 and 2011. Christchurch has proven its resilience to nature's attempts to shake the city and has been able to rebuild in stages, with full urban regeneration, modern architecture, and green spaces to be enjoyed by visitors and residents alike.

Hagley Park sits at the heart of the city and is New Zealand's largest urban space at 407 acres, with the Avon River meandering through. You can easily ride around it and park up by Victoria Lake in the shade. From here the stunning Botanic Gardens, Canterbury Museum, Arts Centre, Art Gallery, and Riverside Market are all within walking distance.

Around Christchurch and Banks Peninsula are numerous rides that can be done in a day, check out the **Detours to the Port Hills, Scargill and Leader Valley** if you have the time.

Mike Pero's Motorcycle Gallery is a stunning collection of two-wheeled beauties primarily from the 70s, 80s and 90s, lovingly displayed six minutes from Christchurch airport and is a guaranteed trip down memory lane for any biker.

Kaikōura is a spectacular seaside township where the mountains meet the ocean and provide an eco-tourism destination like no other. Famous for its resident giant sperm whales, Dusky dolphins and fur seals, all of which can be viewed year-round. Whether you choose to observe from the safety of a tour boat on the water or view from above in a helicopter or plane the options are plenty.

Take a ride around the rugged Kaikōura Peninsula or up the main street to grab some locally caught seafood or fish and chips to eat on the beach and you will feel relaxed in no time.

Hidden within the Southern Alps is the alpine village of Hanmer Springs. Boasting award-winning thermal pools and spas, adventure activities, nature trails, and offering wine and food options from the local region, make Hanmer Springs a fabulous destination to explore.

Start Your Engines!

CHRISTCHURCH TO KAIKŌURA

Named the 'Alpine Pacific Triangle' for its three fantastic destinations while being able to ride from the Southern Alps Mountain Range to the Pacific Ocean in a day. Starting the ride from Christchurch follow State Highway 1 heading north to Kaikōura through farmland and undulating countryside. Just after riding through the town of Amberley you will begin to see the landscape change and be surrounded by vineyards on either side. The iconic Waipara Hills Winery on your right will signify entering the Waipara Valley, and if you are a keen wine connoisseur then you will spot numerous well-known labels along this route. Many of these, such as Waipara Springs and Black Estate, have on-site restaurants and are well worth a visit to the cellar door to pick up a bottle or two to take home.

Enjoy the sweeping bends through the Hurunui District and over the Hurunui, Leader and Waiau Uwha Rivers. From here you are following the Alpine Pacific Touring Route all the way to Kaikōura. After crossing the bridge over the Conway River you are in for a treat as you start to climb up and around the Hundalee Hills. This part of the ride is magical and one of the highlights of the route. There are multiple switchbacks and tight turns on your way, but only one or two passing lanes for slow traffic so keep your fingers crossed you don't get stuck behind a camper or truck and you will get to enjoy this high grin factor ride. All of a sudden, the azure blue of the Pacific Ocean sneaks onto the horizon, followed by a series of challenging hairpin bends to lead you back down to sea level.

When the road starts to flatten out, if the ride didn't take your breath away, then the vista that awaits you certainly will. This unbeatable coastal ride takes you alongside the deep blue sea on one side and the towering mountains on the other. This stunning stretch of road was closed in 2016 due to a magnitude 7.8 earthquake and was rebuilt to reconnect Kaikōura with its steady tourism flow once again. Riding past multiple bays and marine reserves, keep an eye out along the coastal rocks for ones that may move, as a multitude of fur seals call these waters home and can be seen basking in the sunshine or playing in the rock pools below. Stop for a photo but not too close as they may have pups and are very protective and territorial animals.

Coming closer into view is the Kaikōura Peninsula, stretching out into the ocean, and on the other side is your destination. On a clear day, the distant Kaikōura Ranges will be visible and may be dusted with snow for that perfect picture postcard New Zealand scenery. Park up at your accommodation or the township's main street and enjoy exploring this superb seaside location and famous local highlights. Iconic Kaikōura favourite, Nins Bin is an unassuming rustic roadside caravan a short ride north of Kaikōura. This is a must stop for freshly caught and cooked crayfish smothered in garlic butter and overlooking the Pacific Ocean is a true Kaikōura experience. Live music at the Strawberry Tree in the evening is a great way to end your day and whale watching tours or seal spotting along the coast for a half or full day trip makes Kaikōura an unforgettable destination.

KAIKŌURA TO HANMER SPRINGS

When heading inland to Hanmer Springs there are two route options. Rather than heading back the way you came (back down State Highway 1) take the Inland Kaikōura Road instead to avoid the traffic and experience some top-notch and challenging riding. This inland road takes you alongside rivers, through valleys, and around those ever-present, sweeping, South Island bends. Route 70 emerges at the small township of Waiau, turn right and follow Rotherham Street over the Waiau Uwha River. The last stretch of Route 70 ends at the Amuri Plain when you join up with the Alpine Pacific Touring Route again on State Highway 7.

Turn right to head further inland to the hills and ride beside sheer cliffs adjacent to the stunning Waiau River, topped off with the spectacular snow-capped Southern Alps peeking through in the distance.

Turn right to follow the signs to Hanmer Springs at State Highway 7A. You'll see various activities advertised such as bungy jumping, jet boating or rafting. Ride over the iconic narrow Waiau Ferry Bridge, elevated 32 m above the river overlooking the magnificent Hanmer Springs Valley. Winding your way down into the valley, open your visor and breathe in the fresh pine scent from surrounding forest-covered hills before reaching the tree-lined centre of this beautiful alpine town.

Hanmer Springs was discovered in 1859 by pioneer William Jones. News of these natural hot waters spread and thermal bathing soon became popular for its restorative qualities. So much so that a sanatorium was built to house patients, and later the Queen Mary Hospital, a military hospital, which is no longer in use. The resort and surrounding town now boast multiple thermal pools, hydro slides, private pools and saunas as well as a luxury spa, restaurants, shops and activities for visitors, all set in magical alpine surroundings. So take off your heavy riding gear, grab a towel and go for a soak after such a superb day of riding.

HANMER SPRINGS TO CHRISTCHURCH

After reluctantly departing beautiful Hanmer Springs from State Highway 7, rejoin the Alpine Pacific Touring Route on SH7 heading south to Christchurch. Watch your speed from Culverden, as this 13.7 km stretch of road is the longest straight section of highway in New Zealand and numerous tempting straights on this route mean the throttle can seemingly twist by itself. Your speed will creep up before you know it and you may unintentionally get to meet the friendly, local constabulary.

Enjoy the ride through the eye-catching limestone rock formations and look out for Frog Rock and Seal Rock on your way through the bends. Sweeping through forest plantations and vineyards of the Hurunui you reach Waikari, the destination of the Weka Pass vintage steam train. This historic railway still offers visitors a ride from Waipara to Waikari and is a great bonus trip for any transport or automotive enthusiast.

As you travel through the smaller towns, the terrain turns from rolling hills to the flatter farmland landscape of the Canterbury Plains, passing sheep and dairy farms on either side.

After another tempting and well-policed straight, you'll reach the end of the Alpine Pacific Touring Route and State Highway 7 will rejoin State Highway 1 at Waipara. Turn right following signs to Christchurch and you're homeward bound.

Biker-friendly stops along the way

Fossil Point Cafe and Gallery — 1 Valley Road, Greta Valley 7387
Waipara Hills Winery — 780 Glasnevin Road, Waipara 7483
The Hurunui — 1224 Karaka Road, State Highway 7, Hurunui 7385
Waipara Springs Winery and Restaurant — 409 Omihi Road, Waipara 7483
Kaikoura Seafood BBQ Kiosk — 55 Fyffe Quay, Kaikōura Peninsula, Kaikōura 7300
Nins Bin — State Highway 1, 6, Kaikōura 7400
Strawberry Tree — 21 West End, Kaikōura 7300
Weka Pass Railway — 113 Glenmark Drive, Waipara 7483
Mike Pero's Motorcycle Gallery — 1 Hawthornden Road, Avonhead, Christchurch 8042
Smash Palace — 172 High Street, Christchurch Central, Christchurch 8011

Scenic highlights along the way

Hundalee Hills
Kaikōura Ranges
Alpine Pacific Highway
Kaikōura Peninsula
Hanmer Springs Thermal Pools
Whale Watching
Weka Pass Railway

Why this is such a great ride

Multiple fabulous destination options make this route a flexible trip that can be altered by extending or shortening to suit your duration and preferred riding time. Both alpine and coastal riding with well-maintained and twisty roads make this route a great choice for any road trip ride.

Detour 1
The Port Hills/Banks Peninsula

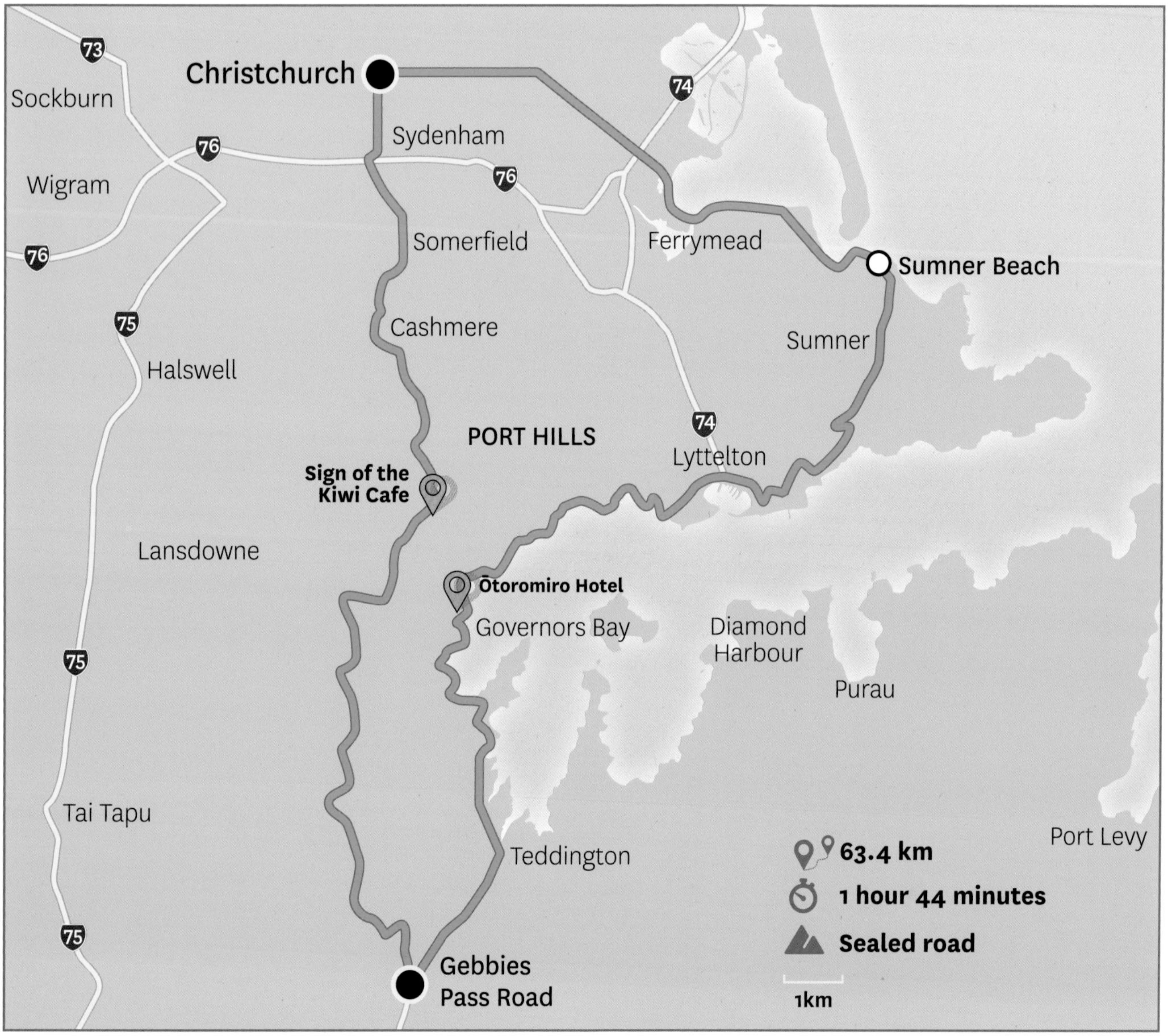

This challenging detour includes multiple bends and switchbacks on narrow cliffside and rural roads with the additional bonus of breathtaking views of Christchurch's Port Hills and Banks Peninsula. From Christchurch City, head east to Sumner Beach and climb up to the Port Hills via Evans Pass Road and down into the harbour town of Lyttelton, with its friendly local atmosphere. Enjoy the endless twists and turns as you ride around Cossair, Cass, Rāpaki and Governors Bay. The Ōtoromiro Hotel is a great biker-friendly stop here with a spectacular view over the peninsula.

Continue following Governors Bay Teddington Road through the hills then when you reach the flat, turn right at the Wheatsheaf Tavern following signs to Gebbies Pass.

After approximately 3.2 km, turn right up to Summit Road and continue to climb up into the hills through fields of livestock and windswept trees and tussocks, surrounded by spectacular 360-degree views. Stop at Sign of the Bellbird and Sign of the Kiwi for the best views and a well-earned coffee or ice cream at the top of the hills before your ride back down into the main town.

Detour 2

Scargill Valley

This detour is a well-known trip for local riders coming from Christchurch and is a great little shortcut between the two state highways. With the Star and Garter Pub in Waikari at one end, and the Fossil Point Cafe in Greta Valley at the other, there is a hot coffee or cold beer waiting at each end, making this ride a great excuse to take the bike out for a spin.

Detour 3

Leader Valley

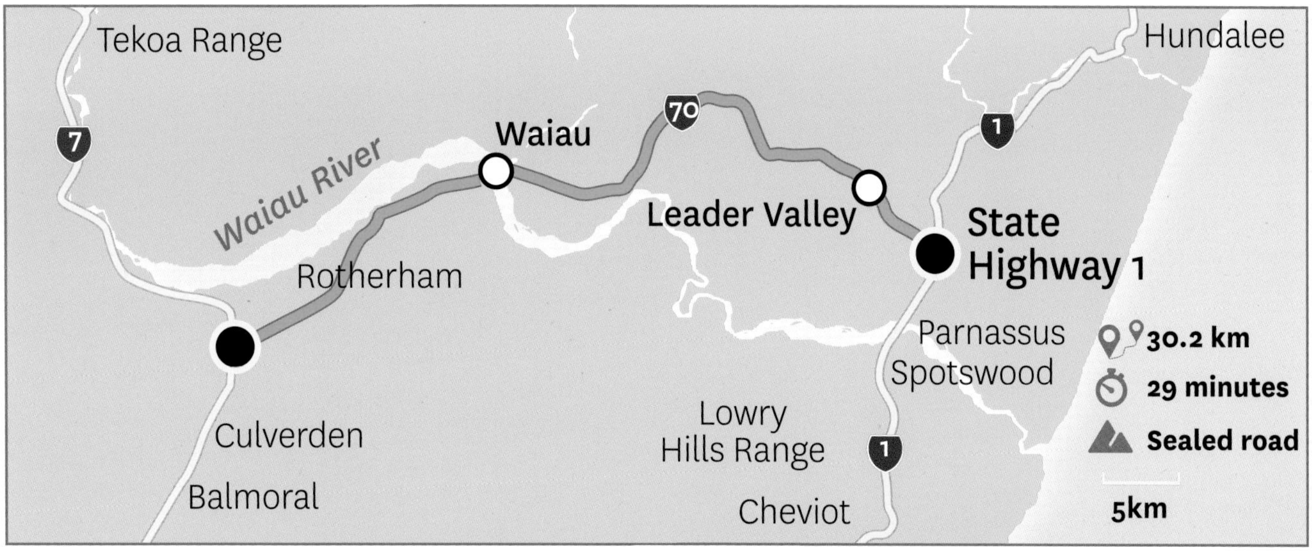

This detour is usually included in the Alpine Pacific Touring Route as the shorter route to Hanmer Springs. You'll leave State Highway 1 just north of Parnassus and follow the sign to Waiau and Hanmer Springs. This fun little detour ride will follow the Leader River for a short stretch before you enjoy the undulating hills and farmland of Canterbury backroads through to Waiau where you meet back up with Route 70 and the Inland Road heading to Hanmer.

10. Lewis Pass — Twin Passes Ride No.1

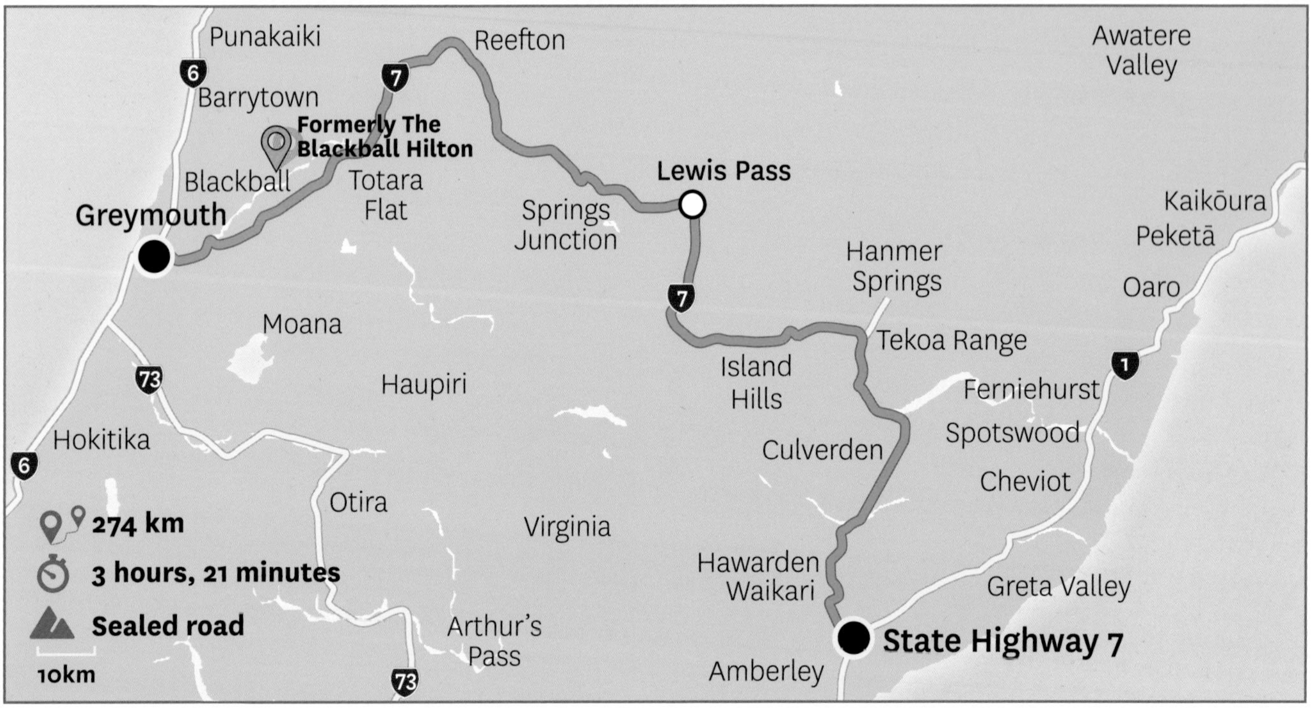

Route Overview

Starting this route from the West Coast means this trip can be linked with the Arthur's Pass Twin Passes ride and is a great multi-day adventure. Equally as magnificent either way, this trip can be split into one or two days with a potential detour stopover in Hanmer Springs.

Greymouth is the largest town on the West Coast, located at the mouth of the Grey River and end of the Grey Valley. The town and its river were named after Governor Sir George Grey in 1846. With a rich history during the gold rush era in the 1860s the town's population increased exponentially with the arrival of immigrant prospectors and settlers to the area. Shifting its sights to coal mining, Greymouth Port became a hub for timber and coal exports. The completion of the railway between the East and West Coast meant a faster, more economical connection. The TranzAlpine rail journey still travels this route today.

The Lewis Pass is the northernmost pass on the South Island and is pure delight for any biker. With its dramatic mountainous road cutting through the spectacular Southern Alps, and following the serpentine sweeps of the Buller River, this road is alpine riding at its finest.

The Lewis Pass is named after the British surveyor Henry Lewis and has an elevation of 907 m. Connecting the overland routes in the centre is Springs Junction. A welcome midpoint and offering fuel stations to top up the tank.

An alternative end point to this trip is the alpine village of Hanmer Springs. Nestled within the mountains, this small but incredibly popular destination offers a great place to relax and unwind after your trip.

Start Your Engines!

If you're riding the Twin Passes this could be your second trip over the magnificent Southern Alps. The scenery changes constantly, depending on weather patterns and seasons, and makes for a thrilling bucket list trip for any rider.

There are numerous detours which will extend the duration, add a stopover, or simply give you better riding options if you are looking for even more excitement adding to this already epic road trip.

Departing Greymouth, you will be following State Highway 7, signs to Reefton and Christchurch.

Check out the **Detour to Blackball** or **Punakaiki and Great Coast Road** if you have the time.

With the vast expanse of the Grey River to your left, as you ride through the Grey Valley, the gentle undulations of the road give you glimpses over the river then bring you back down to follow the railway tracks.

Glorious sweeps and curves that follow the river before dropping down into low lying farmland from Stillwater all the way to the delightful historic town of Reefton.

Check out the **Detour via the Shenandoah and Maruia Falls** if you have time.

Reefton has a rich, proud, and impressive history. In 1888, being the first town in the Southern Hemisphere to boast electric power earned it the title the 'Town of Light'. Reefton's history is proudly displayed in its well preserved 19th century buildings along its main street and is well worth hopping off the bike to explore. The Bearded Mining Company is located on the main Broadway and is a replica of an old miner's hut. Complete with bearded locals on site to chat about the town's mining and gold rush history is both an amusing and educational stop.

Immediately after leaving Reefton, the road begins to climb, and the landscape becomes lush and forested. This stretch of stunning twists and bends is the Rahu Saddle, and the grin will become permanent as you lean into these alternating long sweeps and tight twists while you snake your way beside the Īnangahua River.

Soon you will be surrounded by a remarkable podocarp forest, with an abundant green canopy stretching out over the road, each branch clambering for more sunlight. Fern fronds reach out from the roadside like adoring arms as you ride through this unspoiled paradise, cruising happily all the way to Springs Junction where the stunning open valley comes into view once again.

If you are riding this route in the cooler months, or in the evening, watch the road for ice in shaded areas as your elevation is around 685 m here on Rahu Saddle. The temperature can drop quickly, making for uncomfortable riding, so keeping an extra layer handy is always a good idea when riding these alpine passes.

Springs Junction is a welcome midpoint for a leg stretch, with a fuel stop and public facilities available. Further along, as you follow the Maruia River, you pass Maruia Hot Springs with its natural geothermal springs and overnight accommodation if you wanted to break up the trip.

Approximately six kilometres riding to St James Walkway is the Lewis Pass great divide. You will be crossing from the West Coast into Canterbury and will spy the telltale red tussocks of the Hurunui District as the rolling road ebbs and flows gracefully through the pass and into the gorse dotted valley below.

Riding past vast sheep and cattle farms through Poplars Range will mean the Waiau Uwha River now joins you on your left before you reach Tekoa Range and the turn-off to Hanmer Springs following Highway 7A.

Check out the short **Detour To Hanmer Springs** if you have the time.

The secluded alpine township of Hanmer Springs boasts thermal hot pools as well as magnificent walking tracks, adrenaline-filled activities such as bungy jumping and white water rafting to name a few. A popular tourist destination, this busy town has many accommodation options as well as restaurants, shops, and adventure activities for everyone. As its name suggests, the thermal hot springs at Hanmer are a wonderful way to relax and unwind and a great way to treat yourself after a long ride. This town is definitely worth the extra detour and stopover.

Continuing your journey along State Highway 7 the road speed drops to an 80 km limit due to high crash rates. This reduction in speed doesn't take anything away from the final stretch though, and you will enjoy the hairpins and mountainside riding back down to the low-lying farmlands. If you are linking this ride with the Alpine Pacific Triangle trip then you will be turning off left at State Highway 70 following signs to Kaikōura. Reaching the Amuri Plains, this flat stretch of straight as you enter and exit Culverden is well-policed and it's easy for your speed to creep up.

After crossing over the Hurunui River, you will find some popular places close by to stop and take in the local atmosphere. The historic Hurunui Hotel appears on your left. This iconic spot is a great place to stop with on-site hotel, cottage, and campsite accommodation as well as a restaurant and bar. Further along in the small town of Waikari is the Star and Garter Hotel.

The road begins to climb and the buzz kicks in again as the road twists and turns through magnificent limestone rock formations creating an alien landscape and strangely shaped cliffs. Look out for the local favourite 'Frog Rock' on your left.

You eventually link up with State Highway 1, the longest road in New Zealand that stretches the length of both the North and South Islands. From here you can turn right and head south to Christchurch, or left will take you north to Kaikōura, making this a great ending point to choose your next adventure.

Detour 1

Blackball

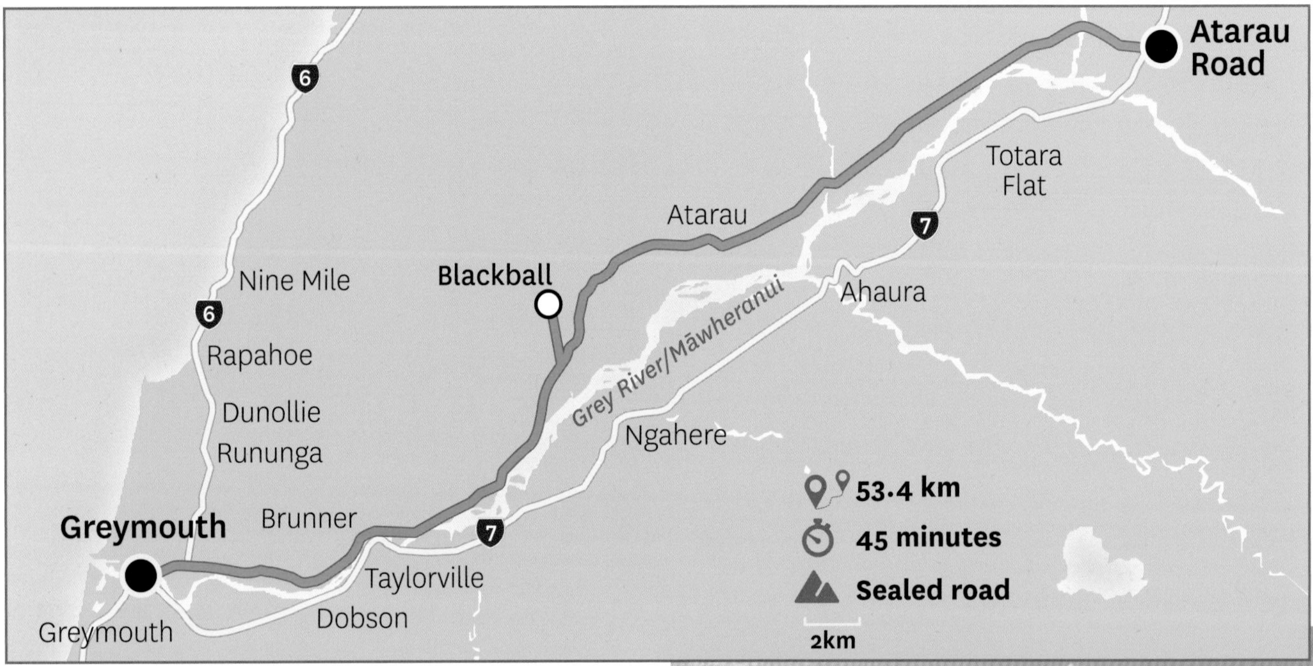

This little back road detour cuts through rural New Zealand and follows the Grey River on the other side, stops at a historic mining town with iconic pub and joins back to the original route of State Highway 7.

Leaving Greymouth, join up with State Highway 6 over the Grey River then turn right following signs to Westport. Shortly after, turn right following the sign to Blackball. Continue following Taylorville Road then, before crossing over the bridge, veer left to follow the Taylorville-Blackball Road for another ten kilometres before a sign to Blackball will mean turning a sharp left curve before reaching the main street.

This quirky little town is known as the birthplace of unionism and the New Zealand Labour Party. Labourers took on the mining companies in 1908 to extend their break time. The locally run museum is full of information about this town and its colourful past.

The iconic pub 'Formerly the Blackball Hilton' received its new name following the threat of a lawsuit from Hilton Hotels in 1992. Taking this with a pinch of salt, this much-loved grand building is a popular biking destination for riders all over New Zealand. With quirky crafts, gourmet meats, and friendly locals, Blackball is a brilliant detour.

Formerly the Blackball Hilton

Detour 2

Punakaiki and The Great Coast Road

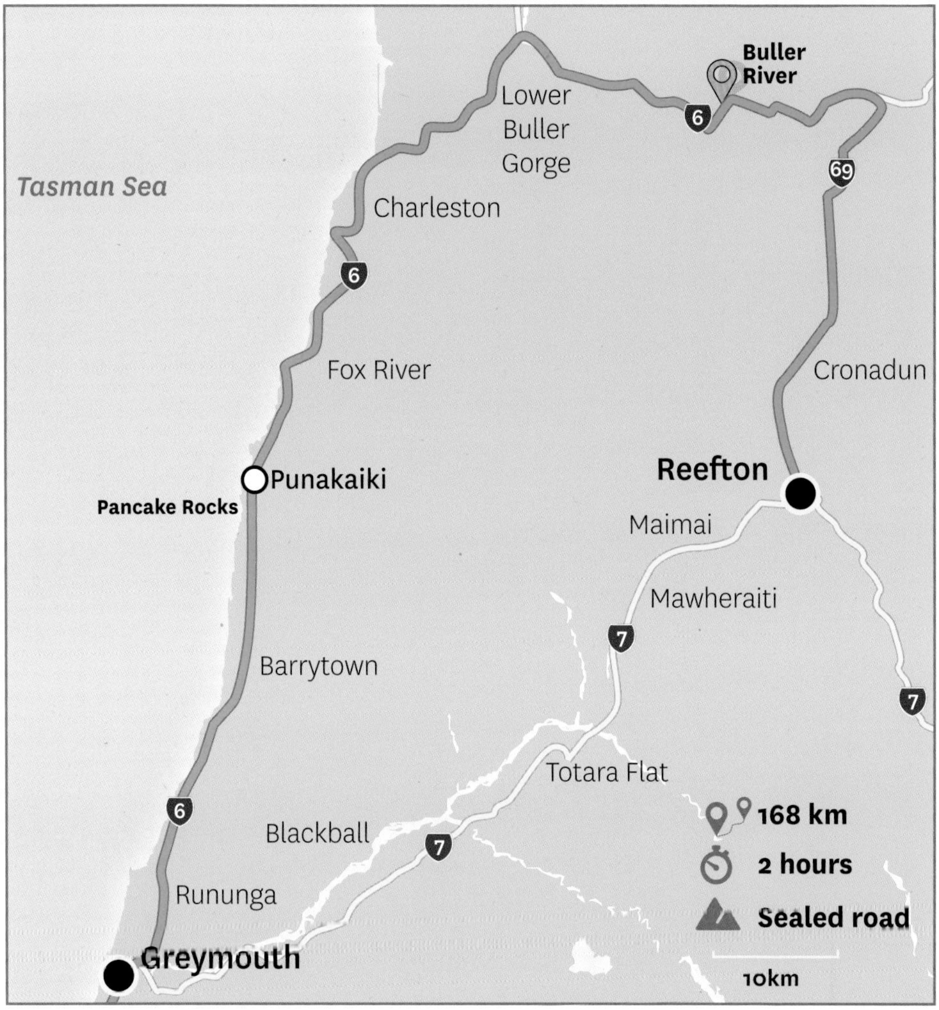

Add in some extra twists and hairpins as well as scenic stops on this breathtaking detour. Heading north on State Highway 6 will bring you to Punakaiki. Kick down your stand and park up at the Pancake Rocks and Blowholes and take the 40-minute stroll around the scenic rainforest walk to look out at the Tasman Sea. View waves crashing in through the pancaked rock formations, creating steam-like puffs of sea spray from multiple airholes created by the sheer force of the ocean and moulded over time. Following the incredible coast road on State Highway 6 then turning inland through the Lower Buller Gorge you'll be grinning all the way on this magical detour to Reefton where you rejoin State Highway 7.

Biker-friendly stops along the way

Red Post Cafe Culverden — 2 Highfield Street, Culverden 7392

Hurunui Hotel — 1224 Karaka Road, State Highway 7, Hurunui 7385

The Star Hotel — 11 Weka Pass Road, Waikari, North Canterbury 7420

Formerly The Blackball Hilton — 26 Hart Street, Blackball 7804

Scenic highlights along the way

Buller River
Reefton, Town of Light
Frog Rock
Waipara Wineries
Punakaiki
The Great Coast Road
Maruia Falls
Hanmer Springs

Why this is such a great ride

This route ticks all the boxes. With spectacular twisty roads, easy and challenging riding all neatly tied up in a bow, with the jaw-dropping beauty of the Southern Alps scenery as the cherry on top. This route is also accessible from many different directions across the South Island so adapting your trip to include this magnificent part of New Zealand is easy.

Detour 3
Shenandoah/Maruia

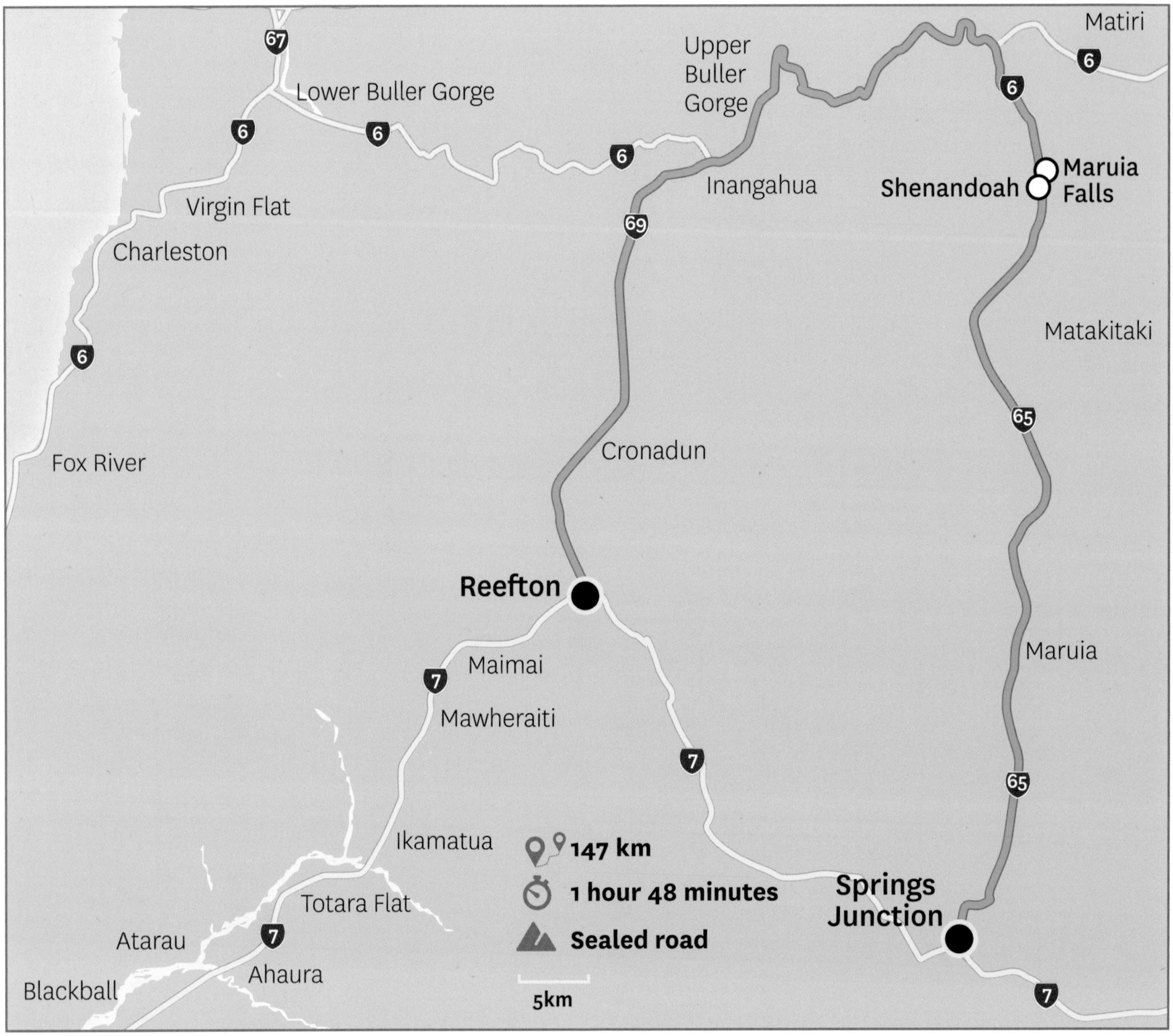

Extend your ride by a few hours, riding north from Reefton and following State Highway 69 to Īnangahua.

The road joins up with State Highway 6 and includes the fabulous twisty hairpin bends of the Buller River surrounded by mountains and dense forest.

The twisty roads around Buller Gorge are the highlight at the top of this loop ride, before turning right to join State Highway 65, following signs to Springs Junction and Christchurch.

Riding along the magnificent Shenandoah Highway you will pass Maruia Falls. Stop and take the ten-minute walk to see nature's handiwork. Following an earthquake in 1929 the river was diverted after a landslide forced it to cut a new path over an old riverbank, creating the current falls.

The long, sweeping bends on this highway will keep the smile on your face before the road joins back with State Highway 7.

Hanmer Springs

Detour 4
Hanmer Springs

A short but worthwhile detour to this stunning alpine village, Hanmer Springs is the perfect place to unwind after a long day in the saddle.

Leaving State Highway 7 for 7A, this is part of the Alpine Pacific Touring Route. With thrill-seeking activities and adrenaline-fuelled options available for everyone, Hanmer Springs is a great stop on this fabulous ride. First cross the Waiau Ferry Bridge. Visitors regularly bungy jump from here and you may even pass over while they launch themselves off.

You're treated to spectacular views across the Hanmer Basin and out across the Waiau Uwha River as you wind your way down to the alpine village.

The natural thermal pools and spas are a popular tourist attraction, and being surrounded by snow-capped mountains and towering redwoods it's easy to see why. With plenty of accommodation options, restaurants, shops, nature walks and adventure activities, this detour is a must-do.

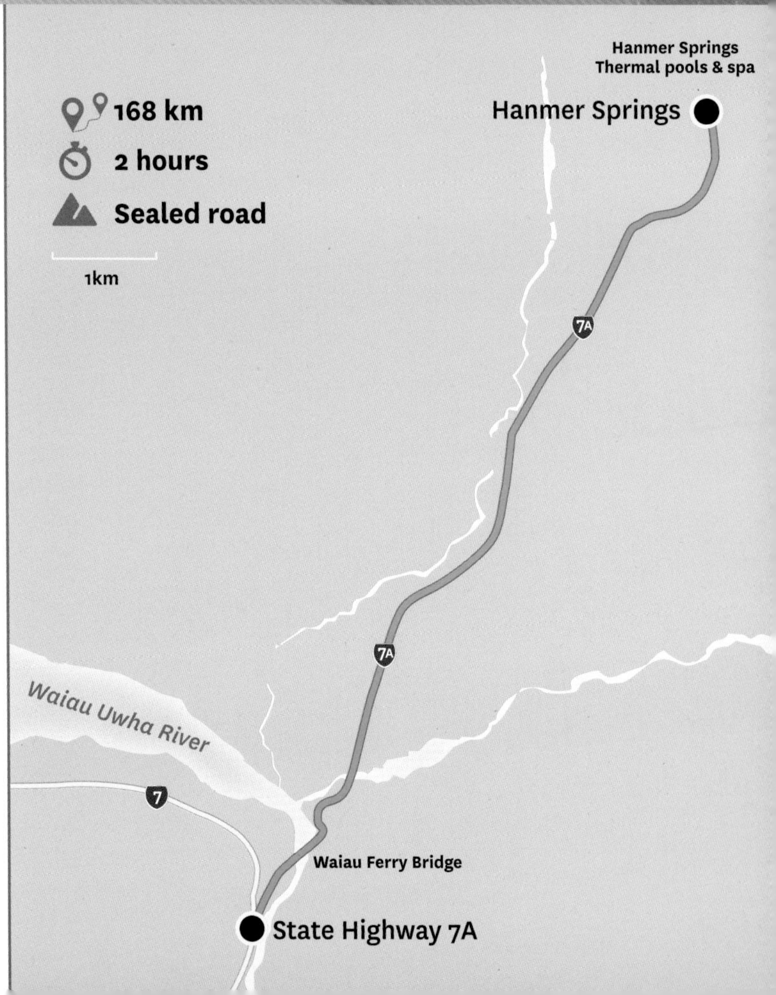

11. Great Alpine Highway — Arthur's Pass — Twin Passes Ride No.2

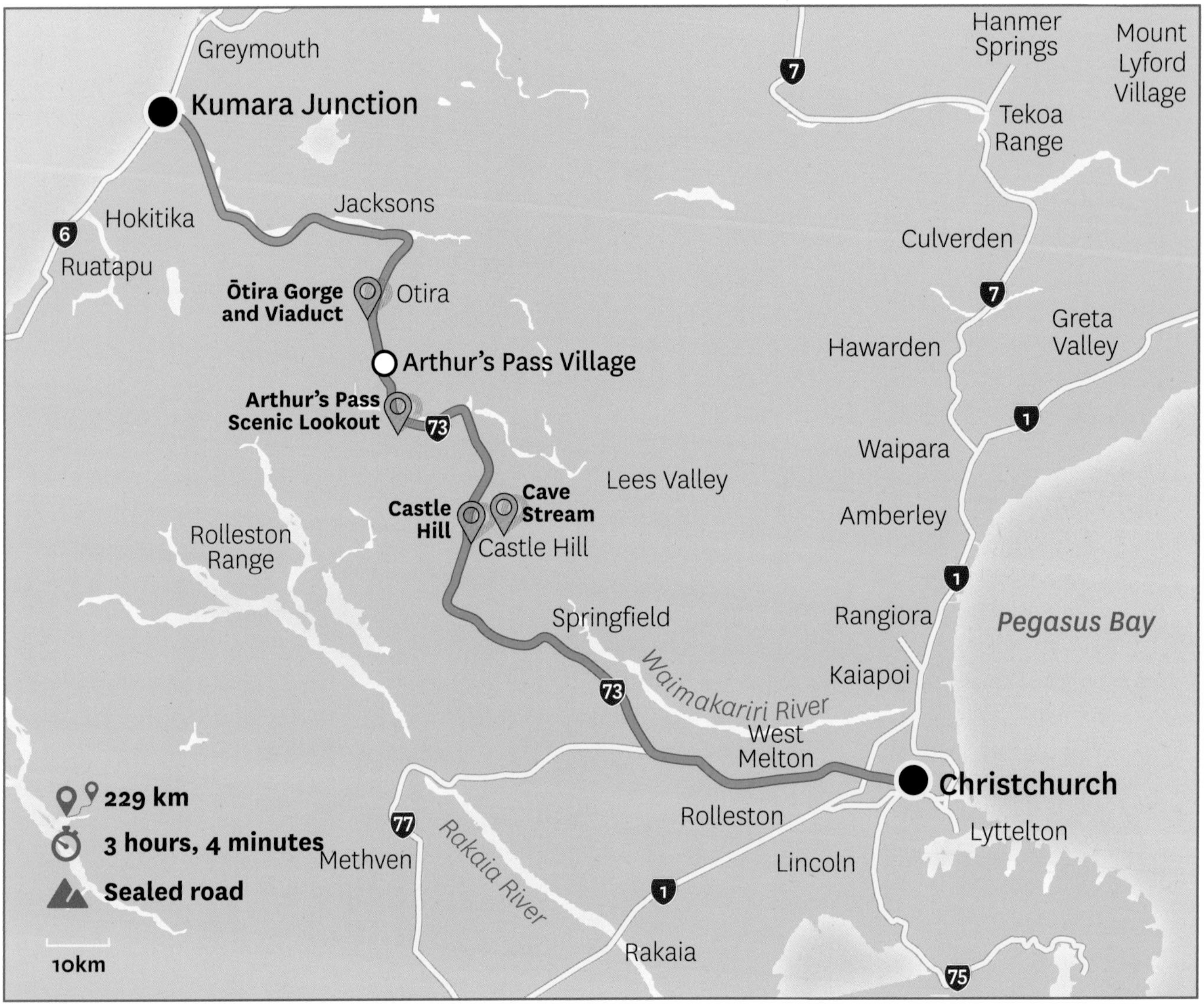

Route Overview

Having the Southern Alps mountain range dividing New Zealand means riding from east to west, alps to ocean is easily doable in one spectacular day. There are two passes that join the east coast to the west coast in the South Island, Arthur's Pass and Lewis Pass (check out the Lewis Pass trip in this book). Both passes offer some of the most challenging, scenic and enjoyable riding in New Zealand. The option to join these two passes together in a multi-day road trip means double the grin factor while you zigzag your way across the country from one side to the other. Riding on well-maintained roads, you will traverse braided rivers and gorges, surrounded by stunning mountain vistas. The history of engineering involved in the crossing of Arthur's Pass is an impressive one. Arthur's Pass is named after Arthur Dobson, a British explorer, surveyor, and engineer, who was commissioned to search for a passable way to cross from the Waimakariri River to the West Coast. Sped up by the gold rush boom, Arthur Dobson had found the pass previously used by Māori was the most suitable, and the construction of Arthur's Pass began in earnest to link the goldfields of the West Coast to the Canterbury Plains. After the Ōtira Railway Station was opened in 1900, followed by the Ōtira Tunnel in 1923, travellers could access the area by train. Today the TranzAlpine Railway is a fantastic way to view this stunning national

Ōtira Viaduct

treasure and travel over the main divide to Greymouth via Lake Brunner. 1999 saw the completion of the Ōtira Viaduct. A welcome and incredible feat of engineering, it replaced a treacherous stretch of road previously taken through the pass. Arthur's Pass National Park is a drawcard for intrepid travellers looking to challenge themselves in the unspoiled beauty of this magnificent location nestled in the backbone of New Zealand. With hiking trails and short walks dotted throughout the area, this could mean a stopover mid-way might be on the cards.

With an elevation of 739 m, Arthur's Pass Village sits between rugged and raw scree-covered mountains in the summer and in winter turns into a snow-covered picturesque wonderland. During the cooler months it's advisable to check the road closures as the Pass does close when conditions are treacherous. If you're riding in the cooler weather, be vigilant of icy road shadows and grit or gravel around corners.

Popular with visitors enjoying outdoor pursuits such as fishing, camping, hiking and four-wheel driving, this road is well used and kept in good condition by road crews.

Whether riding this route from east to west or west to east, you are in for a fabulous adventure. Riding through flame-coloured, tussock-covered landscapes, alongside the icy blue of vast braided rivers and watched over by magnificent snow-capped mountains, you will wind your way through the valleys and bends of the Great Alpine Highway. With a rider's grin on your face you can tick it off the bucket list and know you are undertaking one of the greatest rides in New Zealand.

Start Your Engines!

Beginning from Christchurch and heading west on the flat patchwork of the Canterbury Plains, fuel up at any of the small villages as you follow signs for State Highway 73 — West Coast via Arthur's Pass. If you're a pie connoisseur like most bikers, you won't need an excuse to pull over and put your stand down at the world famous, in New Zealand, Sheffield Pie Shop for a quick bite.

The next town along is Springfield and you might spot the giant pink donut on your right, a nod to Homer and *The Simpsons* television show.

The first part of the Great Alpine Highway is flat and winds its way slowly through farmland before the road begins to cut through hills and valleys. Before long the mountains will rise on either side and you will ride over double and one-lane bridges that criss-cross the Kowai River. The road begins to climb and the long, sweeping bends that make this trip a dream for bikers start to make themselves known.

Further along is Lake Lyndon, followed closely by signs to numerous ski fields. Porters, Mt Cheeseman, Broken River and Craigieburn are all popular destinations for snow sports and adrenaline seekers during the winter months. Riding at a slow, steady incline reveals a dramatic alien-like landscape and one of the most popular stops on the Great Alpine Highway. Castle Hill conservation area makes for a great stop as well as providing a great backdrop for stunning photography. Take the ten-minute walk up to these monolithic limestone geological formations, some towering up to 50 m high. These incredible boulders and rock faces are a magnet for climbers, whether it be professional, recreational, or simply for the young at heart.

Further along State Highway 73 is a town of the same name; Castle Hill offers accommodation and a base for exploring the area, with Cave Stream being one of the drawcards. A fabulous one-hour caving experience which can be achieved by inexperienced cavers with the right equipment and proper research before heading in. Riding alongside Broken River, passing Lake Pearson, and crossing Cass River, eventually leads the road to the Waimakariri River. One of the largest in Canterbury, this vast braided river begins in the Southern Alps and flows south-east to the Pacific Ocean. The undulations and large, sweeping bends, as you follow the icy water on this stretch of road, will prove testament to this road being one of the best in New Zealand.

When you arrive at the iconic Bealey Bridge, the one-way bridge crossing where the Waimakariri and Bealey Rivers meet, you are well and truly in the middle of the spectacular Southern Alps. The road begins its incline and the landscape changes to the telltale beech forest of the west coast fauna. Train tracks of the TranzAlpine Railway will join you to your right as you ride alongside the Bealey River, signifying your arrival into Arthur's Pass Village. Drop your speed and head for Arthur's Pass Store for a well-earned leg stretch.

Watch out for kea around the village. Being alpine parrots, these birds usually live above the snowline but will come down to civilisation where there is the possibility of easy food. They are intelligent and will happily land on your bike and proceed to pick apart your seat or rubber grips with their extremely sharp talons and beak. Where possible, cover your seat with your jacket or make sure you can see your bike if you stop here.

There is fuel at Arthur's Pass Village, but it's limited and for this reason tends to be expensive. Offering numerous stunning forest tracks, and with waterfall walks dotted around the area, make this mountain town a great overnight stop or pass through option. As you ride out of Arthur's Pass the signature windy coast roads and hairpin bends make an appearance, teasing more of what is to come when you cross over to the great divide to the west.

From Temple Basin you will be able to see the Arthur Dudley Dobson memorial obelisk on the horizon on your right. This point marks the divide of the regions and where Canterbury meets the West Coast.

Twisty roads and a spectacular view of the Ōtira Gorge emerge to bring you onwards and over the Ōtira Viaduct. Before reaching the viaduct, on your right, follow signs to the lookout for a fabulous view of this incredible feat of engineering and to see what you will soon be riding over. Ōtira Viaduct is 440 m long and has a gradient of 12 per cent. Take care if the weather isn't at its best, as the force of the wind through the gorge gets very strong here and gusts after passing trucks are an added risk factor. Riding over the viaduct, scree run-off and densely forested mountains are cut through by the Ōtira River thundering below before you ride beneath the Ōtira Gorge Rock Shelter — protection from falling rocks, boulders and water run-off.

Snaking your way along and across the Ōtira River, this road is pure delight all the way to the tiny settlement that shares the same name. Coming in to view on your right is the Otira Stagecoach Hotel. Constructed in 1865 to accommodate travellers, and the growing gold mining population, this fabulous, quirky, biker-friendly stop has accommodation, a cafe and licensed bar on site and is full of antiques and a wealth of local history that makes it well worth a stop.

Biker-friendly stops along the way

World Famous Sheffield Pie Shop — 51 Great Alpine Highway, Sheffield 7681

The Wobbly Kea Cafe — State Highway 73, Arthur's Pass Village 7875

Otira Stagecoach Hotel — Otira Hotel, State Highway 73, Westland, Ōtira 7875

Scenic highlights along the way

Arthur's Pass Lookout

Castle Hill

Ōtira Gorge and Viaduct

Why this is such a great ride

Riding over the Southern Alps of New Zealand via one of the mountain passes is one of the best experiences imaginable for any motorcyclist. With no urbanisation, no traffic lights, no roundabouts, no traffic, and spectacular scenery everywhere you look, this gorgeous empty ribbon road means you'll be in top gear all the way.

Surrounded by the Southern Alps, enjoy the riverside riding all the way to Jacksons. Check out the **Detour to Lake Brunner** here if you have the time.

Soak in the scenery as you ride over the last few one-lane bridges before the mountains give way to civilisation as the landscape flattens and houses begin to emerge from beech forest. Flax-lined roadside will accompany you through to Kumara. Finally meeting up with State Highway 6 at Kūmara Junction. Turning left your journey will take you south along the coast to Hokitika, or turning right you head north to Greymouth.

Check out the Lewis Pass trip in this book and join two legendary Passes together for an incredible extended trip and tick off two of New Zealand's best roads. These twisty mountain passes showcase some of New Zealand's best roads with the spectacular Southern Alps as a backdrop, and you are guaranteed to have a grin from ear to ear.

Detour
Lake Brunner

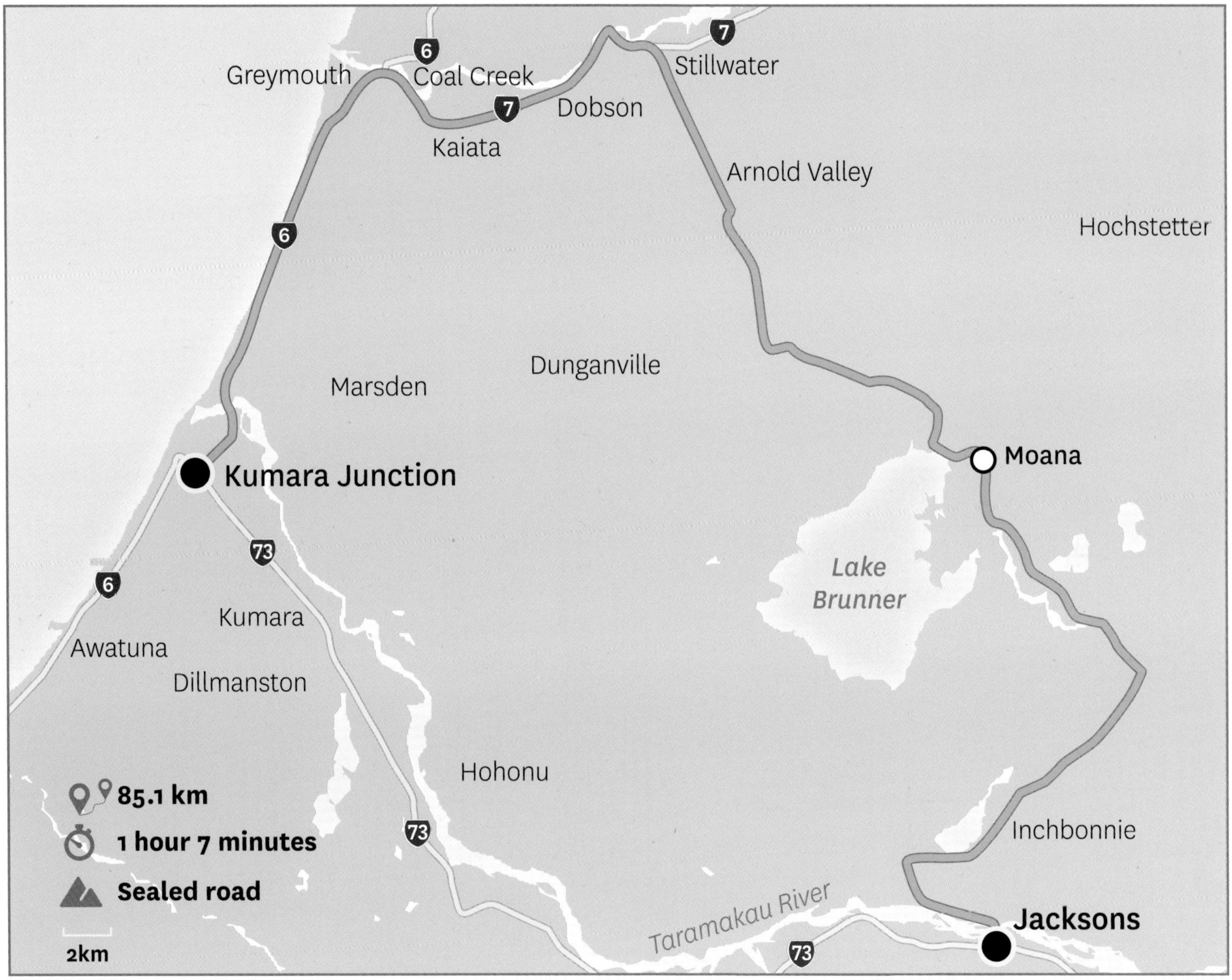

Adding an extra hour to your trip, turn-off at Jacksons from State Highway 73 on the Great Alpine Highway. Turn right onto Lake Brunner Road following signs to Moana via Lake Brunner. A popular holiday destination, this area attracts locals and visitors alike. Recreational activities like fishing, swimming, hiking and boating draw people looking to enjoy this stunning lake and its natural beauty. The TranzAlpine Rail journey also stops at Moana, the only settlement at Lake Brunner. Leaving Moana, Arnold Valley Road follows the Arnold River and joins State Highway 7 at Stillwater. This scenic detour gives you the option to head to Greymouth (turn left) or follow the highway to Lewis Pass and makes it a great shortcut if you're doing the Twin Passes trip as one.

12. The Port Hills and Banks Peninsula

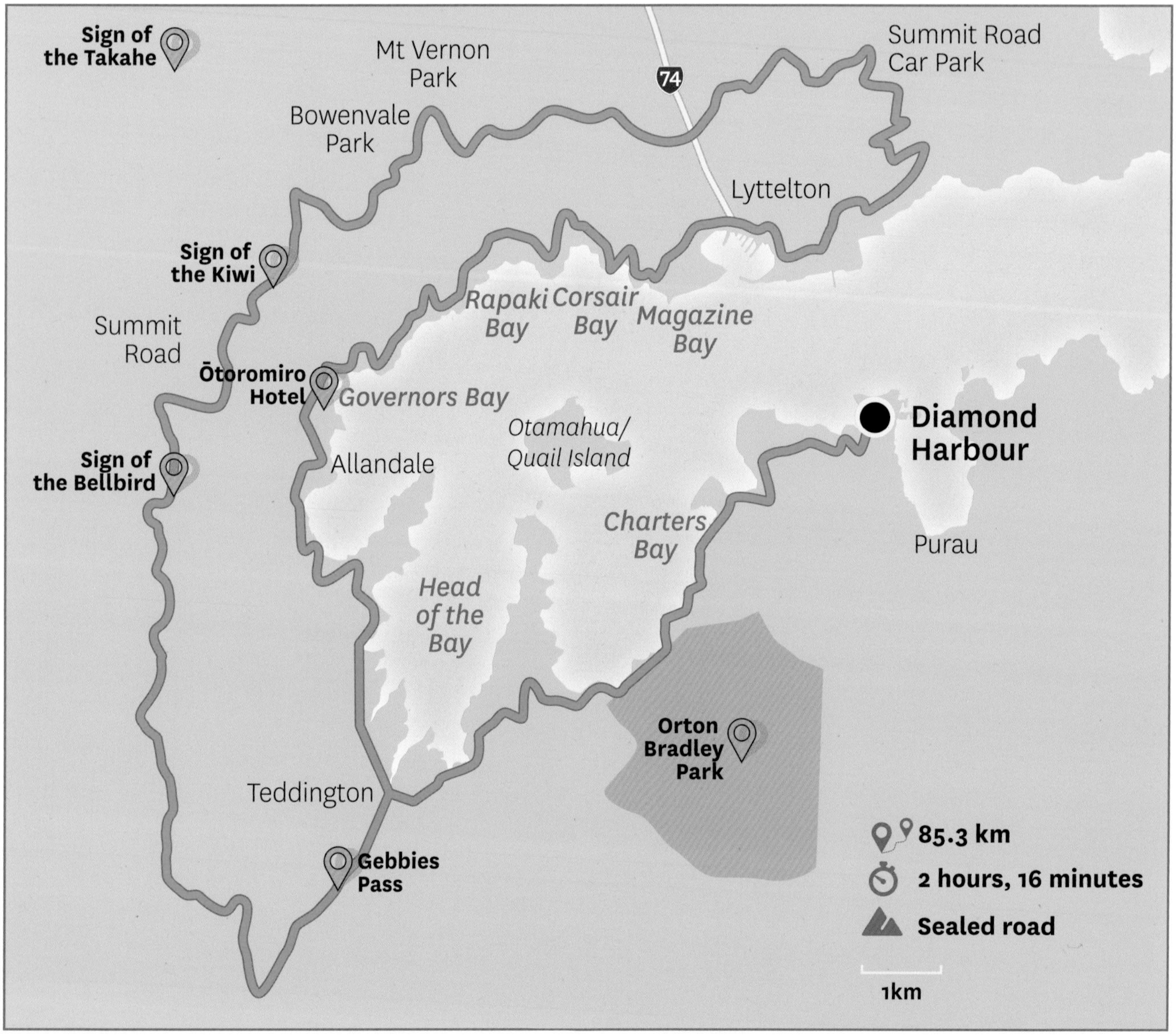

Route Overview

The Port Hills of Christchurch provide an impressive backdrop for the urban city environment. Towering between the city and Lyttelton Harbour, they are easily accessible by vehicle and on foot and attract locals and visitors year-round.

You only need to look at the highlighted map to see what this route is all about. Twists, turns, hairpins and incredible waterside riding all wrapped up in one scenic parcel.

When mapping New Zealand on the ship *Endeavour*, Captain James Cook originally thought the land he saw was an island, and named it 'Banks's Island' after Joseph Banks, the expedition's botanist. Only for the mistake to be realised and rectified in 1806 when it was in fact concluded to be a peninsula.

A unique and striking land mass, Banks Peninsula itself is the product of two extinct volcanoes which originated at Lyttelton and Akaroa. This ride will take you around Summit Road, which snakes its way around both sides of the crest of the Port Hills offering the rider spectacular 360-degree views of the Canterbury Plains on one side, then the peninsula bays and out across to the Pacific Ocean on the other.

Sign of the Kiwi is a great middle point to begin this trip and accessible by more tight twists up the hill to get you started. The cafe here also offers a welcome reward of coffee and ice cream after your trip. Alternatively, start from the port town of Lyttelton. The largest port in the South Island, this bohemian harbourside township

Banks Peninsula

can be accessed easily from Christchurch either over the hill from Sumner or from Christchurch through a tunnel. Packed with options for a great day out with restaurants, markets, shops, and quirky street art. This harbour town is also the site where the original four ships landed from England with settlers, so it holds historical significance for the region.

This route continues around to Diamond Harbour on the opposite side, giving you a full vantage point to show you how far you've ridden around the peninsula.

As you look across the bays you will see Ōtamahua/Quail Island in the middle. This island can be accessed by a short scenic boat cruise and has an interesting history. Previously a colony for leprosy sufferers when Europeans first settled in Canterbury, the island was also the site where explorers Captain Scott and Captain Shackleton trained their sled dogs before heading to the Antarctic.

The Summit Road includes a mixture of single, narrow roads and double lane roads, and the surrounding land is both public and farm land, so you will cross some cattle stops/cattle grids. Loose sheep and cattle are dotted around the hills so be vigilant for loose animals as well as other motorists. Being a farming road also means a few unwanted potholes and road mess so keep an extra eye out.

The Port Hills' summits rise up to 500 m above sea level in some places and it's not uncommon to be riding amongst the clouds. The temperature can drop quickly as well, so make sure you pack an extra layer just in case.

There are multiple places to stop, pull over and get some incredible photos of this dramatic landscape, or if you are simply wanting a challenging ride to test your clutch control then this is the one.

Start Your Engines!

Start this route whichever way you want to. If you start this ride from Lyttelton it means you experience the Lyttelton Tunnel. This engineering marvel has been the link between Christchurch City and the port of Lyttelton since 1964. You emerge at a roundabout overlooking the docks. Turn right along Simeon Quay then turn left on to Brittan Terrace following signs to Governors Bay. The roads are fairly narrow here with parked cars and still quite busy with traffic so get used to the turns as you start to climb.

Twist your way around the bays visible on your left: Magazine Bay, Corsair Bay, Cass Bay and Rāpaki Bay are all popular local swimming spots and it's easy to see why. These clear and still waters provide perfect mooring for boats, as well as offering safe recreational facilities for visitors.

The road undulates around the tussock covered and rocky coastline. Dropping down through your gears the road starts to climb again and you'll arrive at Governors Bay, its prominent historic Ōtoromiro Hotel and restaurant positioned to your right and overlooking a spectacular panoramic view of the harbour. This historic hotel was established in 1870 and is a popular destination for local bikers.

Continuing on, you reach Teddington where the road drops back down to sea level. At this junction the Wheatsheaf Tavern on your right is another favourite stop for bikers in the area. Between the tavern and the old blacksmith forge on your left is where you'll turn right on to Gebbies Pass Road, following the sign to Motukarara and Akaroa. The Blacksmith Shop was established in the 1980s and is well worth a visit if it's open.

Though a short stretch of road, Gebbies Pass has some delightful, long, sweeping bends and all too soon you crest the hill and will need to turn sharp right up Summit Road, but you will be forgiven if you kept going past and down to the valley to enjoy more bends before turning around and coming back to the turn-off.

Be aware there is a cattle grid to ride over as you enter Summit Road as this area is still farmed and has loose stock which roam the hills, so keep an eye out as you ride around. The road is also narrow and without barriers and in cooler months, or after rainfall, can become icy and treacherous.

The landscape alters as the elevation changes, and this ride curves around tussock, flax and bright yellow gorse covered rocky outcrops, fields, and patches of forest. The Canterbury Plains on one side and Lyttelton Harbour on the other creates the most magnificent backdrop for this summit ride.

Passing over multiple cattle grids and through scenic reserves will bring you to Sign of the Bellbird. Pull over at the car park on your right for one of the best views in Christchurch. On the opposite side of the road is the site of one of the stone rest houses bult in the 1900s which provided shelter for travellers.

There are multiple walking tracks which zigzag their way up, down and over the Port Hills, the most well known being the Crater Rim Walkway. This four kilometre walk starts from Sign of the Kiwi, a little further ahead on your right, and ends right here at Sign of the Bellbird so the traffic, foot traffic and bicycle traffic may start to increase from this section of the route.

Sign of the Kiwi is another stone rest house designed in the arts and crafts style. Its cafe here is a popular destination to stop for a coffee or ice cream before heading off on your next adventure. Be vigilant and stop at the intersection here as the four-way crossroads are somewhat concealed and the traffic coming from your left and right has the right of way. This route takes us straight ahead to continue following Summit Road and riding below the iconic 'Sugarloaf' communications tower. This iconic tower provides Christchurch with its television and radio frequencies.

As you ride along the narrow road, the Canterbury Plains stretch out as far as you can see to your left. They end at the magnificent Southern Alps and on a fine day you can see them clearly. Christchurch City sprawls out below you as you climb up and into the clouds. Riding closer towards the Pacific Ocean, you may notice the wind pick up and the tussocks in surrounding fields will be a good indication of what's to come. This landscape is quite exposed which makes it a magnet for paragliding and wind sports.

Further along you ride beneath the Christchurch Gondola, a popular tourist attraction which gives visitors a chance to view the incredible beauty of Christchurch and the Canterbury Plains from above.

As the road ahead begins to descend, you are treated to a clearer view of the Pacific Ocean and the sweeping curve of Pegasus Bay, before rounding the corner to see the seaside township of Sumner below. Check out the **Detour to Sumner** Beach if you have time.

Summit Road ends at the next crossroads. Make sure you come to a complete stop here as this intersection is a fairly fast and blind corner. Check out the **Detour to Godley Head** if you have time.

Biker-friendly stops along the way

Ōtoromiro Hotel and Cafe — 52 Main Road, Governors Bay 8971

Wheatsheaf Tavern — 554 Governors Bay, Teddington Road, Teddington 8971

Sign of the Kiwi — Summit Road, Governors Bay 8971

Scenic highlights along the way

Diamond Harbour
Sign of the Kiwi
Sign of the Bellbird
Sign of the Takahe
Orton Bradley Park
Lyttelton Harbour
Banks Peninsula

Why this is such a great ride

This is a challenging ride along an elevated, twisty stretch of road. Continuous bends will have you on the edge of your seat. Breathtaking views across Banks Peninsula and across the Canterbury Plains are an added bonus on this fabulous, isolated road. Tight turns and effortless sweeping corners make for an incredible ride in the Port Hills.

Port Hills

Detour 1
Sumner Beach, Scarborough Beach, Taylors Mistake Beach

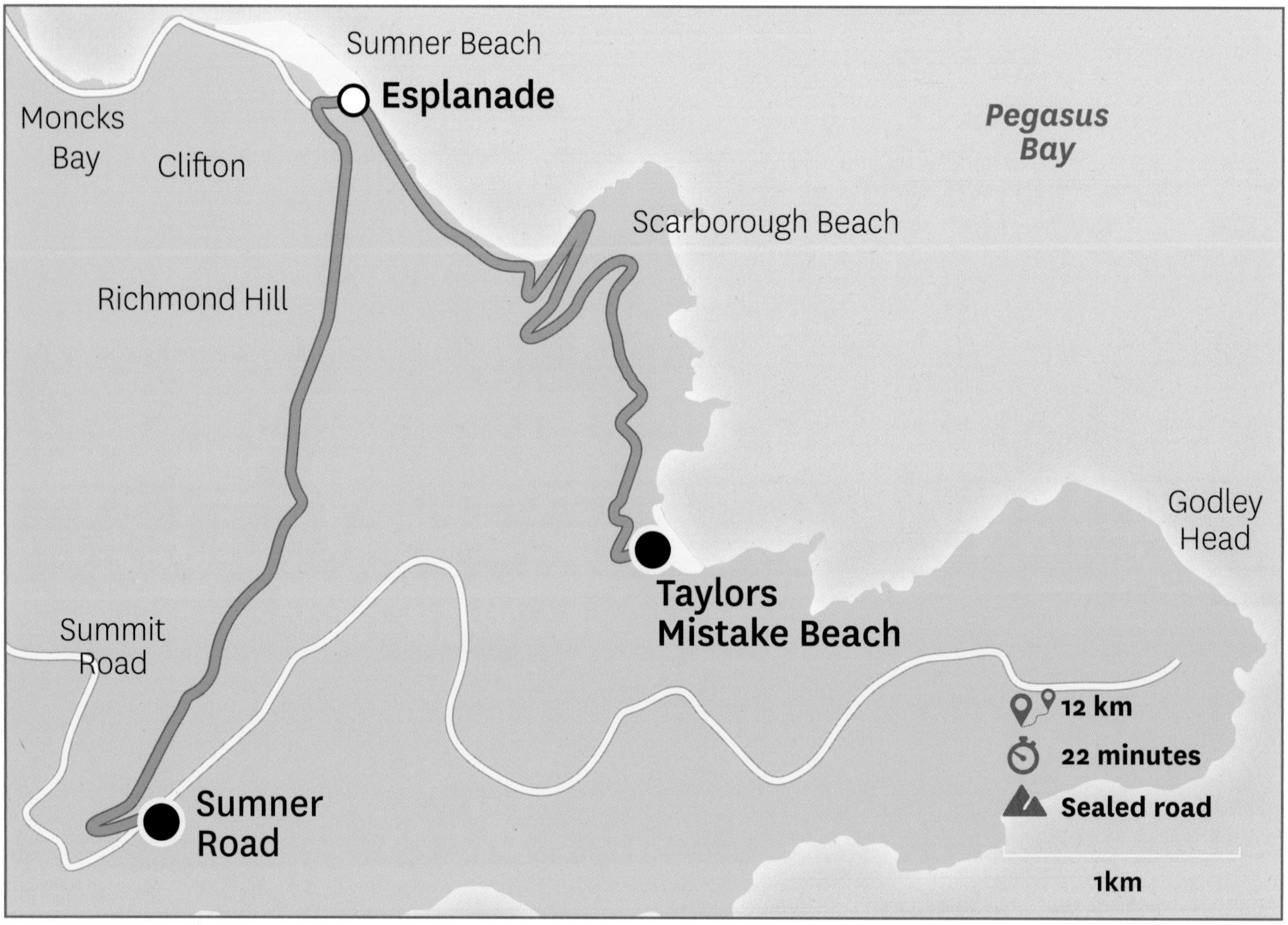

Heading down the hill on Evans Pass Road and joining Wakefield Avenue, this road emerges into the pretty seaside village of Sumner. Follow the road around and turn right on to the Esplanade where you will see the golden sand and Cave Rock to your left. A great place to stop and soak up the sun or grab an ice cream on a hot day.

Along this detour are three beaches that are popular with locals for relaxation and recreation, as well as surfers and surf schools for those who want to learn.

Riding further around will bring you to Scarborough Beach and its promenade, ending at the iconic clocktower. Turn left on to Heberden Avenue and begin the climbing ride up and over the hill, zigzagging your way along the rocky cliff. These roads are narrow so watch out for other vehicles.

This detour ends at Taylors Mistake Beach car park.

Detour 2

Awaroa/Godley Head and Gun Emplacements

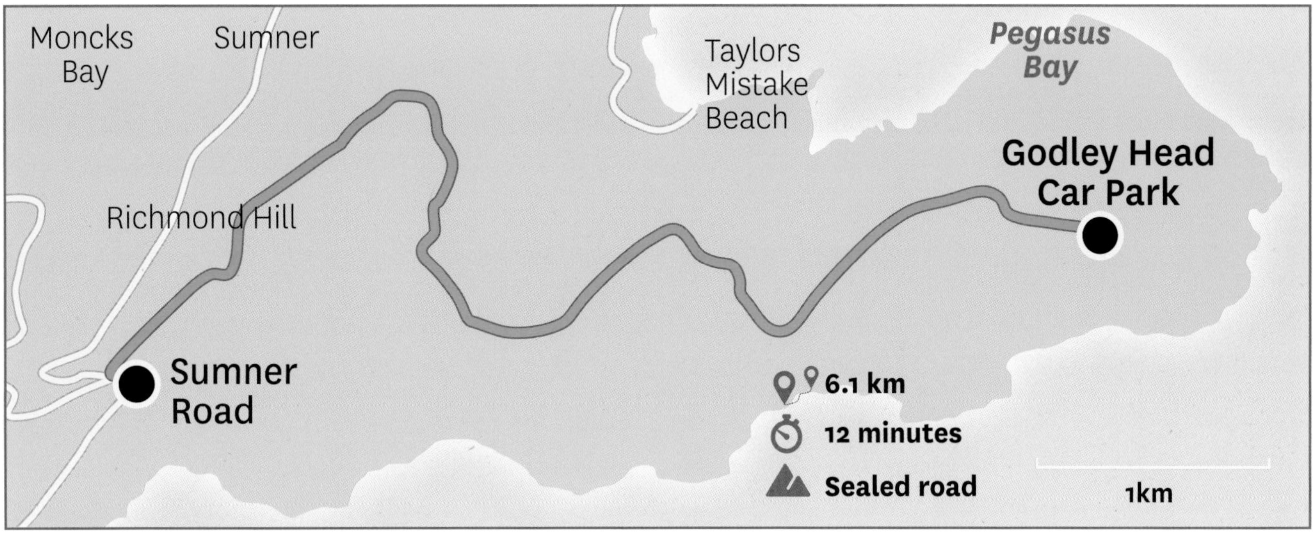

If you have time up your sleeves for some extra scenic riding, at the crossroads from Summit Road, follow Godley Head Road. This single, narrow road winds its way around the hill high up into Scarborough Reserve to overlook the sweep of Pegasus Bay and overlooking Sumner Beach below. Watch out for oncoming vehicles, follow the road around the tussock and grass-covered landscape. On your left you'll see Taylors Mistake Beach. This area off the road to your left is also the launch place of local paragliding enthusiasts and people wanting to make the most of this beautiful area by seeing it from the skies above.

There are multiple walks around this rocky headland, if you're looking to explore, and you'll see a number of signs indicating their start points. This detour ends at Godley Head car park and you can take the short walks to the gun emplacements and coastal defense battery which were built in 1939.

Lyttelton Harbour

13. Christchurch to Akaroa

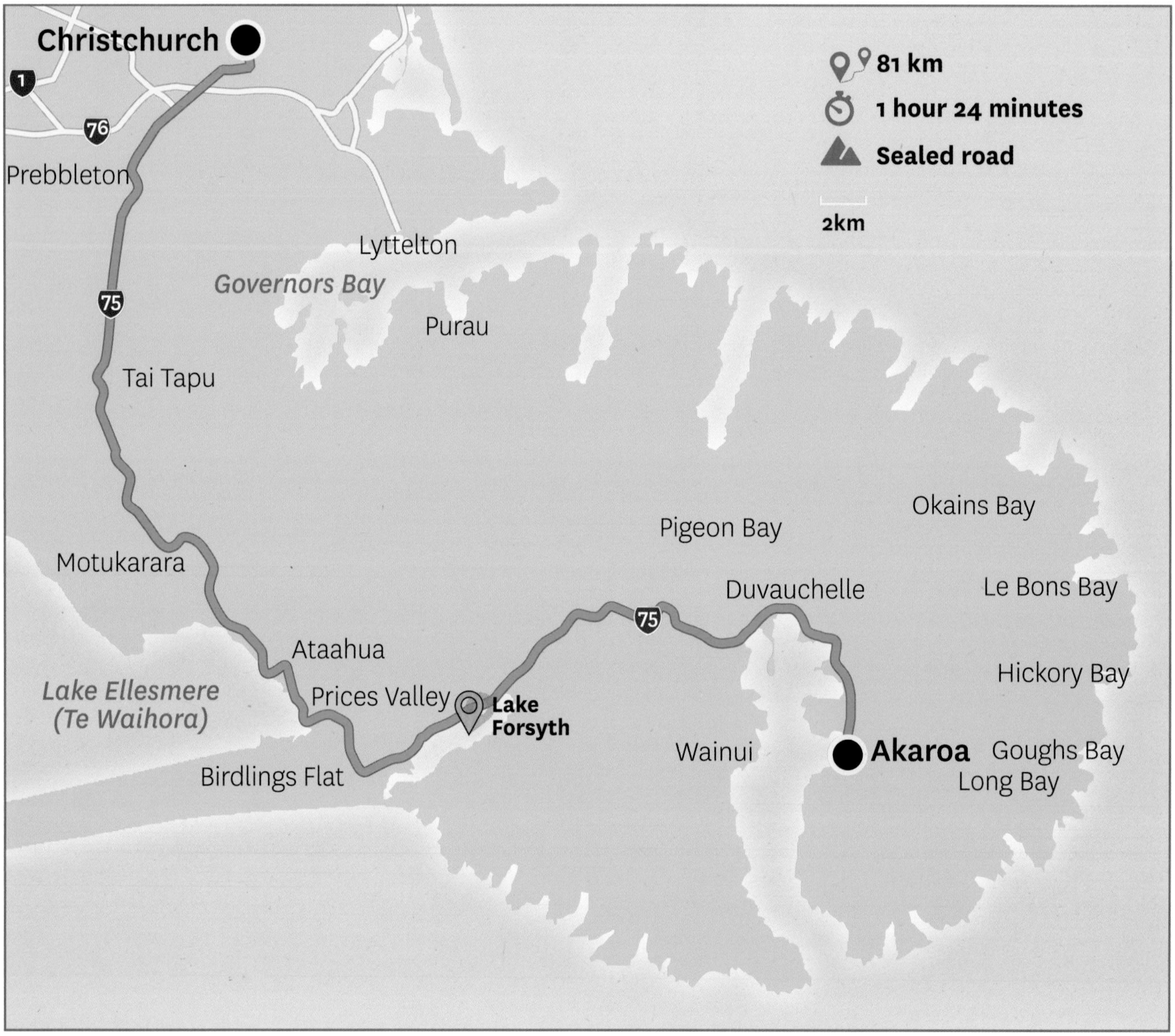

Route Overview

This road trip can also be extended by adding on the Port Hills route at the beginning of this trip. Creating a whole day of twists and turns and scenic riding that will have a grin permanently stuck on your face and the fresh ocean air in your lungs.

As a central base, Christchurch is a great place to start many of the road trips included in this book. There are many day trips from the Garden City that can be extended easily to overnight rides and two-day adventures. This route to Akaroa is a great example of just that. Known by locals as a favourite 'there and back again' destination to ride and grab a quick feed of fish and chips or a pie overlooking the Akaroa Harbour while also getting a good dose of twisty, challenging, and stunning riding included both ways.

There is one main road which services the Banks Peninsula, and this now has a lower speed limit due to being a high-crash area. With some long, straight stretches and long, sweeping bends, it's easy for your speed to creep up unintentionally on the first section of this route.

You will be riding with the vast Canterbury Plains stretching out to your right before spotting Lake Ellesmere/ Waihora. State Highway 75 veers sharp left around the cliffs at Prices Valley and Birdlings Flat and you will be treated to the magnificent sight of Lake Forsyth/Wairewa. These two immense lakes hold

Akaroa Harbour

great ecological and historical cultural significance for local Māori and 'mahinga kai' which highlights the value of ecosystems as a means of producing food and sustaining the environment it comes from.

Banks Peninsula is a landscape of volcanic origin with Akaroa Harbour at the centre. Rocky cliffs curtain the peninsula and numerous bays boast spectacular beaches and coves just waiting to be explored.

In 1840 the French first settled in Akaroa's sheltered harbour. You will notice the French influence dotted around everywhere, from street names to shopfronts and annual festivals, this stunning seaside town is proud of its heritage.

Akaroa Harbour and surrounding headlands are also home to incredible wildlife, including the world's smallest dolphin, Hector's dolphin. This threatened dolphin is a drawcard for tourists and boats cruise the harbour looking to sight these inquisitive mammals, as well as offering dolphin swims and other nature- and water-based adventures.

This road trip makes its way around the base of the Port Hills, and from Little River begins an ascent upwards through the twists and turns that make this route such a top-class ride. Added to spectacular views, seaside riding to a destination that is biker-friendly all-year round make this trip a fabulous road trip.

Start Your Engines!

If you are beginning this trip from Christchurch, follow signs out of the city for State Highway 75 to Akaroa, through the town of Halswell and the picturesque country village of Tai Tapu. Both are good places to top up your tank with fuel before you head out to Banks Peninsula as watching the fuel gauge the entire trip won't be much fun.

Check out the **Detour via Summit Road/The Port Hills** if you have the time.

The Christchurch-Akaroa Road boasts some fabulous sweeping bends around the base of the Peninsula and when you reach Motukarara you will see a sign to Diamond Harbour and Lyttelton via Gebbies Pass. The turn-off further down on your left is where you would rejoin the road if you take the detour or link up with the Port Hills route. Or you could opt to take this detour on your way back if you have some extra time. Continue around the bend to the right to head towards Akaroa before you follow alongside the water with the Plains and Lake Ellesmere on your right.

The sharp left turn at the end will open up your view to the stunning and often mirror-calm Lake Forsyth/Wairewa before reducing your speed to reach the small village of Wairewa/Little River. There is a fuel station here if you need to top up the tank, as well as gift shops, galleries and cafes, and is a favourite stop for bikers to grab a coffee and a bite to eat before climbing up and over the hills.

Still continuing along State Highway 75, riding through the picturesque tree-lined streets will signify the start of your ascent and to get ready to enjoy the next seven kilometres of twisty switchbacks and tight hairpin bends.

The recommended cornering speed signs are a great

way to gauge the upcoming corner, as well as knowing your own speed limit and which gear you're going to be comfortable in, making for a fabulous climb all the way up to Hilltop.

Just before you reach the Hilltop Tavern, check out the **Detour via Summit Road** if you have time.

Rounding the crest of the hill you will see the Hilltop Tavern on the left with its fantastic backdrop overlooking the bays below. Pull over here to take in this incredible view and stretch your legs before dropping down the gears and enjoying your picturesque descent into the first of four stunning bays.

The ride dips and climbs in and out of Barrys Bay, Duvauchelle Bay, Robinsons Bay and Takamatua Bay before reaching Akaroa. Enjoy stunning waterside riding as you skirt your way around the crater of an extinct volcano and past secluded inlets.

When the masts of numerous sailboats come in to view you have reached your destination of Akaroa Harbour. Follow the main streets of Rue Lavaud and Rue Jolie through the town and take a right on to Bruce Terrace before joining up with Beach Road. This one-way waterfront street offers the best views out across the bay and the local bikers park up opposite the fish and chip shop and Bully Hayes. Grab a drink, a bite to eat and relax enjoying the view of the harbour and any other bikes that turn up. This friendly biker's destination is a great spot to meet fellow riders.

Along the promenade are gift shops, restaurants, cafes, galleries, sandy beaches, and the iconic Akaroa Lighthouse. This street is also the main place to book any excursions you may want to try while here in nature's playground. Famous for swimming with dolphins, nature cruises, sailing, hiking, culinary delights, arts and crafts and incredible scenery, Akaroa has something for everyone so you may want to extend this road trip. The best part is, you get to ride over all those twists and turns on your way back.

Biker-friendly stops along the way

White Rabbit Garden Cafe — 1683 Christchurch-Akaroa Road, Gebbies Valley 7672

Little River Cafe — Christchurch-Akaroa Road, Little River 7591

Akaroa Fish and Chips — 59 Beach Road, Akaroa 7520

Bully Hayes Cafe and Restaurant — 57 Beach Road, Akaroa 7542

Scenic highlights along the way

Hilltop Lookout

Lake Forsyth

Banks Peninsula Bays

Akaroa Harbourside

Why this is such a great ride

This route is known for the incredible tight twists as you climb up and over the hilltop from Little River all the way to Akaroa. A fabulous ride to test your gear skills and enjoy the destination as well as the ride itself. With multiple detours available this is a great route to meet fellow riders who are all enjoying the trip for the same reasons.

Detour 1
Lyttelton/ Governors Bay

For a more scenic start over to Akaroa, this detour will add an extra hour on to your trip but well worth the extra time. Start by following signs to Sumner from Christchurch, then climbing up to Summit Road and over the Port Hills (check out the Port Hills Ride in this book for more details) and down to Lyttelton Port.

Following signs to Governors Bay, with the stunning harbour on your left, you'll be turning right just after the Wheatsheaf Tavern at Teddington and following signs to Gebbies Pass.

The Pass has some great twists and hairpins which is a great precursor for the bends on your trip to Akaroa.

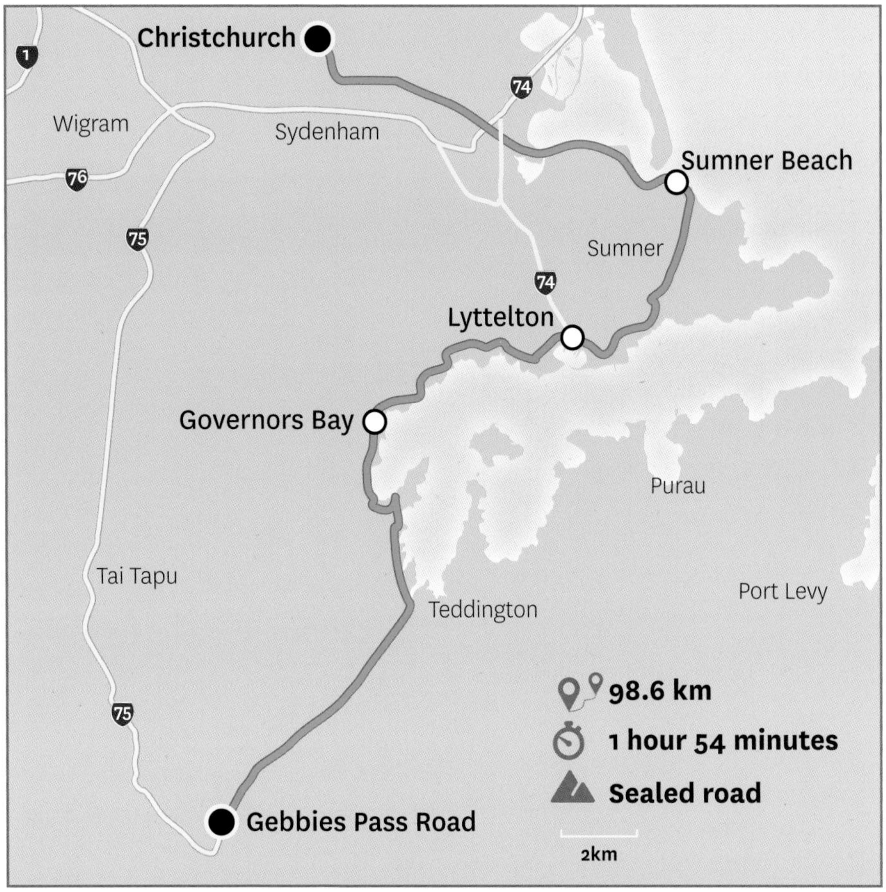

Detour 2
Banks Peninsula/ Akaroa Summit Road

Adding an hour or so to your ride, the Summit Road Tourist Drive winds its way around the rim of Banks Peninsula, giving unparalleled views over Akaroa Harbour, the Eastern Bays and out to the Pacific Ocean.

Join this detour from State Highway 75 just before Hilltop Tavern or from Long Bay Road, Akaroa. Follow signs for 'Tourist Drive'. Riding through open farmland and scenic reserves along this twisty, narrow road, passing very few people, it's easy to forget there are other vehicles on the road. Enjoy the peace and incredible scenery on this relatively traffic-free detour.

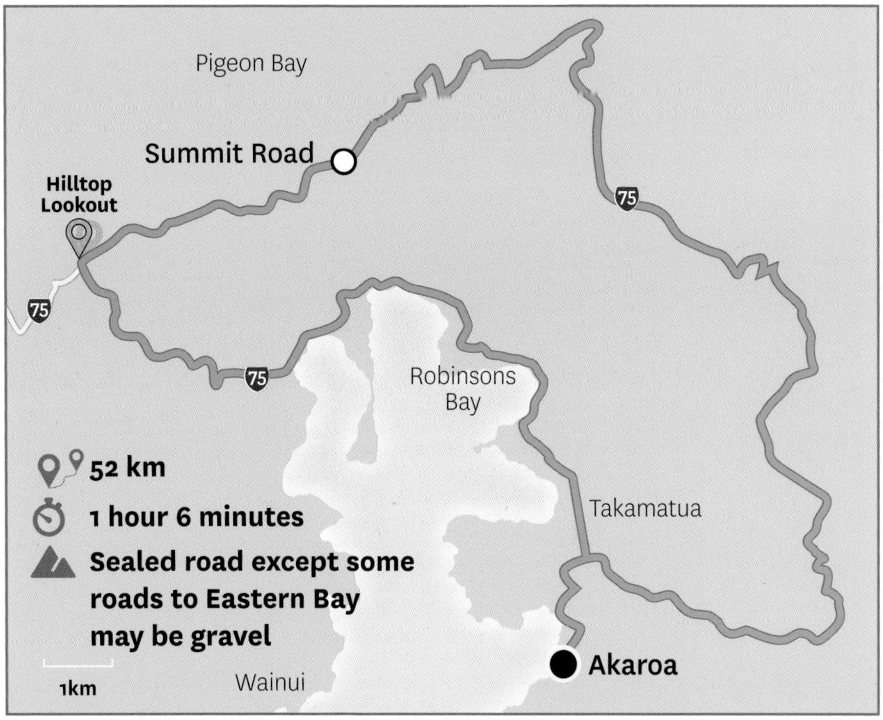

14. Queenstown to Franz Josef Glacier via Crown Range and Haast Pass

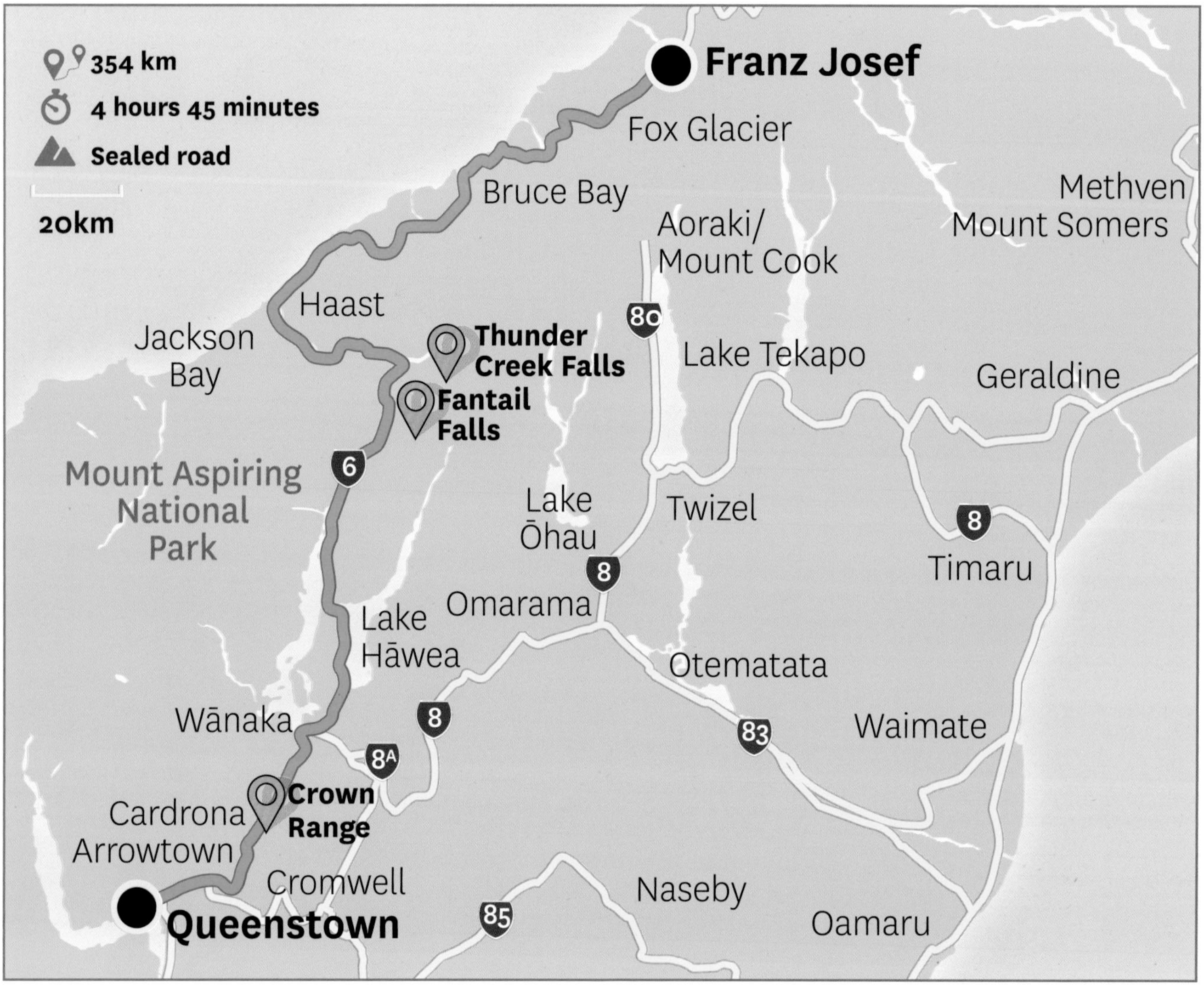

Route Overview

This trip is breathtaking whether you are riding in from the south or north. If you have had a few days to explore or relax in the adventure capital of the world, Queenstown, and are heading back north then you will be itching to get back on the bike and will have earned yourself this adrenaline-filled day of riding through some of New Zealand's most spectacular scenery.

Mountain ranges, tussock-covered hills, crystal blue lakes, braided rivers, valleys, rainforest, and fern-covered cliffs will be your constant companions today. The scenery will change from one to the other in the blink of an eye and will keep you on the edge of your seat the entire trip as you ride through the Queenstown Lakes District to connect with the Westland coast.

You will be riding through some fabulous small townships so if you have the time, stop for coffee, a pie or whitebait pattie (in season, this tiny fish is a West Coast delicacy) and have a chat with the locals. West Coast hospitality is well known and your bike and travels will be a great conversation starter.

Highlights of this trip include riding the magnificent Haast Pass, The Neck, Lake Hāwea and Lake Wānaka. Wānaka is a great place to stop and catch your breath after you park up at the lakefront. This mountain town in the winter transforms to a mecca for those looking for fresh powder for snow sports. This region boasts some of the best skiing in the Southern Hemisphere

Lake Hāwea

and is surrounded by the ski fields of Cardrona, Treble Cone, and further south to the Remarkables ski field. Another highlight is every two years sees this picturesque town flooded with aviation enthusiasts who travel here from all over the world for 'Warbirds over Wanaka'. The skies are filled with heritage aircraft for a weekend of incredible airshows and wartime displays not to be missed.

The West Coast is known for its wild weather and as you ride north through 'The Neck' the terrain will change to lush green rainforest. Keep your fingers crossed for good weather for this trip as it is truly breathtaking being able to see the vast landscape and superb 360-degree vistas. Even if the weather is less than favourable and you do get some rain, the upside is that the surrounding mountains will gift you with hundreds of cascading waterfalls with the increased rainfall. You'll soon forget the wet and cold as you ride through this dramatic landscape.

One of the best parts about riding in New Zealand is breathing in that fresh mountain air and the scent of rainforest will permeate through your helmet and add to the full emersion of this incredible ride.

Start Your Engines!

Leaving Queenstown, the towering presence of The Remarkables mountain range will be in your wing mirror as you ride out of town. Make sure you fuel up at either Queenstown or Wānaka as you head out, as petrol stations are few on this first stretch of the West Coast and you will want to be focusing on the riding, not your fuel gauge on this route. If you are taking the detour via Arrowtown, you add another hour on to your trip.

State Highway 6 is the main road in and out of Queenstown and is usually busy, especially at the roundabout in Frankton and the airport. Be vigilant here as there will be tourists who are new to New Zealand roads hiring cars and looking around at the scenery rather than for bikers.

Head out of Queenstown following SH6, over the Shotover River Bridge to pass Lake Hayes.

There are two ways to ride from Queenstown to Wānaka. Choose either via the Crown Range Road or through Cromwell beside Lake Dunstan. Although shorter, the Crown Range Road is more of a challenge on a motorcycle and a great bucket list ride. Check out the **Detour via Cromwell** if you need to.

To follow the Crown Range Road, ride past the turn-off to Arrowtown until you see the sign to Cardrona and Wānaka via the Crown Range. This ride follows the Alpine Scenic Route and is New Zealand's highest main road at an altitude of 1,121 m.

During the winter months this road is often closed due to ice and snow and the temperature drops very quickly. Check the road conditions, heed any ice warnings, and watch out for grit and gravel at the sides of the road. Remember that tourists in campervans also use this road and they tend to drift over the centre-line sometimes to overcompensate for the tight corners. Give yourself enough room on your side of the road to allow for any oncoming vehicles on the bends.

As you turn sharp left at Arrow Junction the road immediately starts to climb over the Crown Range via a series of incredibly tight hairpin bends and you may like to stop briefly at the top to look back at the view across Queenstown to The Remarkables in the far distance. As you ride higher over the Range you may notice the temperature drop considerably and the scenery will become more dramatic as you are now up at cloud level. There is another lookout at the summit where you can stop for a photo and even consider doing the ride back down the other way, and you wouldn't be the first biker to do so.

The Crown Range Road continues to offer glorious long sweeps and bends as you descend down into the Cardrona Valley. The historic Cardrona Hotel offers that all important 'been there, done that' photograph. A well-earned break should be on the cards either here or at your next stop at Wānaka. Cardrona Valley Road will take you all the way to Wānaka and its deep blue lakefront shores. A good idea would be to top up your tank with fuel here, as there is only one fuel station at Haast, and it may or may not be open. Wānaka is a great place to stop overnight as there is plenty to do in and around this stunning lakeside township; visit the National Transport and Toy Museum, Warbirds and Wheels, Puzzling World and many other great attractions all in one place.

Ride onwards and along State Highway 84 out of Wānaka, before turning left to join State Highway 6 and following signs to Lake Hāwea and the West Coast.

Breathtaking riding today alongside Lake Hāwea and some of the most spectacular scenery in New Zealand. Undulating roads, perfect corners and ever-changing vistas make this route a real treat. Stop at Lake Hāwea Lookout point before your throttle hand starts twitching again as you eye the road ahead. As you skirt this magnificent lakeside road you reach 'The Neck', so named as this stretch of road snakes between the alpine lakes of Lake Hāwea and Lake Wānaka.

After the next fabulous 30 minutes of pure biker bliss, the landscape will begin to change from red tussocks to rainforest-covered mountains that tower overhead as you enter the Haast Pass. Makarora River will keep you company to your left as you wind your way through the lush, forest-covered valley road. Makarora Country Cafe is a great quirky place to grab a coffee and take a break surrounded by car license plates, flags and farm equipment decorating the walls. Continuing on, Haast River appears to your right, and you cross the one-way bridge over the thunderous, cascading rapids of the Gates of Haast, signalling your arrival through the gorge to the untouched Jurassic landscape of the West Coast. These crystal-clear waters are a drawcard for tourists for fishing and hiking. There are multiple forest walks and viewpoints along this route, the Blue Pools, Fantail Falls and Thunder Creek Falls are all popular places to take in the real, untouched West Coast. Crack open your visor as you ride and breathe in the pure rainforest air. If you look up and around the valley cliffs, thin silver waterfalls cascade down the sides of the mountains like webs across the landscape. If the weather is less than perfect and you get some rain, expect the falls you see to double in size and number. Keep an eye out for surface water here as the rainforest water run-off sometimes flows across the road, making for a beautiful, dramatic, yet challenging ride.

There are plenty of single-lane bridges on this route and it is popular with tourists in campervans, caravans, and coaches. Be vigilant when crossing these bridges as sometimes it's easy to miss the sign indicating who has the right of way.

The roads are narrow along here so when cornering, the safest way to ride is to stay as far left on your side of the road as possible, as other vehicles can sometimes drift over the white line simply because they have a wide turn, need more space and the driver may not be as confident on tight turns. The 'recommended corner speed' signs are helpful on this ride and are a great gauge as to what kind of corner to expect.

As you reach the Haast River Viewpoint this incredible braided river really shows itself off as you ride the sweeping bends through the Middle-earth landscape. Recognised internationally as a UNESCO World Heritage Site, this spectacular part of New Zealand is home to rare and endangered animals such as the kiwi and takahē, and encompasses ancient fauna including beech trees, mosses, and podocarp trees.

Signs of civilisation will start to appear as you ride into the village of Haast. Stop at the Hard Antler for a well-earned rest and famous welcoming West Coast hospitality. If you arrive during Whitebait season, try the local delicacy of Whitebait. Whitebait

Riders on the Crown Range

fishing season on the West Coast is from the start of September to the end of October and is an important commercial and recreational resource on the West Coast. The Department of Conservation regulates consents and monitoring.

Back in the saddle after a well-earned break takes you back on to Haast Highway 6 and over numerous deep azure rivers. Look out for 'Ship Creek' and take a stroll down the boardwalk to a secluded beach. Remember you are in the territory of the 'sandfly' now and these pesky tiny black insects bite and leave an itchy bump, not much fun when you're riding along! Insect repellent is recommended here on the West Coast.

As you ride further along State Highway 6, the high grin factor begins in earnest. Multiple tight, twisty turns constantly dip inland and back out to the coast again. This constantly changing landscape is a reminder why this is one of the best motorcycle touring rides in New Zealand.

As you ride towards the glacier townships of Fox Glacier and Franz Josef Glacier, you are in good company with Aoraki/Mount Cook looming in the distance over to your right. Both towns offer exceptional visitor attractions such as helicopter flights

Biker-friendly stops along the way

Cardrona Hotel — Cardrona Valley Road, Cardrona 9382

Cardrona Distillery — 2125 Cardrona Valley Road, Wānaka 9382

National Transport and Toy Museum — 891 Wanaka-Luggate Highway, RD 2, Wānaka 9382

Warbirds and Wheels — 11 Lloyd Dunn Avenue, Airport, Wānaka 9382

Hard Antler Bar & Restaurant — 5 Marks Road, Haast 7886

Scenic highlights along the way

Arrowtown Historic Village

Crown Range Lookout

Lake Wānaka

Lake Hāwea

Blue Pools, Fantail Falls, Thunder Creek Falls

Lake Matheson

Why this is such a great ride

The Crown Range is a challenging ride; hairpin bends and riding New Zealand's highest sealed road is one to tick off the 'must do' list. Followed by stunning lakeside riding until you reach the rainforest. Dramatic landscapes with perfect riding roads snaking through the mountains will keep the grin etched on your face.

with snow landings, hot pools, and even a wildlife centre where to view New Zealand's national bird, the kiwi, up close. Both towns are great places to stop for a well-deserved rest after a long day riding one of the most incredible roads in New Zealand. If you are leaving your bike outside overnight in Fox Glacier or Franz Josef Glacier, keep an eye out for kea. These alpine birds are extremely intelligent and love to pick apart objects for fun, especially motorcycle seats.

A wonderful ride from start to finish, you have more incredible roads to explore as you ride further up the coast.

Detour 1

Queenstown to Wānaka (via Cromwell)

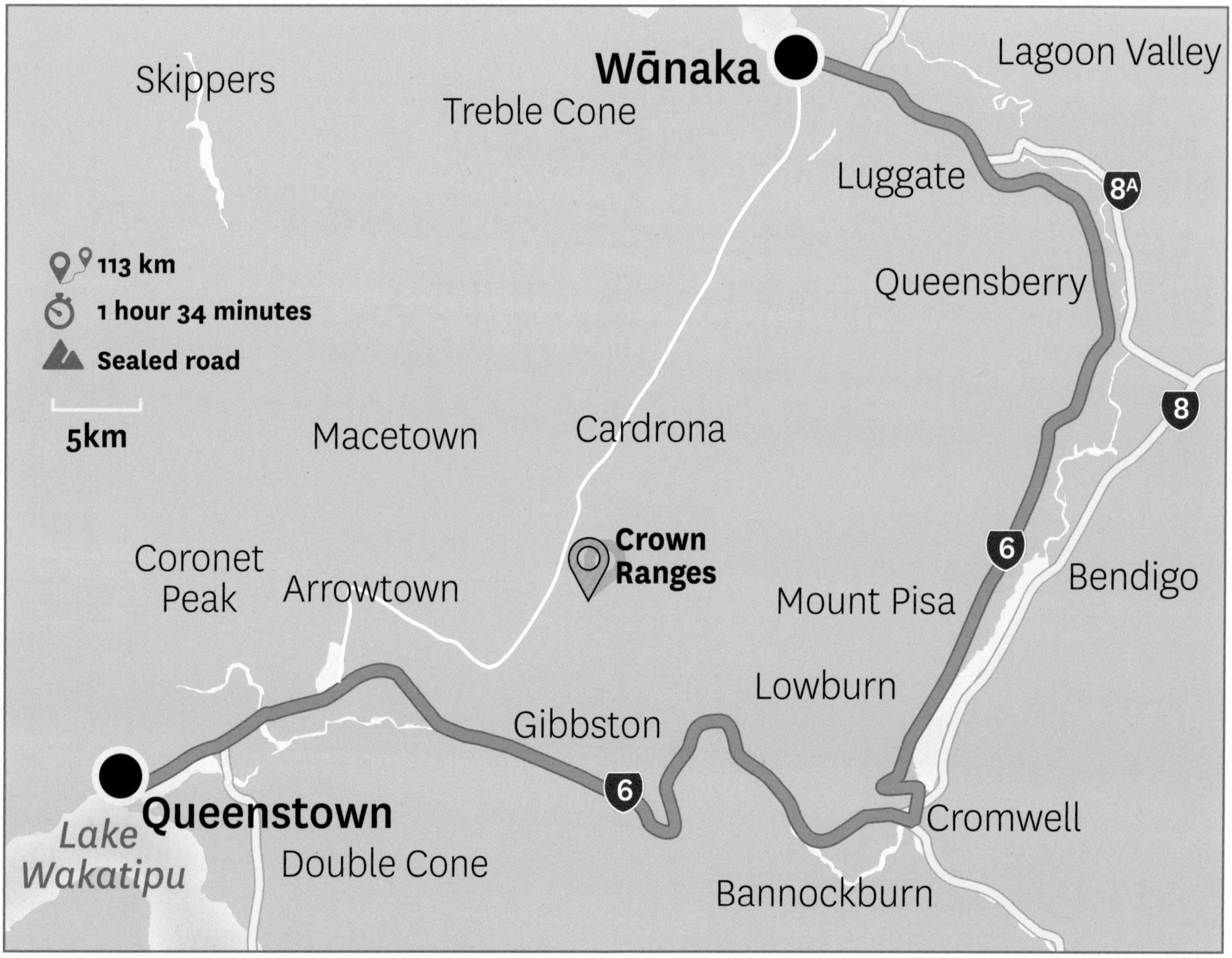

If you're wanting a less challenging start to your day, or the weather is looking less than pleasant and you wish to omit the Crown Range, you can head to Wānaka following State Highway 6 signs to Cromwell.

This ride follows the magnificent Kawarau River and passes the original AJ Hackett Kawarau Bungy Centre. Whether you are feeling brave yourself, or just want to witness the bravery of others, this is a great place to stop and see why Queenstown is considered the adventure capital of New Zealand.

This stretch of road is superb. Enjoy the ride winding your way through the vineyards of Gibbston Valley to Cromwell. This lakeside town was established by miners hoping to strike gold in the surrounding mountains. Goldfields Mining Centre, before you enter the town, is a great way to learn more about this area's gold rush history. Cromwell's Historic Precinct is located on the shores of the Clutha River if you want to explore before continuing alongside Lake Dunstan on State Highway 6 all the way to Wānaka.

Detour 2

Queenstown to Wanaka (Loop via the Crown Range)

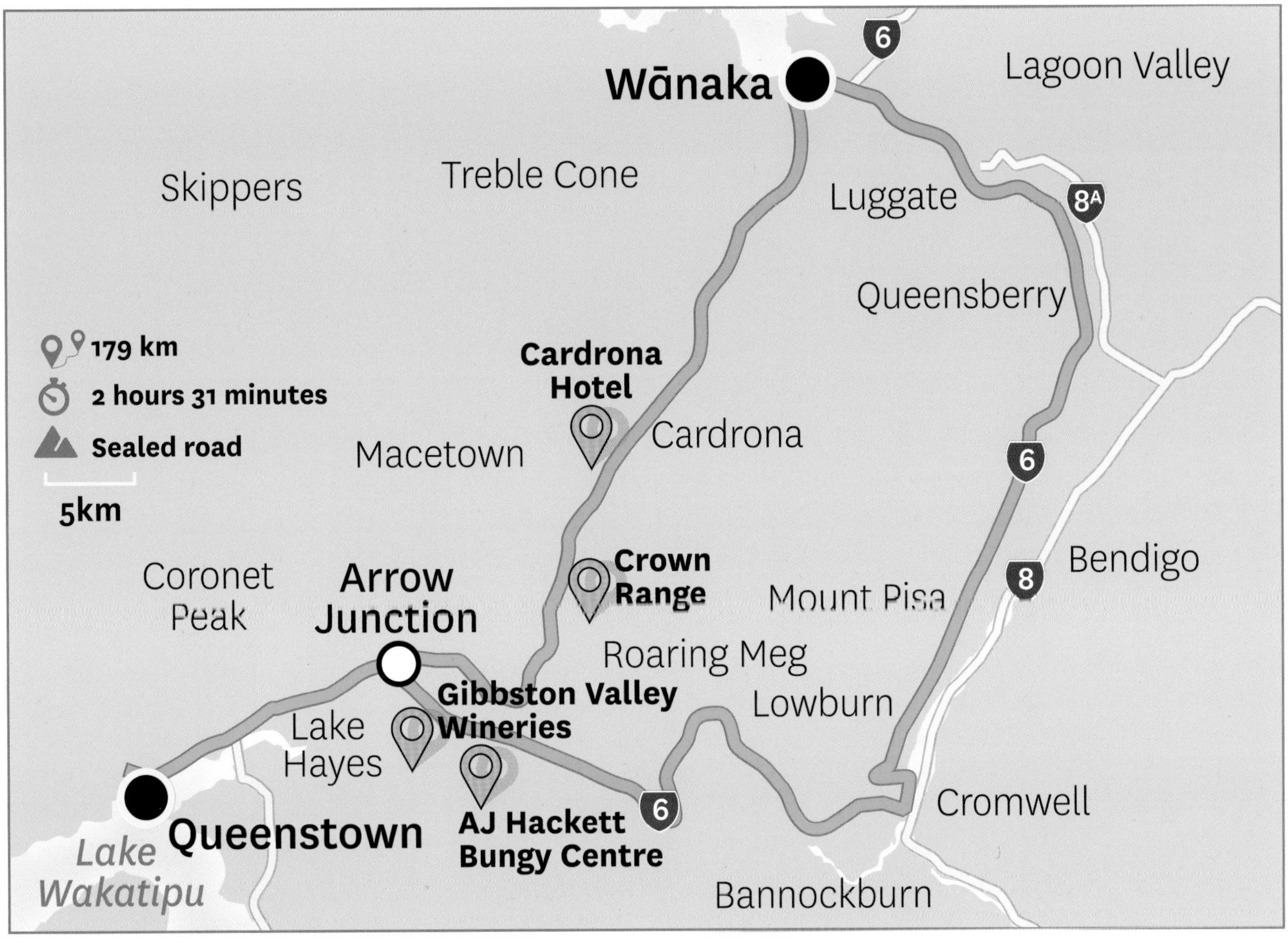

If you've got a little time off in Queenstown for an extra ride, this loop offers a little bit of everything — the adrenalin-pumping challenge of the Crown Range road; lake-side riding along Lake Dunstan followed by a run through the Kawarau Gorge and a great finish through the Gibbston Valley with its award-winning wineries.

Activities options along the way are bountiful; the Cardrona Distillery, wine or cheese-tasting, and bungy jumping at A J Hackett's Original Bungy Jumping Bridge at the Kawarau River.

Looping back out of Wanaka simply follow State Highway 6 to Cromwell and back to Queenstown.

Crown Range Lookout

15. Aoraki/Mount Cook and Lindis Pass

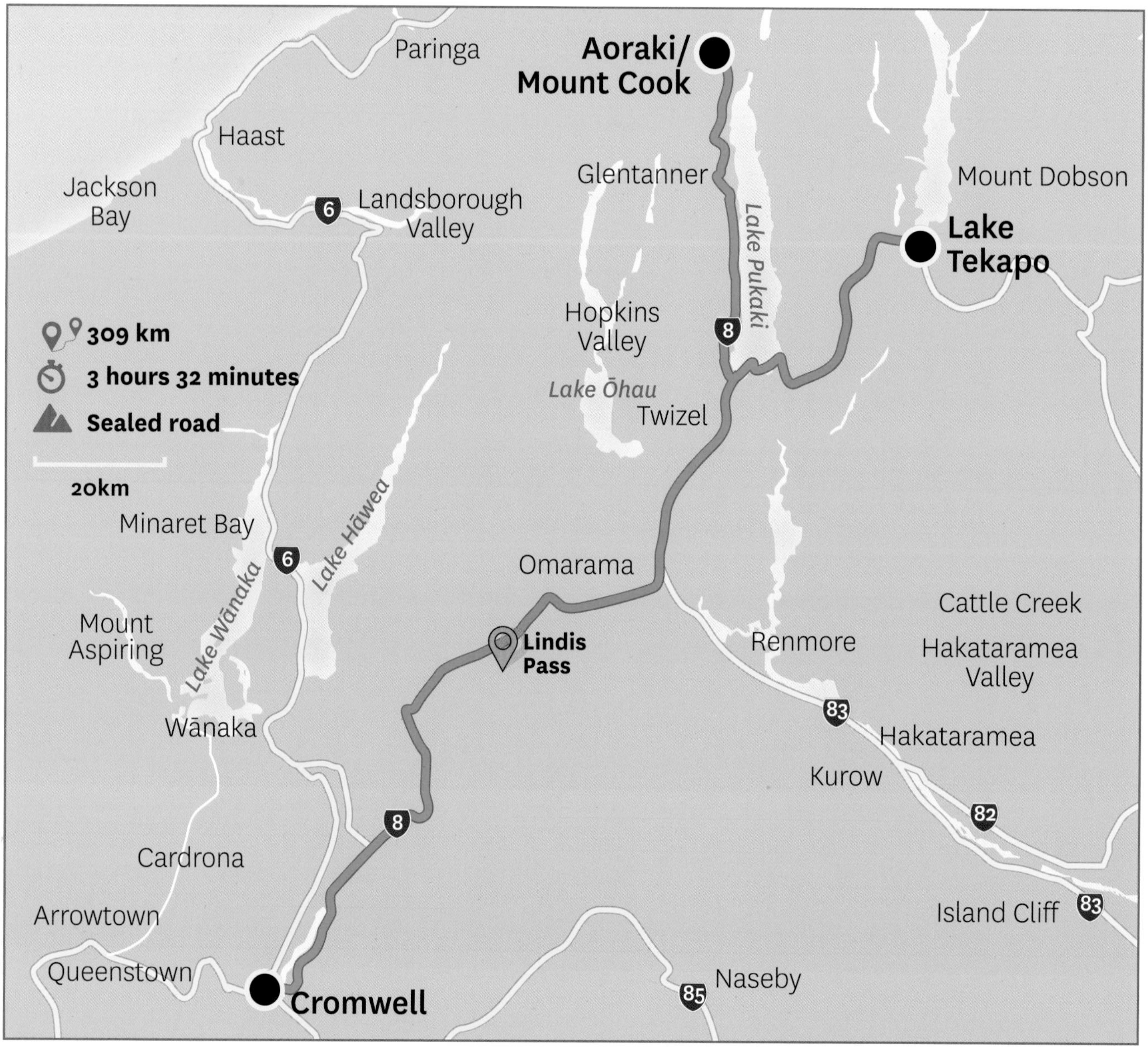

Route Overview

This route takes the rider along the spectacular Southern Alps that spine New Zealand's South Island. This incredible mountain range stretches almost the length of Aotearoa and its highest point is Aoraki/Mount Cook. This route begins in Lake Tekapo, the heart of the Mackenzie Region. Set against a stunning alpine backdrop and glacier blue lake, this township offers a range of activities for those wanting to relax and unwind in the hot pools overlooking the lake or discover and learn at the local planetarium, all whilst being set in a protected area of exceptional scenic beauty.

The Aoraki Mackenzie International Dark Sky Reserve is the largest of its kind. This unspoiled reserve attracts visitors, astronomers, students and enthusiasts all year round as light pollution is low, making the skies above exceptionally clear. The Dark Sky Experience planetarium at the lakefront offers visitors an educational and interactive experience, and Mount John University Observatory can be seen perched high above the town if you are wanting to get up close. This working observatory has unsurpassed 360-degree views of breathtaking scenery across Lake Tekapo and Mackenzie Basin. You can ride up to the summit and visitors can pre-book tours to experience the telescopes for themselves and learn more about the

The road to Aoraki/Mount Cook

skies of the Southern Hemisphere. The Astro Cafe at the top of Mount John also boasts the very best views while you drink your coffee.

The Mackenzie Region sits in the middle of the South Island and is home to New Zealand's highest mountain, Aoraki/Mount Cook, 'the cloud piercer'. With an elevation of 3,724 m and surrounded by rugged peaks and glacial lakes, the peak is always dusted with snow and Aoraki/Mount Cook National Park boasts a range of walking and hiking tracks suitable for all ages and fitness levels.

You would be forgiven for wanting to extend your time in this area; with its never-ending list of activities such as hiking, fishing, hunting, glacier experiences, scenic flights, skiing and stargazing, you're spoilt for choice. Seen in most tourism pictures, Aoraki/Mount Cook is a national icon and towers above the skyline as the road leading up to it runs beside the glacial blue of Lake Pūkaki. This magical picture of New Zealand's long, sweeping roads with alpine backdrop is a 'see it to believe it' moment and is what makes it one of New Zealand's best motorcycle roads.

Mount Cook Village is small but offers accommodation options should you wish to stay here. The Hermitage Hotel showcases educational experiences such as the Sir Edmund Hillary Museum, a 2D and 3D theatre and planetarium on site. Scenic flights with snow landings are also a great way to view this spectacular landscape from a bird's eye view.

Emerging from the Mackenzie Basin into the Lindis Valley you'll be excused for thinking you're in a different county as the terrain changes around every bend. The environment is sparse and covered in tussocks and grasses as far as the eye can see. The Lindis Pass has an altitude of 971 m and in the winter months is often covered with snow. With its fabulous motorcycle roads snaking through epic, breathtaking scenery, this route will get that biker grin showing in no time.

Start Your Engines!

Heading west with the incredible ice blue of Lake Tekapo on your right and the Southern Alps in your wing mirrors, follow State Highway 8 out into the vast plains of Mackenzie country once again.

Endless grassy fields stretch on for miles either side of the road, before reaching the foothills as you ride through the Mackenzie Basin. Follow the straight stretch of highway for 6.5 km to ride over part of the Tekapo hydro canal system that also weaves its way through these grasslands and sheep stations. These hydro canals are also a drawcard for keen anglers as large trout and salmon can be caught from the banks of the canals.

With such a vast expanse of landscape around, you will spot any potential rain clouds rolling in over the mountain tops. The welcome long, sweeping bends and slight incline signify your arrival at Lake Pūkaki and you are treated to a sneak peak of the glacier blue lake before cresting the rise to view this spectacular alpine lake in all its splendour. Even in summer the surrounding mountains here are often dusted with snow, making for dramatic and breathtaking scenery as you cruise the twists and turns alongside the lake. There are numerous viewpoints along the road as well as the main Punatahu Visitor Centre and car park at the top of the lake where you can learn more about this culturally significant area of the South Island. If you are lucky enough to visit on a clear day, you will be treated to a magnificent view across to the very end of the lake where Aoraki/Mount Cook rises in the distance.

Turn off to follow State Highway 80 and signs to Aoraki/Mount Cook National Park. Eleven kilometres further along the road is Peter's Lookout, which offers unsurpassed views across the turquoise blue of Lake Pūkaki. This is the most iconic view of Aoraki/Mount Cook you may have seen in adverts and travel books, with its winding road snaking alongside the water's edge. This road for bikers is one of the best. Continuing on from the lookout you can expect to follow the gentle curves along Mount Cook Road which is overlooked by the Ben Ohau Range. Reaching the end of Lake Pukaki, where it finally merges with the Tasman River and the Hooker River, fed by numerous glacial lakes. For those that are able, there are stunning hikes and camping huts dotted around the mountains for both novice and experienced trampers alike. If you intend doing one of these walks, make sure your motorcycle is either parked somewhere safe, or with a cover over it, as kea frequent the area and may end up damaging your bike with their sharp beak and talons.

Riding through the Tasman Valley surrounded by the Southern Alps is breathtaking, and when you arrive at Mount Cook Village look over to your right. If the weather is clear you'll have a magnificent view over to Aoraki/Mount Cook, the highest mountain in New Zealand. Head to the main visitor centre in the heart of the village or immerse yourself in one of the on-site educational experiences offered at The Hermitage Hotel.

Retrace your route back alongside Lake Pukaki and enjoy the views on your return ride to rejoin State Highway 8. Eventually crossing the Twizel River into the Mackenzie region's largest town, Twizel, 'Town of Trees'. Offering a range of accommodation to suit every budget, this town is surrounded by magnificent mountain ranges and is a great place to base yourself if you want to explore the area more.

You will ride past fields of merino sheep as you glide through the Ahuriri Valley, through Omarama and into the Waitaki District. Check out the **Detour around Lakes Benmore and Aviemore** if you have the time.

Tussock-covered landscape and rugged, grass-covered hills, as far as the eye can see, denotes your arrival into Central Otago and the start of the Lindis Pass Scenic Reserve. Often covered in snow in the winter months, this mountain pass has an elevation of 966 m and a slight incline as you slowly climb and curve your way around this spectacular route to the scenic lookout. The road then descends into the snaking valley below for some incredible mountain and valley riding, with great visibility if you need to pass large trucks or caravans.

Emerging from the mountains, the Lindis River appears on your right and the landscape becomes dotted with trees as the road follows the river flowing through the superb twists and turns of the Lindis Valley. Looking down over the surrounding farmlands, experiencing the undulating road and ever-changing scenery, will leave

Biker-friendly stops along the way

Three Creeks Store — 2119 State Highway 8, Burkes Pass 7987
Mount John Observatory — Godley Peaks Road, Lake Tekapo 7945
The Astro Cafe — Godley Peaks Road, Lake Tekapo 7945
The Wrinkly Rams — 24-30 Omarama Avenue, Omarama 9448

Scenic highlights along the way

Lake Tekapo
Church of the Good Shepherd
Mt John
Lake Pukaki
Aoraki/Mount Cook

Why this is such a great ride

With such an iconic pit-stop on the way through this route, you will be treated to two of New Zealand's best rides. Riding beside spectacular Lake Pūkaki, this road is full of sweeping bends with Aoraki/Mount Cook as your backdrop. The excitement doesn't stop there; with only one road in, it means you get to ride this stretch of road coming back the other way. All this before taking on the incredible Lindis Pass, an altogether vast landscape broken up by a fabulous road which is a joy for any rider.

you breathless and it's easy to see what makes this one of New Zealand's best motorcycle riding roads.

Following State Highway 8 through Tarras, you may spot the Clutha River to your right. This picturesque body of water turns into Lake Dunstan at the southern end of Cromwell which marks the end of this route. Enjoy the waterside riding before turning right to State Highway 8A and Cromwell or Queenstown or straight on to Alexandra and Dunedin.

Detour 1

Hydro Lakes Ride — Benmore Dam and Lake Aviemore

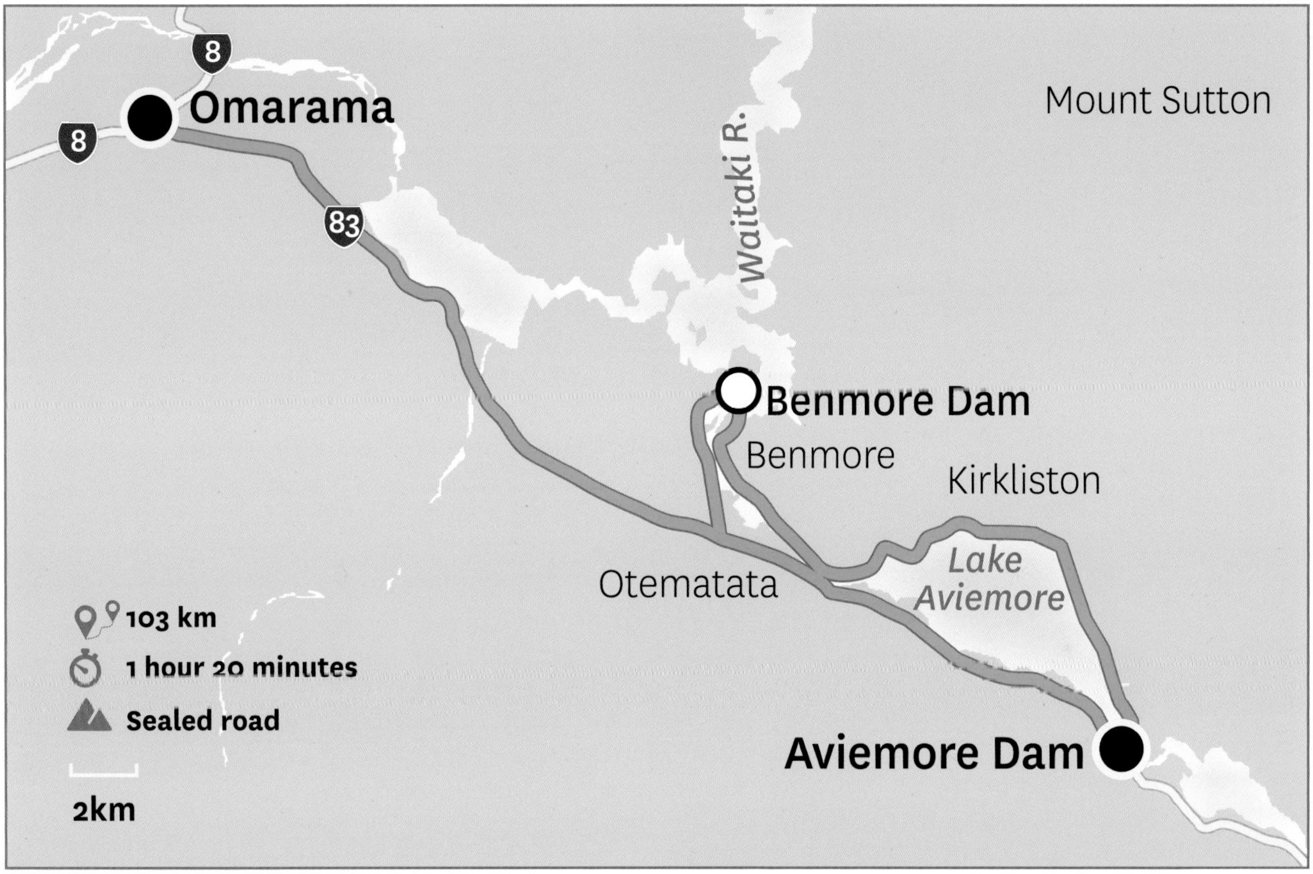

If you're wanting a quick, scenic, twisty detour on your way down south, check out the artificial hydroelectric lakes and iconic dam on your way.

From Omarama, follow State Highway 83 and signs to Kurow and Oamaru for 23 km before turning sharp left on to Loch Laird Road and the sign to Benmore Dam. Ride along this pretty poplar-lined road, beside the Waitaki River, all the way up to the top where you can pull over and park up to take in the spectacular view from atop Benmore Dam. Benmore is New Zealand's largest man-made lake and the dam the largest earth-fill dam.

As you ride over the dam you continue along the Waitaki River until it expands into Lake Aviemore, a popular camping and recreation spot for locals.

The engineering marvel, tree-lined twists and waterside riding make this a fun detour on this route.

16. Ride to Paradise (Queenstown to Glenorchy)

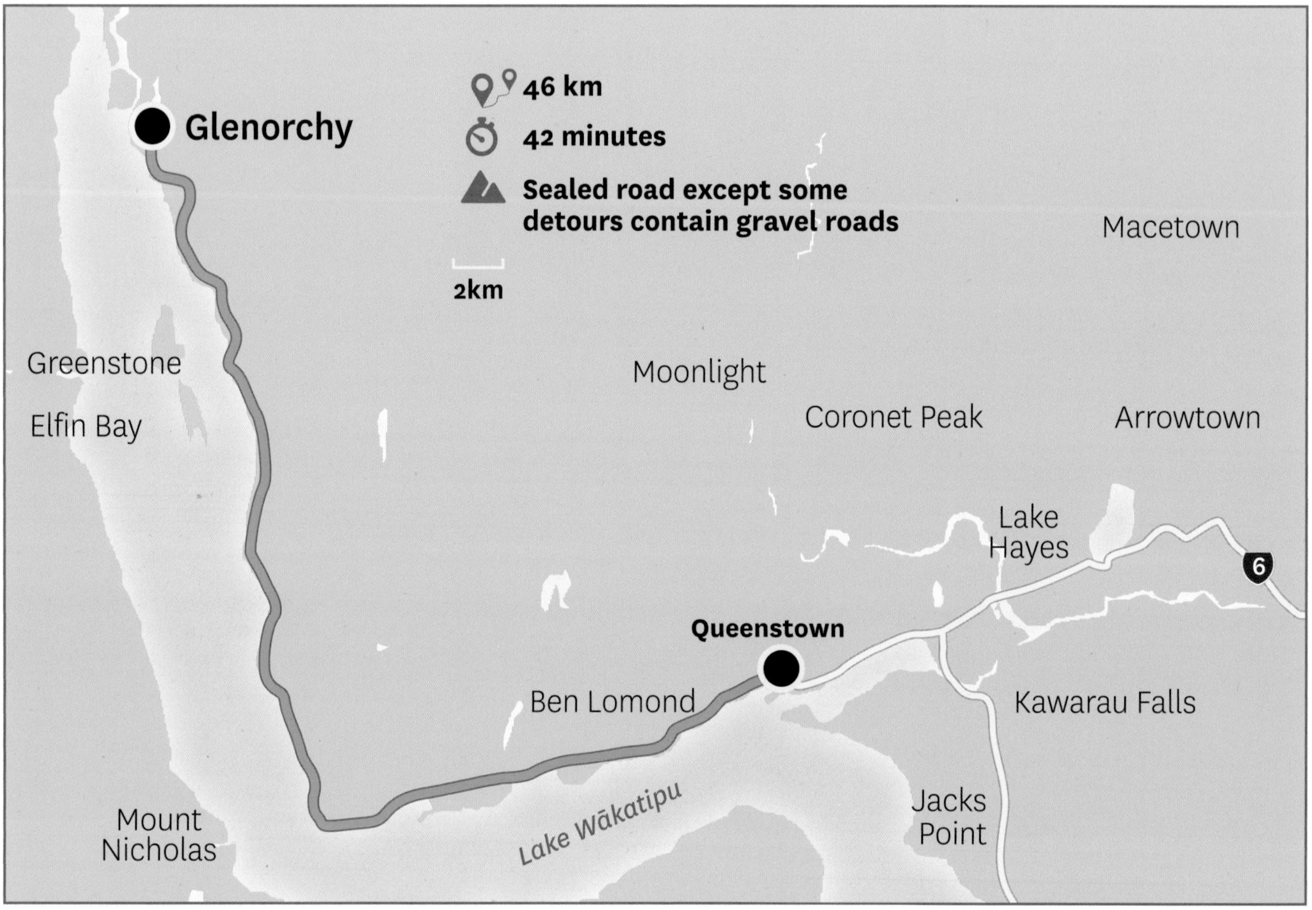

Route Overview

Known as the adventure capital of New Zealand, Queenstown is a destination that will not disappoint, and you will want to spend more than just a day here to make the most of all the area has to offer. Whether you choose to take part in the adrenaline-filled activities of bungy jumping, white water rafting or jet boating (to name but a few), or decide to relax and enjoy the local historic towns, award-winning wineries, ride the gondola or luge, or simply stroll along the lakefront, there is something for everyone here in this picturesque part of New Zealand.

Named after England's Queen Victoria, Queenstown lies at the edge of Lake Wakatipu. New Zealand's longest lake at 80 km, Lake Wakatipu is fed by five rivers which makes the water level fluctuate often and flooding a very real concern for its inhabitants. Three hundred and eighty metres deep, Lake Wakatipu is the main source of fresh water for the township and is accessible by scenic cruise, jet boat, kayak, and of course the iconic *TSS Earnslaw* steamship.

Lake Wakatipu is overlooked by the magnificent and aptly named The Remarkables mountain range. One of only two ranges (the other being the Rockies) to run directly north to south, The Remarkables is a ski resort during the winter months, providing yet another spectacular outlet for thrill seekers.

Queenstown is a great place to use as a base to explore the region, and riding around the area is a treat. A 20-minute ride will take you to Arrowtown, a historic gold-mining village which, in the autumn months, sees an influx of tourism as its surrounding tree-covered mountains turn from green to spectacular gold and red in a mesmerising blanket of colour. The incredible ride to Cromwell will take you over the Kawarau Gorge beside the river, and you will pass the original bungy jumping location of legendary thrill seeker AJ Hackett. Stop and watch the jumpers or, if

Glenorchy curves

The road to Paradise

you're brave enough, take the leap yourself.

Queenstown and its surrounding areas were used as the vast landscapes of Middle-earth. There are a few locations on this road alone, such as the 'Ithilien Lookout' at 12 Mile Delta, and 'Lothlorien' at Paradise further along from Glenorchy. Lord of The Rings fans can pick up a location guide and ride to seek out the accessible sites that were used for the film sets.

Traffic does get very congested in Queenstown during peak season, so of course always be on the lookout for campervans or cars who don't take that extra second look for bikers.

This ride to Glenorchy certainly ranks in the top five best in New Zealand and will have you easily wanting to do it all over again. At 45 minutes each way, the grin factor is off the charts as you ride beside the deep blue of the lake before reaching your destination, buzzing. If you ride outside of peak hours, you'll avoid getting stuck behind other vehicles which will make the ride all the more rewarding.

With its effortless, sweeping bends, this is one ride you will wish would go on forever.

Start Your Engines!

As you start your ride out of Queenstown on the main street, Shotover Street, you will notice some iconic local and tourist town favourites. The AJ Hackett Bungy Centre is on your right, the home of the bungy jump, where you can book your adrenaline-filled adventure depending on your bravery and ability. Fergburger is world famous for epic inventive burgers, late night hunger-craving fulfilment and usually has a queue out the door. On your right, look up towards the towering mountains and you'll see the Skyline Gondola slowly carrying passenger pods up to the peak. From the top you have the most stunning views of Queenstown and the surrounding Remarkables mountain range. The Luge ride at the top is a must to satisfy your inner child. With 900 m of banked corners, tunnels, and dippers, you will be wanting to try a few more turns before you leave.

To your left, across the lake, Cecil Peak and Walter Peak are the visible mountains and you may spot the *TSS Earnslaw* steamship puffing smoke as it slowly glides across Lake Wakatipu. This iconic ship is part of Queenstown's history and has been lovingly maintained since 1912. Carrying visitors daily across to Walter Peak High Country Farm to be treated to an interactive farm show with sheep shearing.

As you follow the road around you may get the feeling you're riding through one of Sir Peter Jackson's *The Lord of The Rings* movies all the way in to Glenorchy township.

There are a few cafes and shops as well as accommodation options in Glenorchy if you want to stay and explore a little more. First head for the Glenorchy Waterfront Reserve to take it all in. Follow Oban Street (the main street) and turn left on to Mull Street, which will take you to the reserve where you will see the iconic 'red shed' in front of you. This well-photographed shed was once a storage depot for the goods carried by steamship from Queenstown to Glenorchy.

This peaceful lakefront location can be explored easily; take off your heavy bike gear and stretch your legs. If you are after a tasty toasted sandwich, thirst quenching cuppa, or cooling ice cream then The Trading Post or The GYC Cafe have got you covered. You would have passed them on your right as you rode in. Once you're fuelled with coffee or a snack, look around the area and perhaps follow the Glenorchy Lagoon Scenic Walkway, accessible to your right when looking towards the lake. There is a 30 minute or 120 minute option, and the flat walking tracks skirt the Rees River and Glenorchy Lagoon. If you're keen to stay on two wheels, you could always hire an electric bicycle and explore at your own pace. Or, swap two wheels for four legs and try a different kind of horsepower and pre-book a horseback riding trip. Your options are endless.

TSS Earnslaw

Hopping back on the bike, you get to do this ride all over again from a different perspective on your way back. Many riders often do this road multiple times as it's really that good.

Biker-friendly stops along the way

The Trading Post — 13 Mull Street, Glenorchy 9350
The GYC Cafe — 25 Mull Street, Glenorchy, New Zealand
Mrs Woolly's General Store — 64 Oban Street, Glenorchy 9372

Scenic highlights along the way

TSS Earnslaw
Lake Wakatipu
The Remarkables Mountain Range

Why this is such a great ride

The unicorn of motorcycle riding roads, long effortless bends on well-maintained roads, surrounded by stunning scenery; what more could you ask for?

Detour

The Road to Paradise — Glenorchy to Paradise

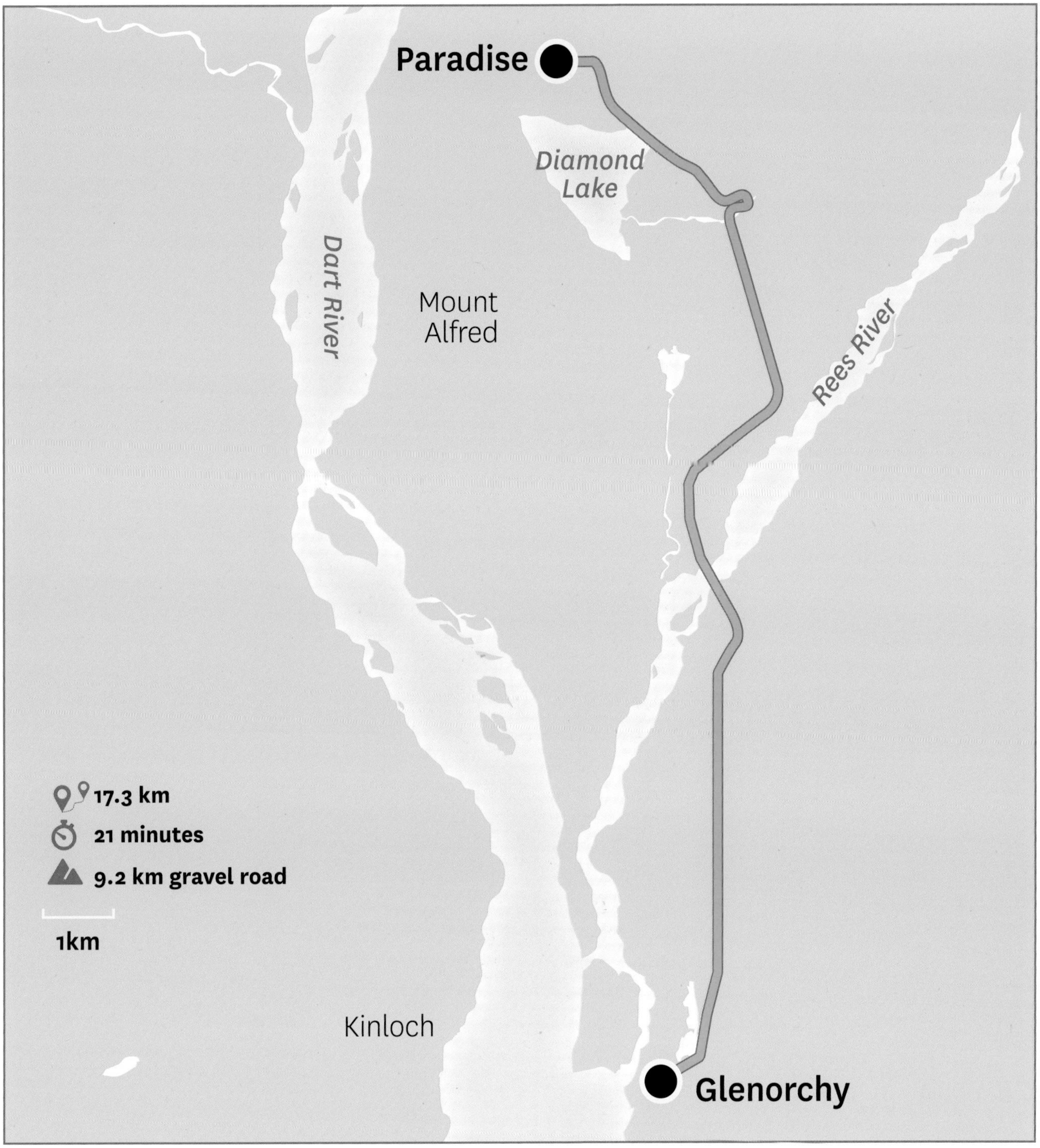

For an extra add-on to this already unbeatable road, if you're looking for something to write home or brag to your mates about, then take this detour to be able to say you've ridden the 'road to Paradise'.

From Glenorchy, follow Mull Street to join up with the Glenorchy-Paradise Road and ride until you cross the bridge over the Rees River. Just after this the road turns to gravel, so if you're confident carry on. You are now literally riding the road to Paradise. You'll ride through rural New Zealand farmland, surrounded by mountains on either side, and you will pass yet another *The Lord of The Rings* location of Lothlorien. You'll eventually find the sign that deserves that all-important photograph of you with your bike to show people you've been to Paradise.

17. Central Otago — Oamaru to Cromwell

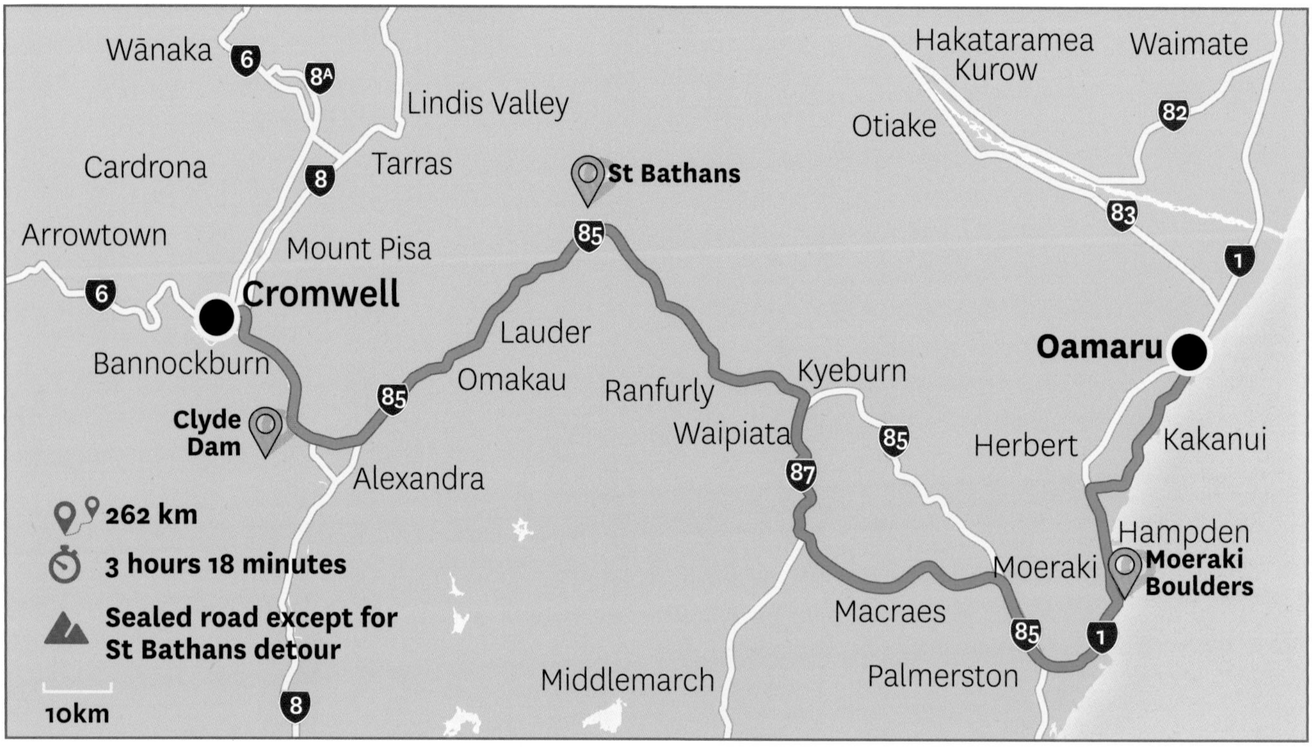

Route Overview

Regardless of whether you ride a cruiser, adventure, classic or sports bike, this trip will take you from the ocean to the alps and will have you grinning from ear to ear all the way. Before embarking on the wonderful motorcycling back roads of Central Otago, this route takes you off the beaten track straight away as you head south from Oamaru alongside the azure blue waters of Kakanui beach and the Pacific Ocean.

Oamaru, your starting point, is well worth exploring before you start your engine. The largest town of the Waitaki District, with a population of around just 14,000, gives you an idea of just how rural this region is. This cute little town boasts a high street full of buildings with bright white limestone Victorian architecture, and an original heritage precinct where you can discover shops, galleries, craft breweries and distilleries. Positioned perfectly between the two, an old Victorian grain warehouse is now the home to 'Steampunk HQ', an amazing and quite unique steampunk museum housing an eclectic array of weird and wonderful rusted art pieces, plus a tantalising light show. For nature lovers there are also two penguin colonies in Oamaru, and each night at dusk you can watch rafts of native little blue penguins coming ashore to roost.

You could be forgiven for thinking that you had gone back in time some hundred years on this route. Heading inland you enter a land of scenic beauty made up of big blue skies, ancient mountain ranges, fast-flowing rivers, and vast areas of sheep-filled farmlands and grasslands. By 1863 this area had become inundated with prospectors when gold was discovered. As you explore this wonderful region you'll be able to see remains of days gone by in the form of historic villages, rusty old gold mining machinery, relics, and old sluicing sites. Gold mining in this region still exists today and you'll be riding through New Zealand's largest gold mine that has created a large landscape reminiscent of a moon-landing movie, situated around Macraes Flat. With multiple detours for exploration into Otago's pioneering past, this fabulous ride finishes at Cromwell, your gateway to the glorious Southern Alps.

Start Your Engines!

Keeping away from the main State Highway 1 and following a few backroads, follow Beach Road south of Oamaru. Beach Road, as the name suggests, provides an absolute beachfront ride with the coast with its golden sandy beaches to your left and incredible views out to the Pacific Ocean. When you reach the seaside

Watch out for the penguins in Oamaru

Central Otago

Macraes Road

settlement of Kakanui, glide around to the right, following signs to All Day Bay and Dunedin. Follow Waianakarua Road to rejoin State Highway 1.

Turning left on to State Highway 1, a ten-minute ride will bring you to Moeraki Boulders, a popular tourist attraction and a great place to stop and walk along the beach to view giant stone spheres which were exposed from the cliffside due to erosion. They now scatter the coastline and make an impressive sight at low tide. Kick down your stand and grab an ice cream at the cafe here overlooking the ocean.

Leaving Moeraki Boulders, check out the **Detour via Horse Range Road if you have the time.** Alternatively follow the stunning east coast until you reach Palmerston where you will turn right on to State Highway 85 following signs to Ranfurly.

Riding inland through rural farmland for the next 15 km, cresting a hill and a sweeping bend, turn left on to Macraes Road following signs to Macraes Flat. The road begins to climb, with some fabulous curves looking out over the Otago vista. The undulations and long, sweeping bends, coupled with great visibility, mean you can open the throttle and enjoy riding this road safely at pace.

The landscape changes rapidly, from an untouched world to a huge earthmoving site plunging down some 200 m into the huge opencast pit of OceanaGold, the largest modern day gold mine in New Zealand. Further on at the township of Macraes you can learn more about the gold rush era, how it affected the area, and even book tours of the gold mine itself.

With the Lammermoor Ranges in the distance, continue along Hyde-Macraes Road with a grin on your face, enjoying the serpentine arteries of the Otago backroads until meeting up with State Highway 87 at Hyde.

Head north on State Highway 87, weaving in and around the hills before reaching the comparatively flat landscape of Kyeburn and rejoining State Highway 85. The incomparable Maniototo Region of Central Otago boasts the impressive Hawkdun and Mt Ida mountain ranges and vast open grassland plains. Meaning 'plains of blood' in Māori, Maniototo refers to the flowing red tussock that once surrounded the area.

Arriving at Kyeburn turn left following signs to Ranfurly. There is a fuel station here if you need to top-up and quaint art deco architecture lines the zigzagged main street. Further north along State Highway 85 the historic Wedderburn Tavern is a great place to kick down your stand for a bite to eat. Built in 1885, this tavern was a welcoming watering hole for coaches and travellers and has an interesting history if you have time to stop.

Staying on State Highway 85, enjoy several hours of non-stop biking bliss via continuous sweeps and bends, with scenic vistas wherever you look. Check out the **Detour to St Bathans and Blue Lake or the Ida Valley if you have the time.** Passing through small towns of Lauder and Chatto Creek will take you through to Alexandra and into the stunning wine country of Central Otago. Turn on to State Highway 8, following signs to Cromwell. Five minutes ride

Biker-friendly stops along the way

Moeraki Boulders Cafe — 7 Moeraki Boulders Road, Hampden 9482
Waipiata Hotel — 29 Main Street, Waipiata,
Wedderburn Tavern — Wedderburn-Becks Road, Wedderburn 9395
Chatto Creek Tavern — 1544 Omakau-Chatto Creek Road, Chatto Creek 9393
The Stoaker Room — 180 State Highway 8B, Cromwell 9310
Highlands Motorsport Park — Corner SH6 and Sandflat Road, Sandflat Road, Cromwell 9384

Scenic highlights along the way

Moeraki Boulders
Shag Point Look Out and Fur Seals
Ophir Historic Bridge
Clyde Dam

Why this is such a great ride

This route is off the main tourist drive around the South Island. Multiple back roads will keep you off the main route for much of the way, and these empty ribbon roads intertwine the Central Otago countryside.

further along, follow the sign to veer off into historic Clyde township to check out this stunning historical location and the engineering marvel of the hydro dam as you depart on your way to Cromwell. Approaching your destination, the ride alongside the mighty Clutha River that flows through the gorge into Lake Dunstan is simply breathtaking. Depending on what time of year you're riding, these surrounding, imposing ranges may be dusted or covered with snow as the altitude increases and you cross over the bridge into the beautiful town of Cromwell.

Detour 1
Horse Range Road

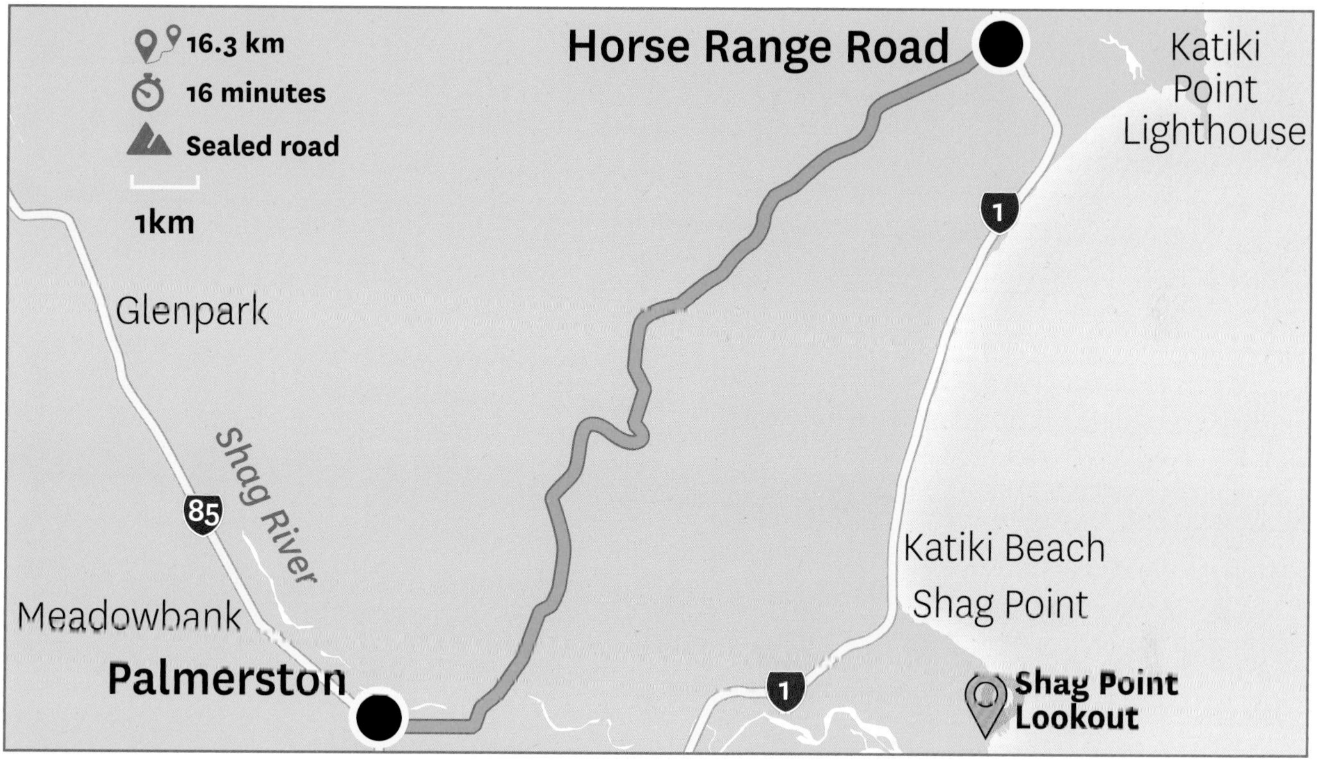

An alternative shortcut to avoid State Highway 1 is to turn off right, three minutes after Moeraki Boulders. Follow the sign to Trotters Gorge on Horse Range Road. This is a five kilometre shortcut of narrow country lanes through Trotters Forge Scenic Reserve. This road has no road markings or safety barriers and should be navigated with caution.

Moeraki Boulders

Blue Lake, St Bathans

Detour 2
St Bathans

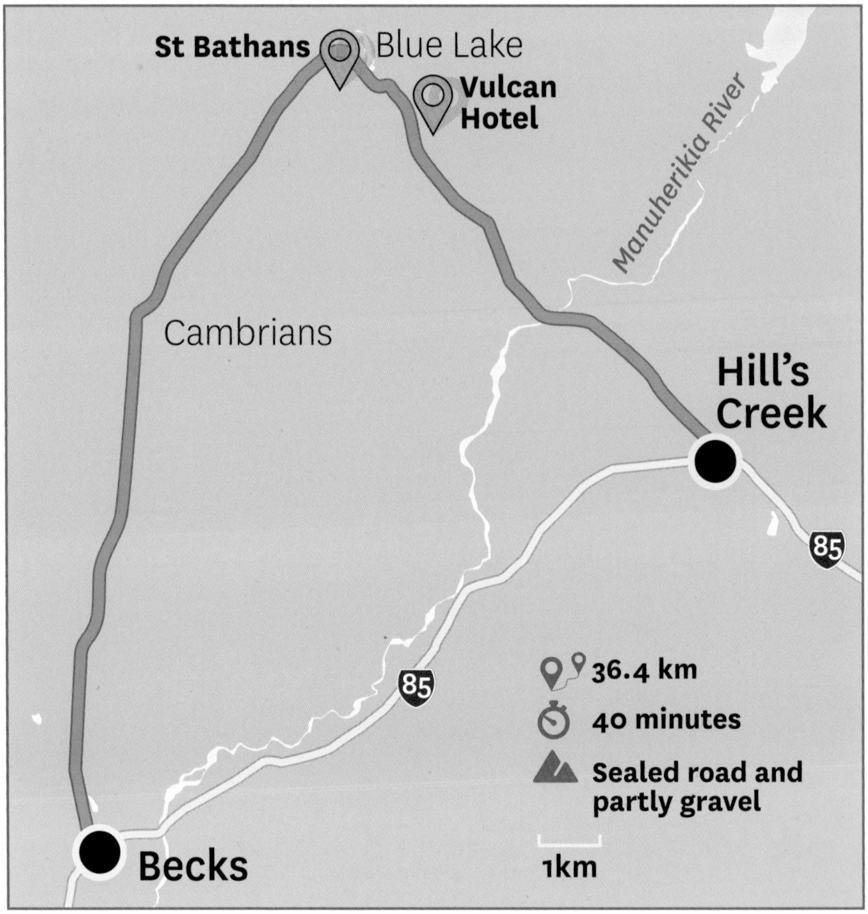

This detour makes for quite an adventure as you leave State Highway 85 at Hills Creek and turn onto the St Bathans Loop Road. Start off on a country lane through farmlands and over the Manuherikia River, until you reach the tiny historic gold-mining village of St Bathans. Park up at the Blue Lake car park to explore this fascinating area with its historic constable's cottage, post office, blacksmiths and bank.

The Vulcan Hotel and pub was first built during the gold rush era of 1869 for the prospectors and their families who settled here in the hope of finding a fortune. Boasting a rumour of being New Zealand's most haunted hotel, with its very own ghost 'Rosie', why not check in to Room 1 and test your bravery with an overnight stay.

Across the road from the Vulcan is the manmade 'Blue Lake'. Around 1873 gold digging was prominent in Central Otago and by the early 1930s miners had created a pit so large it became dangerous for the townsfolk. The pit was abandoned and began to fill with water. Water filtered by the surrounding quartz stone cliffs and minerals gives the lake an ethereal blue colour.

Leaving St Bathans, continue in the same direction on St Bathans Loop Road, but be aware you may encounter a few kilometres of hard, compacted, gravel road instead of tar seal.

Detour 3
Ida Valley

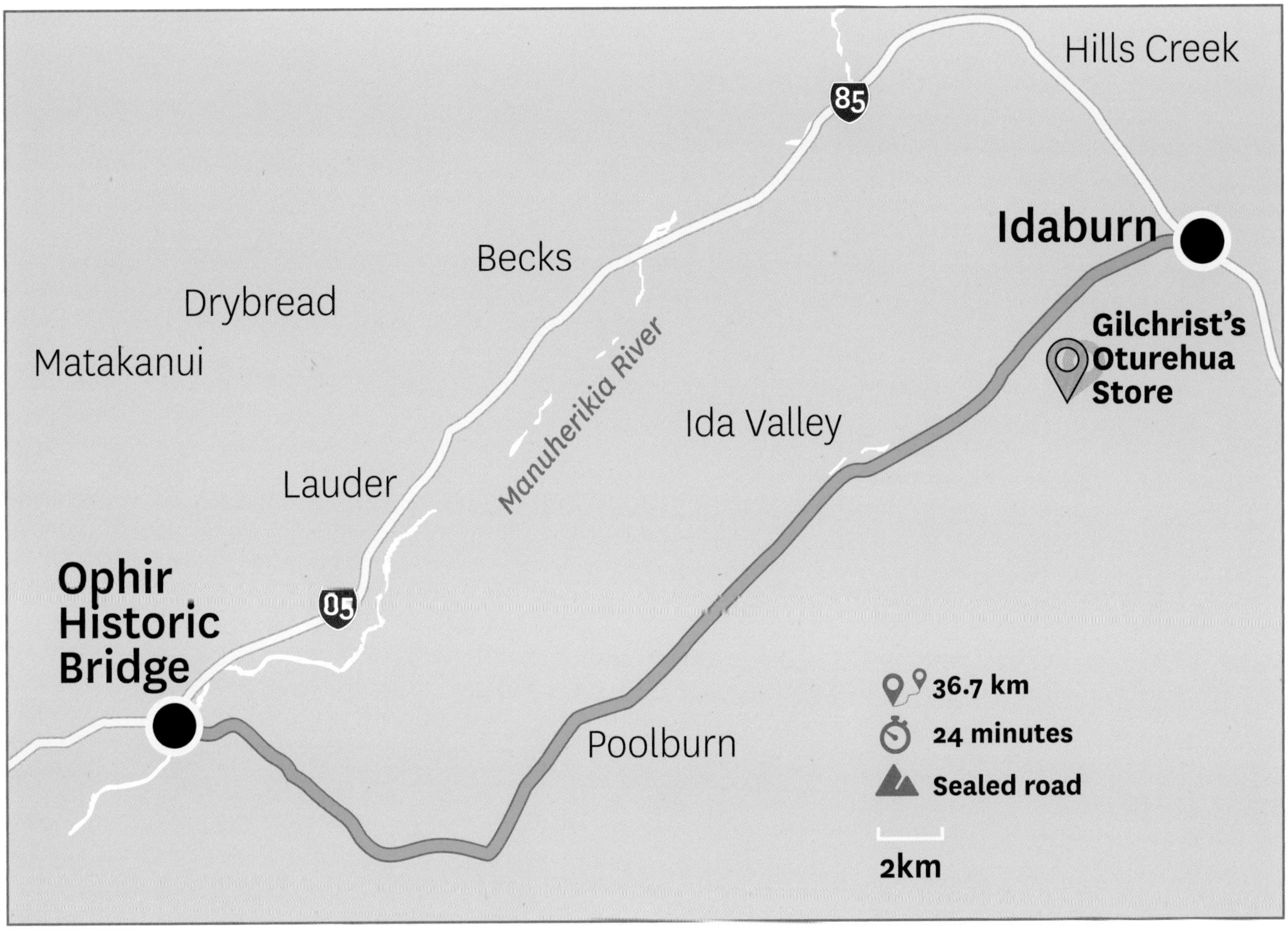

Shortly after Wedderburn turn left on to Ida Valley-Omakau Road, following signs to Ida Valley and Hayes Engineering. Enjoy almost 40 km of empty ribbon road that weaves and wends its way over the Ida Burn stream all the way to Omakau. If you are interested in engineering and pioneering feats of New Zealand there are several stops along this route. Gilchrist's Store, at the tiny 1890s village of Oturehua, and Hayes Engineering Works & Homestead showcase an unchanged era that's history that has been restored and well preserved.

Continue along this excellent road that must have been made in motorcycle heaven, with long sweeps and excellent vistas. When you approach the small village of Ophir, turn left on to Swindon Street before Blacks Hotel. This small detour will bring you to Ophir Historic Bridge. This marvelous piece of engineering is just one of many beautiful suspension bridges that used to straddle Otago's mighty rivers back in the late 1800s. Quite a few remain today, creating interesting tourist attractions. The Ophir Suspension Bridge, however, is still fully operational and quite a magnificent sight with its four tall piers made of solid schist stone on each corner. Ride over this piece of history before rejoining State Highway 85.

18. Devil's Staircase

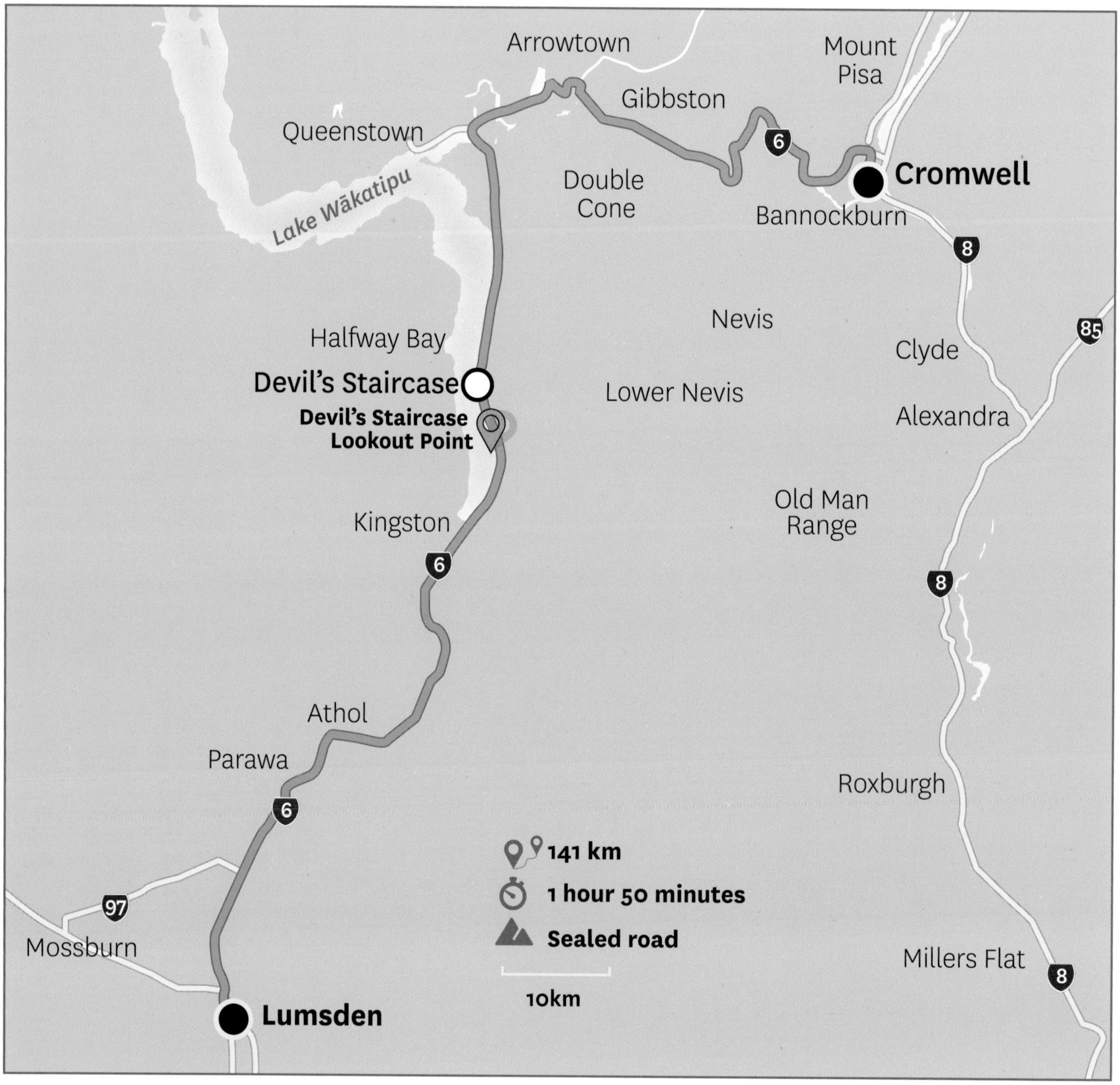

Route Overview

This route, although short in terms of riding time, is one of the most spectacular in terms of scenery and location in New Zealand. Starting and ending points for this trip can be altered to suit and the journey extended in either direction to include this special piece of road. Whether you are heading north or south in summer or winter, this central road is magical.

Previously a gold rush town, Cromwell sits in Central Otago beside picturesque Lake Dunstan and at the junction of the Kawarau River and the mighty Clutha River. The damming of the Clyde and Clutha Rivers to create Lake Dunstan meant that the original old town of Cromwell was flooded. The Cromwell Heritage Precinct showcases buildings that have been lovingly restored from the 1860s and are now artisan businesses. Visitors can walk through history while enjoying the many cafes, galleries and craft stores beside serene Lake Dunstan.

Central Otago wines are famous worldwide, and the surrounding area is covered with vineyards and orchards due to the warm micro-climate of the area, making it perfect for growing fruit. Boasting roadside

Taking a break in Arrowtown

The Devil's Staircase

fruit stalls selling fresh produce and real fruit ice cream, award-winning wineries and local artisan restaurants, this area is perfect for a road trip stop.

Shaped from the times of the gold rush era, the spectacular surrounding mountains turn to gold themselves during the autumn months, as the tree-covered slopes change their colours to match the seasons. There are multiple heritage walks around Cromwell and Bannockburn that tell the tales of its historic gold rush days. For the more active and adventurous, explore by hiking or mountain biking in the tussock-covered mountains, or search for adventure and gold along the banks of the Kawarau River.

For the petrol-heads, speed demons and adrenaline junkies, Highlands Motorsport Park has something for everyone. This world class facility showcases the need for speed, and if you are keen to get off two wheels and on to four then the self-drive attractions might be up your alley. Go-karting, V8 Muscle Car U-Drive options are available, or take it up a gear and strap yourself in for a Supercar Fast Dash or Subaru WRX Experience. Also boasting its own on-site museum with epic machines such as Michael Schumacher's Benetton Formula One car and some of the rarest cars in New Zealand motorsport history, you are in for a real treat.

This route ends in Lowther to give multiple options as to your next riding destination. Head west to untouched Fiordland and explore the magic of Milford Sound, or further into the deep south to Invercargill, or even simply explore the many backroads that stunning Southland has to offer.

Start Your Engines!

Leaving from Cromwell, follow State Highway 6 and Kawarau Gorge Road past orchards and fruit stalls dotted alongside the road. A great excuse to stock up on snacks in your panniers for this trip. With granite cliffs towering over you on either side, you will be riding through Kawarau Gorge, and below you the mighty Kawarau River which drains from Lake Wakatipu to join

Lake Wakatipu waterfront

up with Lake Dunstan in Cromwell. Due to its crashing, cascading falls and white-water rapids, this powerful river is a drawcard for thrill seekers from all over the world and the source of some of the extreme adventure tourism activities that the region is famous for. White-water rafting, jet-boating, and bungy jumping are all right here on your doorstep. Making Cromwell a great place to stay as a base while you explore the region.

From early on this ride is simply glorious; you are escorted like a faithful friend by the ever-present glacier blue of the Kawarau River to your left. As you cruise through the Gibbston Valley, the etchings on the cliffs above show the scars of long-past gold-mining trails and settlements. If you are interested in learning more about this prominent and rugged piece of Central Otago history, stop in at Goldfields Mining Centre for a tour or try your hand at gold panning.

This road is very well maintained and often busy during peak tourism season, so there are a lot of double yellow lines to deter drivers from overtaking on this narrow highway for your own safety. If you do find you're stuck behind the odd camper or slow-going vehicle, there are passing lanes dotted throughout, so you won't be stuck for too long.

After snaking your way through the valley and beside steep bluffs you will emerge at Gibbston, affectionately known as 'Valley of the Vines' and for good reason. Surrounding wineries and cellar doors engulf this stretch of road. Look out for some well-known labels as well as boutique accommodation, stores and restaurants such as Gibbston Valley Winery with its on-site cheesery and deli.

A little further on you will see signs to AJ Hackett Bungy on your right. Turn in for a look and you will see the magnificent Kawarau Suspension Bridge hanging over the canyon. Welcome to the birthplace of bungy tourism. Whether you feel like just watching the action, or if you are feeling brave, then this is the place to live out your extreme dreams. With multiple thrills available to choose from such as the Canyon Swing,

Zipride, Catapult or Bungy, you can test your limits, get your heart racing, and have photographic evidence to prove you have faced your fears afterwards. This is the original home of bungy jumping and the perfect place to tick off the 'been there, done that' all important bucket list.

Continue along SH6 through the valley until you reach Arrow Junction and check out the **Detour to Arrowtown and Queenstown** if you have the time.

The vistas of this incredible district change with every corner you lean into, and you will spot the azure blue of Lake Hayes to your right and The Remarkables mountain range on the horizon, indicating your closeness to Queenstown. After crossing the Shotover River Bridge the urban sprawl becomes apparent as you reach Frankton, the location of Queenstown Airport and the hub of this bustling gateway to Queenstown. The traffic becomes heavier at the Frankton roundabout. SH6A straight on leads to Queenstown and turning left here heads south. Take the first exit left to SH6 following signs to Invercargill and Milford Sound.

This is the Southern Scenic Route and it's obvious to see why. Although this stretch of road is relatively straight, it makes up for it with fabulous scenery. Riding over Kawarau Falls Bridge, and the crystal blue of the Kawarau River, you are gifted with the sight of the jagged pinnacles that make up the defining features of The Remarkables mountain range towering above. This is a world-class ski area in the winter months and attracts powder hunters, fearless freestylers and brave boarders from around the world looking to carve up the snow.

Sneaking into view is Lake Wakatipu with its mirrored reflections. Once you close in to ride beside this beautiful, blue southern lake, the road will really start to begin to become biker heaven. Enjoy riding these long sweeping bends that dip, arch, and curve around the steep cliffs as you climb up and above to overlook the lake.

Approximately 25 km from Frankton you will notice the road cuts in close to the rocks and cliffs on your left. This next piece of road is known as the 'Devil's Staircase' and was so named due to the challenging and laborious rocky bluffs that were to be navigated when the original road was being cut through from Queenstown to Kingston. Further along the road you'll see signs for Devil's Staircase Lookout, which will give you the best view back over to the staircase as well as an epic panorama stretched out in front of you to highlight what this route is famous for. With the dazzling, vast, freshwater lake in the foreground and a dramatic snow-tipped mountain backdrop, you'll want to pull over, kick down your stand and take it all in. Make sure you take some snaps of you and your bike in front of this unblemished landscape before you enjoy the rest of this incredible scenic ride to the small settlement of Kingston.

Turn right into Kent Street and along to the water's edge. This pretty lakeside town is visible on the shores of Lake Wakatipu in the distance and signals the halfway point of this ride. The town was once a busy thoroughfare for both rail and lake transport, ferrying passengers and prospectors throughout the region before the road to Queenstown was completed. Now a quiet stop along the way, Kingston is the home of The Kingston Flyer. This classic vintage steam train was originally built in the 1870s and has weathered demise and revitalisation throughout the years, thanks to the hard work of committed enthusiasts. The train can be booked for private charters and if you're lucky, some public rides on special occasions.

Grab a coffee or snack at the Kingston Cafe and Bar located in the original station, or wander outside to find a shaded spot under a tree on the lakefront to take in the stunning scenery.

When you are back in the saddle, join SH6 again, heading south through the valley. Crossing from Otago into Southland now, you ride past fields of sheep, cattle, and farmland rich in agriculture. This stretch of road is well policed and you will need to drop your speed when riding through the smaller towns of Garston and Athol. The weather in this part of the country is also quickly changeable so keep that extra layer handy just in case.

Forty-six kilometres (approx. 30 mins) from Kingston is the 'blink and you'll miss it' town of Lowther, where this route ends. You will see signs to continue straight with SH6 to Lumsden and Invercargill, or veer off right to continue following the Southern Scenic Route to Te Anau and Milford Sound. The biker-friendly Five Rivers Cafe on the corner of this intersection is the perfect place to decide. If you have already planned your next destination in advance, or if you choose to be spontaneous and see where your wheels take you from here, whether it be Southland or Fiordland, the adventure continues, and you won't be disappointed.

Biker-friendly stops along the way

Highlands Motorsport Park — Corner SH6 and Sandflat Road, Sandflat Road, Cromwell 9384
Five Rivers Cafe — 1724 Mossburn Five Rivers Highway, Five Rivers, New Zealand
Lumsden Hotel — 6 Diana Street, Lumsden 9730
Kingston Flyer — 221 Kent Street, Kingston 9373
Route 6 Cafe — 22 Diana Street, Lumsden 9730

Scenic highlights along the way

Kawarau River and Gorge
Gibbston Valley
AJ Hackett Bungy/Kawarau Suspension Bridge
Lake Wakatipu
Lake Hayes
The Remarkables Mountain Range
The Devil's Staircase Lookout
Kingston

Why this is such a great ride

Riding beside the crystal blue of Lake Wakatipu and beneath the towering jagged Remarkables is jaw dropping in itself. Top that with long sweeping bends and you have a match made in biker heaven. This stunning ride is an added bonus when riding to or from Queenstown.

Detour

Arrowtown and Queenstown

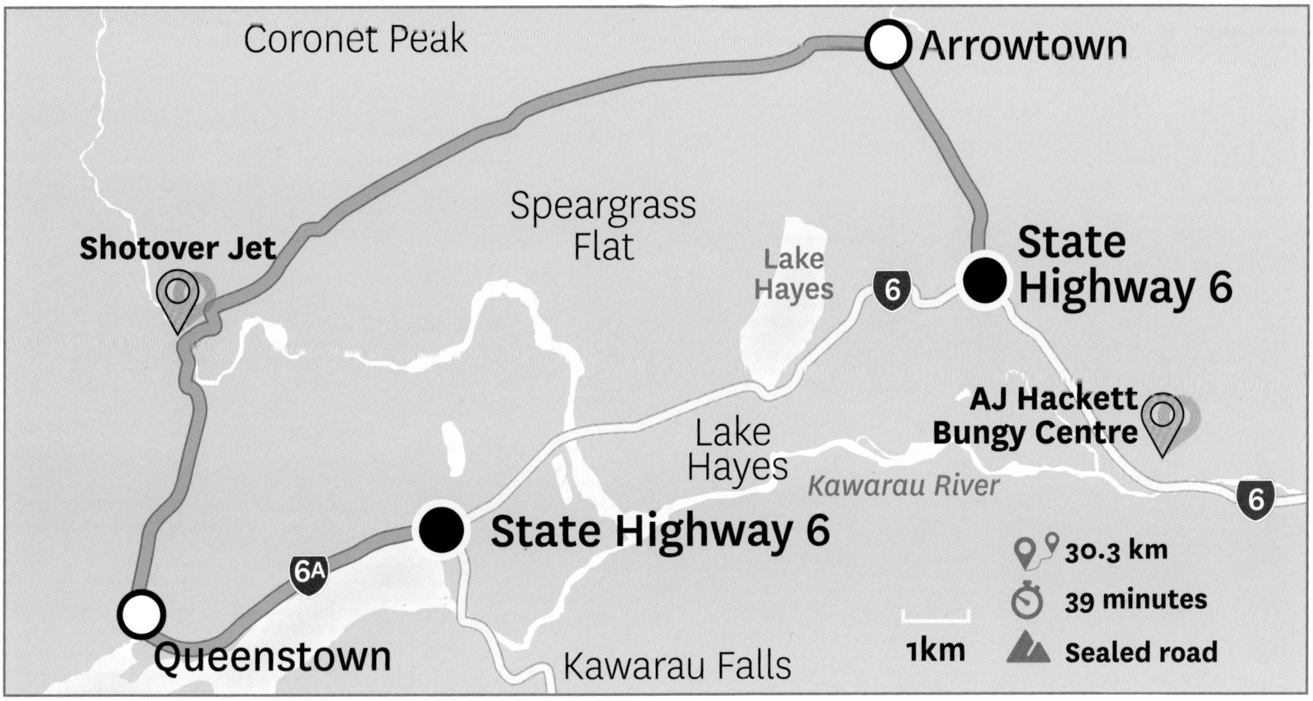

If you are riding from Cromwell, when you reach Arrow Junction, from State Highway 6 turn right to follow signs to Arrowtown. Park up your bike and explore this delightful historic gold mining town. With a fantastic high street of shops, galleries and eateries, from the historic Fork & Tap pub to the local bakery and converted post office, this town is a fabulous stopover if you have time to spare. Following Malaghans Road you are skirting the back of Queenstown under the mountainous gaze of towering Coronet Peak, a favourite ski destination for thrill seekers during the winter months. You will be winding your way through the valley and come across the Shotover River, where the iconic 'red boats' of the Shotover Jets blast their way through the canyons, powered by two 350 Mercruiser V8 engines. Another bucket list adventure to tick off.

Gorge Road will bring you in around the back of Queenstown township and links up with Shotover Street, the main street in Queenstown. Park up your bike and explore the wharf and all the easily accessible activities in this picturesque and bustling tourist town. To get back on track to the main route, follow Frankton Road and signs to Frankton before turning right to rejoin SH6 Southern Scenic Route.

19. Magical Milford Sound — Te Anau to Milford Sound Return

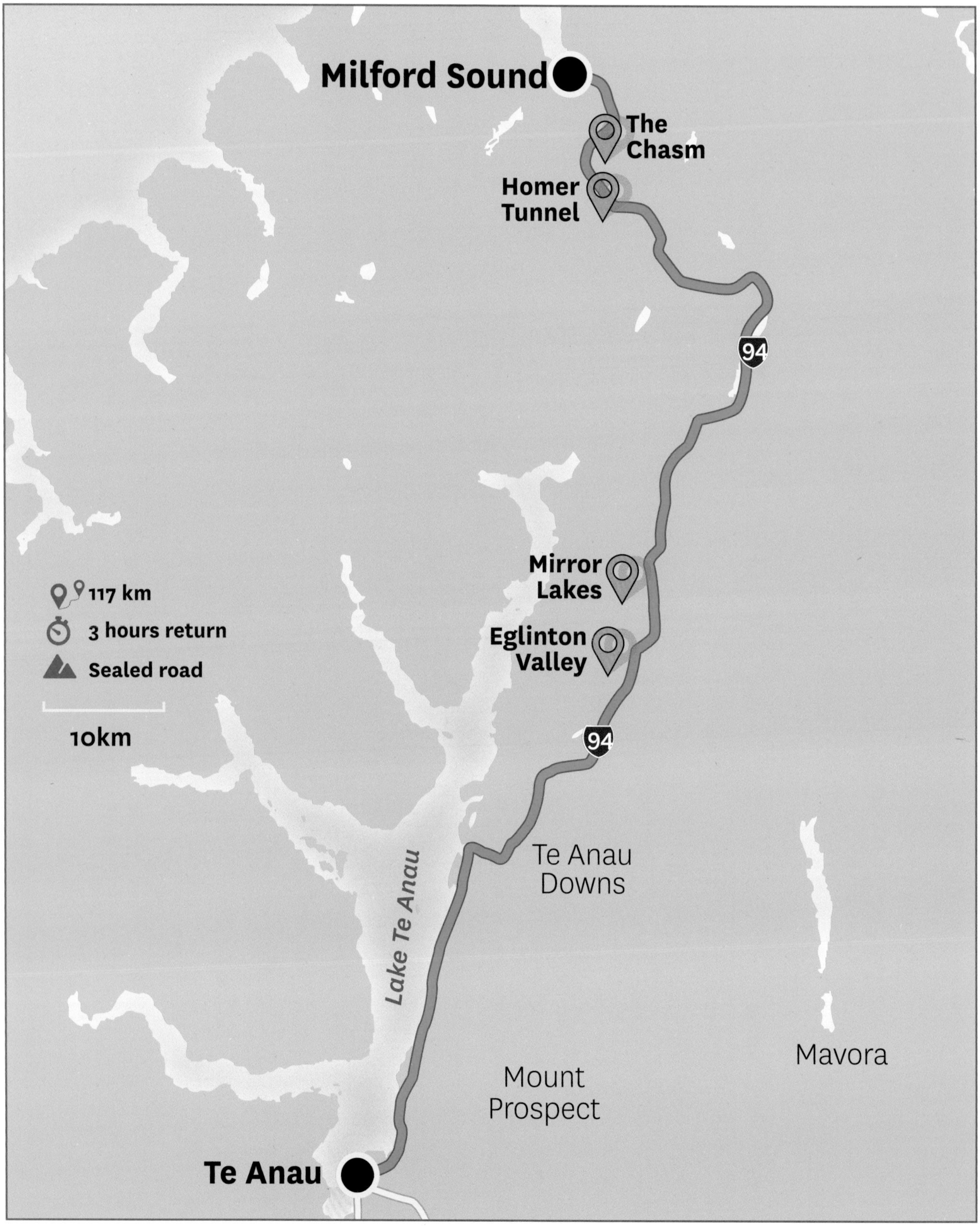

Milford Sound

Route Overview

This bucket list ride begins in Te Anau. Making your way here even before the ride begins, you will be amazed at the beauty of the area, and it keeps getting better.

Located in Fiordland, Lake Te Anau is the largest of the southern glacial lakes and a whopping 65 km long. Steeped in Māori culture, rich with wildlife and boasting unsurpassed awe-inspiring landscapes, it is suggested that Te Anau is a shortened form of 'Te Ana-au' which means 'place or cave of swirling water'.

From the lakefront there are many tours and activities available to visitors, from boat cruises, glow-worm caves and scenic flights, as well as exploring and hiking the local trails. So, if you feel like a day away from the saddle, you're spoilt for choice here in paradise.

Before you leave on this ride, check the weather in Milford Sound itself, and top the tank up with fuel. Despite what its name suggests, Milford Sound is not actually a 'sound', but in fact a 'fiord', as it was carved out by the erosion of an ancient glacial lake.

The weather on the way to, and in, Milford Sound itself is quickly interchangeable and often differs from Te Anau. If you are riding in the cooler months, or it has been raining overnight then there may be a possibility of road closures due to rockslides or avalanches. The road teams along the Milford Highway act quickly, so keep checking frequently as it's likely that if the road is closed it won't be long before it opens up again.

This is an extremely popular tourist attraction and if you choose to leave during prime travel hours there will likely be a fair number of campervans and coaches along the route. The road is narrow in some places so watch out for vehicles coming in the opposite direction that may drift over the centre line, and make sure you are riding well over to the left when cornering to avoid any disasters.

Being one of the wettest places on earth it is

advisable to take your wet weather gear just in case. If you don't mind riding in the wet weather then you won't be disappointed as you'll be rewarded by cascading waterfalls in full flow as you ride through the valley and will even be under cover through some dense rainforest on your way to Milford Sound.

The Milford Highway is not a through road so it has one way in and one way out and there are only a few accommodation options. This ride can be a day trip in and out, broken up by a highly recommended scenic boat cruise in Milford Sound.

The ride to Milford Sound is spectacular. Not only does it tick all the boxes with staple biker needs such as sweeping bends and challenging turns, but add in jaw dropping vistas, rushing waterfalls, lush rainforests and staggering mountains and valleys and you'll see why this makes the ride to Milford Sound one of the best motorcycle rides in New Zealand.

The best thing about this ride is that you get to do it all again on your way back.

Start Your Engines!

You will be exploring the most untouched part of New Zealand and this is a wonderful, but challenging, ride. Take your time as there are multiple places to stop along this magical road that you won't want to miss. Yes, the age-old biker question of 'can I be bothered to take my helmet off each time?' will crop up at numerous points, but most often, the extra effort is worth it, and if you miss something on your way in, you can always stop on your way back out.

The first part of the ride is beside Lake Te Anau which will escort you through to the Fiordland National Park entrance, where the road then follows the Eglinton River to Eglinton Valley., The mountains tower into view and your rainforest riding experience begins. Open your visor and you'll smell the freshness of the ancient lowland beech forest and ferns which creep right up beside the road.

Eglinton Valley is a prime photo stop for tourists so watch out for the odd camper slowing down and stopping suddenly here. This valley was once filled with glacier ice and was carved out slowly over time. It is now covered in golden tussocks and clouds often drop down below the mountains.

A little further down the highway you'll see cars and campers parked up at the 'Mirror Lakes'. These crystal waters reflect their surrounding scenery and the Earl Mountains opposite. At peak tourist times the boardwalks can get quite crowded, so you could even decide to stop here on the way back instead to avoid the crowds.

Enjoy the beech forest riding for a while as you ride over numerous creeks and beside Lake Gunn and Lake Fergus. Fiordland National Park is famous for its Great Walks and if you're a keen hiker then the Routeburn Track entrance is just up ahead. You'll notice the road has slowly been climbing and as the sweeping bends begin to appear here, the biker smile will start creeping on to your face. The forest will open to give you a better view of just where you are, surrounded by sheer cliffs, waterfalls and snow-tipped mountains even in the summer months — magic!

At the end of the valley, you reach Homer Tunnel. Finished in 1954 this is a 1.2 km tunnel which is controlled at either end by traffic lights. While you are stopped and waiting, look out for kea parrots, who may be brave enough to come closer in search of food. These cheeky birds are an alpine parrot, so prefer the colder climate and often stay close to the snowline, but will venture down to try their luck scavenging treats from tourists. They are not dangerous but are extremely intelligent and have sharp beaks and talons, so beware they don't land on your bike as they may pierce your seat or start tugging on important cables.

Take off your sunglasses before you go into the tunnel as there are no lights inside and there is a fairly steep gradient. Emerging from the darkness, you'll be treated to a breathtaking view down through the Cleddau Valley and tight hairpin bends as you descend. Enjoy the rest of the sweeping turns until you reach The Chasm, which is located half-way between Homer Tunnel and Milford Sound. A 20-minute walk to a series of powerful waterfalls, which have shaped the rock over thousands of years, create this dramatic natural chasm.

Milford Sound is your next stop. Park your bike up and take a stroll to the wharf.

Mitre Peak dwarfs the central landscape. Distinguished by its steep, triangular silhouette, it was named after its resemblance to a bishop's mitre (headdress). Cruises will take you right into waterfalls, let you drink from the glacial waterfalls, allow you to spot birdlife, dolphins and penguins or discover the sea creatures from an underwater observatory.

Enjoy the returning ride back to Te Anau and experience the incredible jaw-dropping scenery from a different perspective.

Milford Sound

Biker-friendly stops along the way

The Fat Duck Restaurant & Bar — 124 Town Centre, Te Anau 9600

The Moose Tavern — 84 Lakefront Drive, Te Anau 9600

The Redcliff Cafe — 12 Mokonui St, Te Anau, Fiordland 9600

Scenic highlights along the way

Eglinton Valley
Mirror Lakes
Homer Tunnel
The Chasm

Activities

Cruise Milford Sound
Kayaking
Scenic Flights
Te Anau Sea Plane
Glow Worms
Great Walks

Why this is such a great ride

Add a curve packed, well maintained, two-lane highway to spectacular five-star views the whole way and you've got yourself the ingredients for a route made in biker heaven. Attack this ride early in the morning or late on a sunny afternoon and it simply cannot get any better.

20. The Catlins Ride — Dunedin to Invercargill

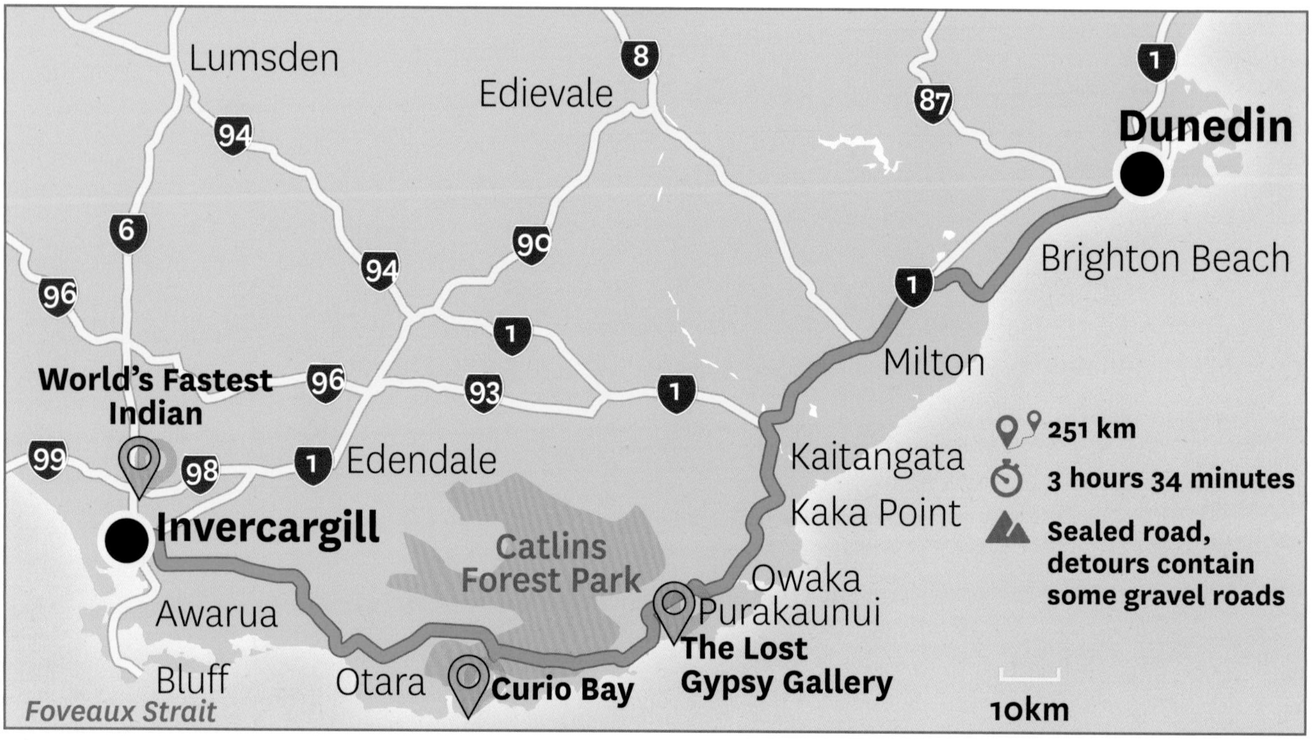

Route Overview

The deep south boasts New Zealand's most wild, untouched, prehistoric scenery, as well as the proud history of its most famous kiwi motorcycling legend, Burt Munro. Burt rode into the history books in 1967 on his Indian Scout and inspired the feature film '*The World's Fastest Indian*', starring Sir Anthony Hopkins.

This unforgettable ride starts off from Dunedin, a city rich in Scottish heritage as well as grand Edwardian and Victorian architecture, and ends in Invercargill, New Zealand's southern-most city. Invercargill is now affectionately known as New Zealand's 'Motorcycle Mecca' and showcases a fabulous classic motorcycle museum of the same name. Kiwis, international visitors, and bike enthusiasts alike, flock to Invercargill each year for the 'Burt Munro Challenge', a motorcycle rally to honour Burt's ingenuity, spirit, and love of motorcycles. The annual event offers fun, fuel-filled events such as drag racing, street racing, speedway, hill-climbing and beach racing and is an event not to be missed by any biker.

If you have time to explore Dunedin for a day or two before you head south, the Otago Peninsula ride is a biker's dream, and will give you an alternative view of Dunedin and Otago Harbour. Riding twists and turns beside the ocean to Taiaroa Head, nature lovers can stop at the Royal Albatross Centre and pre-book other ecotourism attractions at the popular wildlife sanctuaries to see colonies of fur seals and sea lions or yellow-eyed penguins. The return ride then begins to climb up into the hills above (and sometimes into the clouds), where you will find New Zealand's only castle perched atop the peninsula. This spectacular city icon is open for tours, accommodation and evening meals (for guests only), and they regularly welcome riders from all over the world.

The Catlins ride takes approximately three to four hours if you want to get to Invercargill in one day. If you have a few days up your sleeve and able to break up this trip to take in the sights, this will allow you to take your time, ride all the extra detours along the way and you'll be able to explore all that the south has to offer; you certainly won't regret it.

Start Your Engines!

From Dunedin, most tourists take the direct route to

Florence Hill Lookout, The Catlins

Invercargill to save time, but from a biker's perspective, it's more fun to take the long way down and ride the rugged bends of the Catlins coastal road. Heading south from Dunedin, turn off the motorway towards Brighton Road or travel via Saint Clair Beach and head for signs to Brighton Beach.

This slight detour follows the stunning coastline along Taieri Mouth Road, avoids the initial traffic on the motorway, and is a great way to start the trip.

Cross over the Waipori River and past the harbour of little fishing boats. Turn right on to Finlayson Road and head inland to climb your way over the hills for a roller coaster ride back onto State Highway 1 for a short stretch. Balclutha is the gateway to the Catlins and you'll ride over the iconic Balclutha Road Bridge which spans New Zealand's second longest river, the Clutha. Rather than following signs for State Highway 1 to Invercargill, turn left down Owaka Highway and follow signs for the 'Southern Scenic Route'.

Check out the possible detours to Nugget Point/ Tokata Lighthouse or Purakaunui Falls along this stretch of road if you have time and are comfortable riding on gravel.

Just after you cross over the Tahakopa River into Papatowai (blink and you'll miss it), keep a look out on your right for a hidden, quirky, kiwi gem. The Lost Gypsy gallery is world famous in New Zealand and artist Blair Somerville has created a 'fantastic cabinet of obscurities' that will be sure to put a smile on your face. An authentic kiwi experience and a great place to stop, stretch your legs and grab a treat at the Little Rocket coffee cart.

As you ride further south, and should you have a clear day with no wind, you're in for a treat. This rugged part of the country often gets the full force of the ocean gales, and you only have to take a look at the famous leaning trees at Slope Point, the South Island's southernmost point, to understand nature's forces at work here. If you start off your ride on a windy day, just be prepared for it to get *much* worse.

There are multiple sights and stops along this route when you need a break. Cathedral Caves and Florence Hill Lookout will allow you to get the feeling back into your legs as well as taking some incredible snaps to send back home. Check out the **Detour to Curio Bay or Bluff** if you have time.

You know you are getting close to Invercargill as the road begins to straighten out. The landscape gradually changes too, from beech and podocarp native forests to flat wetlands and farmlands. Invercargill is New Zealand's southernmost city and you'll ride past numerous heritage and art deco buildings.

The city's love affair with all things classic motoring is evident with attractions such as Bill Richardson's Transport World with its world-class vintage trucks and classic car displays. If you're into mega machinery and feel like trying your hand operating, digging, or destroying something with a 15 ton digger then 'Dig This' has rides that allow the inner child to come out, no license necessary!

Classic Motorcycle Mecca is a must-see for any biker here in Invercargill. Boasting over 300 motorcycles dating from 1902 the nostalgia may kick in as you get up close and personal to these machines. With displays covering John Britten to Brough Superior and Burt Munro you're in for a real treat. Their on-site cafe, Meccaspresso, also does a mean 'Bikers Breakfast' and is not to be missed!

Invercargill's best kept secret is tucked away in a hardware store on Dee Street; The E Hayes Motorworks Collection has grown from a small shop selling tools into a full-blown display of classic motorcycles, cars and machines. It also has the honour of showcasing the original 'World's Fastest Indian', Burt Munro's 1920 Indian Scout. The collection is free to the public and the bonus, if you're after a wrench or hammer, is that you're in the right place!

Get your photo taken beside Burt's bronze statue in Victoria Park or check out Oreti Beach where Burt would test-ride his latest machine and where *The World's Fastest Indian* was filmed for the blockbuster movie.

If you're lucky enough to visit in February, when the Burt Munro Challenge Motorcycle Rally is on, the city will be swarming with bikers, motorcycles and petrol-heads from all over. This action-packed event won't disappoint, and you'll be sure to receive a warm southern welcome from the people of Invercargill.

With so many places to explore along the way, you have the option to ride through in one day. Or take your time and stop over midway at any local accommodation to really make the most of this incredible part of the country, to take in those special 'off the beaten track' locations that the Catlins has to offer.

Biker-friendly stops along the way

Lost Gypsy Caravan — Papatowai Highway, Papatowai 9586

Tumu Toka Curioscape — 590 Waikawa-Curio Bay Road, Waikawa 9884

Bill Richardson's Transport World — 491 Tay Street, Hawthorndale, Invercargill 9810

Classic Motorcycle Mecca — 25 Tay Street, Invercargill 9810

Niagara Falls Cafe — 256 Niagara-Waikawa Road, Niagara 9884

Fat Bastard ('FB') Pies — 158 Tay Street, Invercargill 9810

E. Hayes Motorworks Collection (The World's Fastest Indian Motorcycle) — 168 Dee Street, Invercargill 9810

Burt Munro Bronze Sculpture — Queen's Park, Invercargill, 9810

Scenic highlights along the way

Nugget Point Lighthouse
Purakaunui Falls
Florence Hill Lookout
Cathedral Caves
Slope Point
Niagara Falls
Curio Bay — Petrified Forest
Bluff

Detour 1
Otago Peninsula Loop

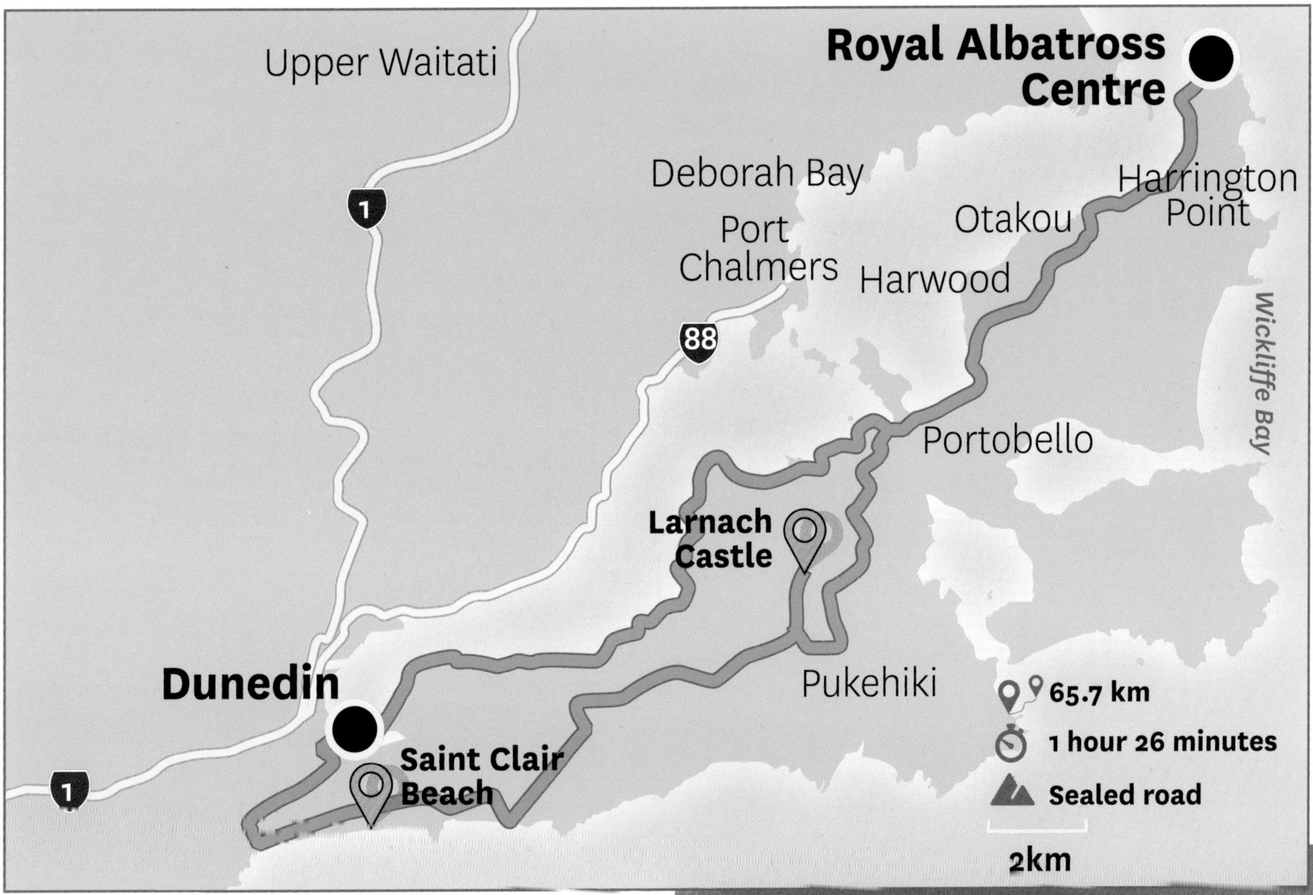

Before you head south, make sure you've explored the Dunedin Peninsula which winds its way along Portobello Road beside the Otago Harbour and its picturesque bays. From Portobello, if you continue along Harrington Point Road you will reach Taiaroa Head, home to New Zealand's Royal Albatross Centre and other ecotourism sites. Turning off at Portobello will take you up Highcliff Road, up twists and turns to Larnach Castle then down towards Saint Clair Beach.

Why this is such a great ride

This route has minimal traffic and it's isolation will make you feel you're the only rider in New Zealand. Southland's best kept secret with multiple places to stop along the way, as you glide around corners you've only dreamed of.

Larnach Castle

Detour 2

Nugget Point/Tokata Lighthouse

Five minutes south of Balclutha at Otanomomo, turn left and follow signs to Kaka Point along Kaka Point Road, then signs for Nugget Point/Tokata Lighthouse. For bikers it is worth noting that at the end of the esplanade the road turns to gravel for 7.5 km before you reach the car park so take care. Park your bike up and take the stroll to the lighthouse for fabulous seascapes and the all-important photo opportunity.

Nugget Point was named by Captain Cook due to the rocks bearing similarities to gold nuggets, and the landscape offers up incredible views at sunset.

On your way back, turn left at the end of the gravel road following the sign to rejoin the Southern Scenic Route. When you reach Ahuriri Flat you will rejoin the Owaka Highway. Turn left and you're again heading south towards the Catlins.

Detour 3
Purakaunui Falls

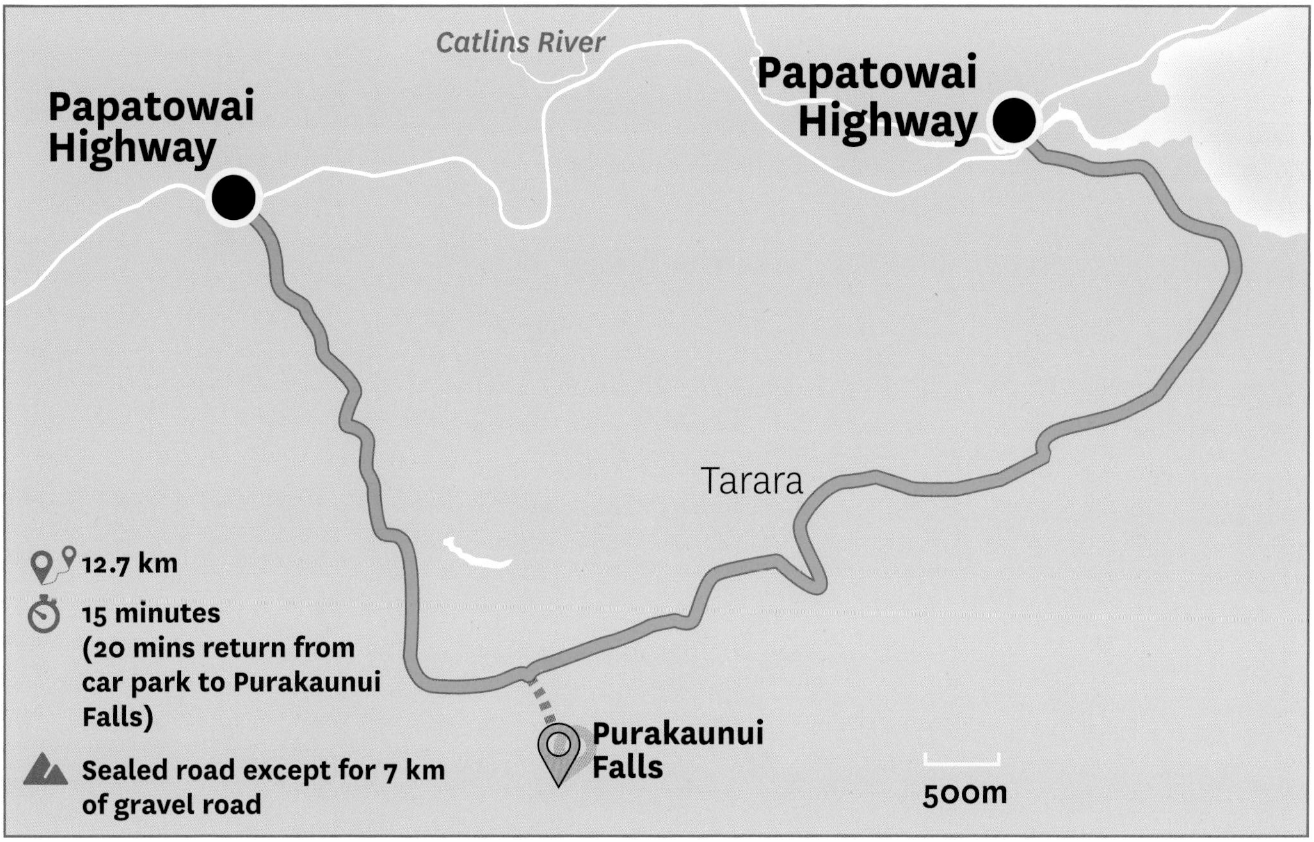

If you're confident riding on gravel roads, just after you cross the Catlins River turn left to follow the sign to Purakaunui Falls. Located just a short forest walk from the car park, this spectacular three-tiered cascading waterfall is one of the most photographed in New Zealand.

Purakaunui Falls

Detour 4

Niagara Falls, Curio Bay and Slope Point

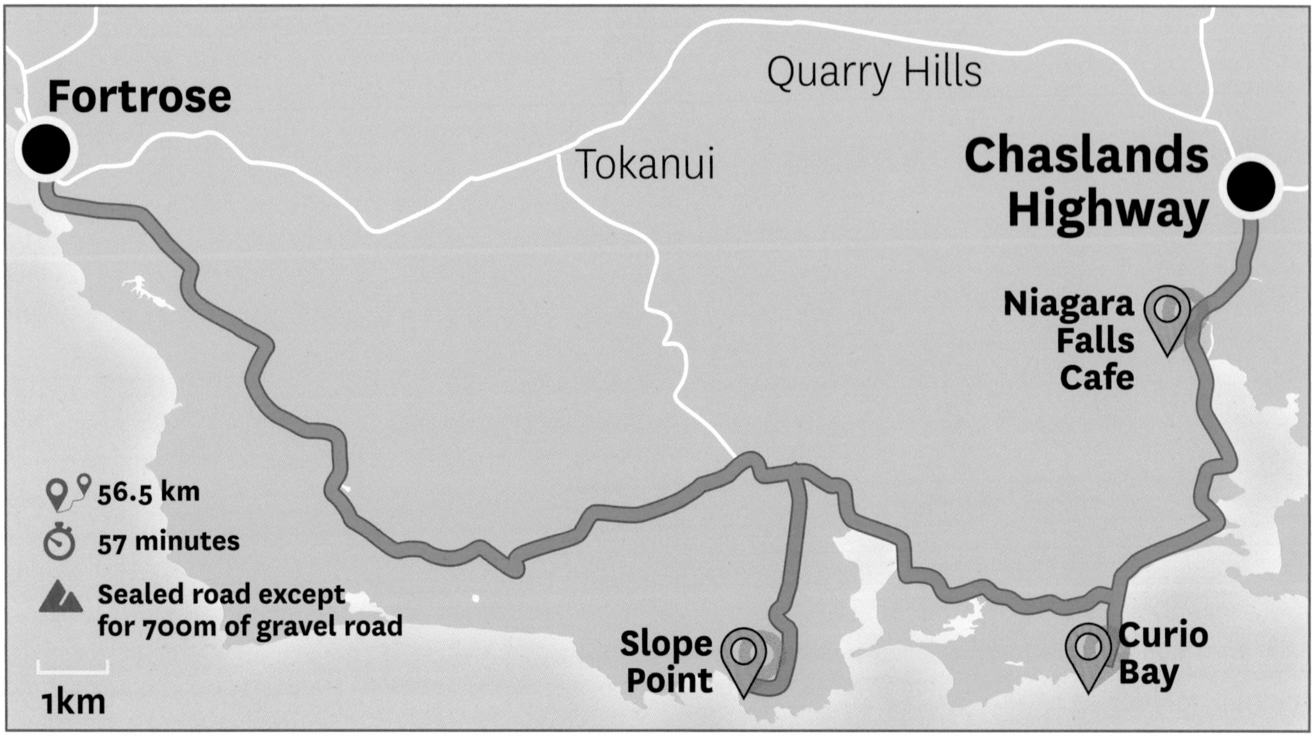

Turning left on to Niagara-Waikawa Road, follow the signs to Curio Bay and if you want to stop for a quirky photo opportunity, New Zealand has its very own Niagara Falls! Niagara Falls Cafe also offers authentic kiwi food and a warm welcome to bikers.

Continue on to the end of the road where a 180 million-year-old petrified podocarp forest awaits you. Tumu Toka CurioScape also offers a welcome coffee break and a place to learn more about the Catlins, its geological formations and history. Slope Point is further along this route and is New Zealand's southernmost point. It is accessible via a 20-minute walk across private farmland.

Stirling Point, Bluff

Detour 5
Bluff, Stirling Point

Just before you turn right and head towards Invercargill is your chance to turn left down Motu Rimu Road to meet up with State Highway 1 and follow the sign to Bluff. Bluff is where State Highway 1 officially begins and winds its way up the entire length of New Zealand, all the way to Cape Reinga in the far north. Famous for delicious oysters and the most photographed signpost at Stirling Point, which points to countries around the world showing their distances from your current location in every direction. Bluff Hill is also the location for the Hill Climb event during the annual Burt Munro Challenge Rally and thousands flock here each year to see riders speed up the hill as quickly as possible, but don't get any ideas!

Acknowledgements

Special thanks to:
Mike Lester
Carole Lester
Hayley Sampson
David Bright
Nathan O'Brien
John Munro
Margaret Munro
Duncan Perkinson
Katrina Bassett

Images thanks to:
Robbie Magasiva
Ralph Griebenow
Hanna Johansson
PJ and Terry O'Reilley
Louie and Kim Hale
Gord Russell
Ian and Susan Wardrope
David and Robyn Watt
Brian and Ros Smith
Daryll and Libby McCaffrey
David Hazzelby
Chris Palmer
Shutterstock
Dreamstime.com
Alan Barsamian
Rahul Panda
Dana and Cheryl Karapita
Beth and Mark Chrimes
Mark Healey
Jeff Harris
Mick Skinner
Allan Dederer
Mick Cranston
Craig Strongman
Dana Delmont
Ed Crowley
Jeosen Cua
Natalia Ramirez
Hanmer Springs Thermal Pool

A White Cloud Book
Published in 2023 by White Cloud Books, an imprint of Upstart Press Ltd

26 Greenpark Road, Penrose,
Auckland 1061
New Zealand

A catalogue record for this book is available from the National Library of New Zealand

ISBN 978-1-77694-035-6

Design and format: Nick Turzynski, redinc. Book Design, www.redinc.co.nz

Printed by Everbest Printing China, on paper sourced from sustainable forests